# Dealing with Dysfunction

INNOVATIVE GOVERNANCE IN THE 21ST CENTURY

ANTHONY SAICH
*Series editor*

This is the tenth volume in a series that examines important issues of governance, public policy, and administration, highlighting innovative practices and original research worldwide. All titles in the series will be copublished by the Brookings Institution Press and the Ash Center for Democratic Governance and Innovation, housed at Harvard University's John F. Kennedy School of Government.

# Dealing with Dysfunction

*Innovative Problem Solving in the Public Sector*

**Jorrit de Jong**

ASH CENTER FOR DEMOCRATIC GOVERNANCE AND INNOVATION
*John F. Kennedy School of Government*
*Harvard University*

BROOKINGS INSTITUTION PRESS
*Washington, D.C.*

The Brookings Institution is a private nonprofit organization devoted to research, education, and publication on important issues of domestic and foreign policy. Its principal purpose is to bring the highest quality independent research and analysis to bear on current and emerging policy problems. Interpretations or conclusions in Brookings publications should be understood to be solely those of the authors.

*Library of Congress Cataloging-in-Publication data*

Names: Jong, Jorrit de, author.
Title: Dealing with dysfunction : innovative problem solving in the public sector / Jorrit de Jong, Ash Center for Democratic Governance and Innovation, John F. Kennedy School of Government, Harvard University.
Description: Washington, D.C. : Brookings Institution Press, 2016. | Includes bibliographical references.
Identifiers: LCCN 2016017500 (print) | LCCN 2016029634 (ebook) | ISBN 9780815722069 (pbk : alk. paper) | ISBN 9780815722076 (ebook)
Subjects: LCSH: Bureaucracy—Case studies. | Public administration—Case studies. | Government accountability—Case studies. | Problem solving—Case studies. | BISAC: POLITICAL SCIENCE / Public Affairs & Administration. | POLITICAL SCIENCE / Government / National. | BUSINESS & ECONOMICS / Human Resources & Personnel Management.
Classification: LCC JF1501.J665 2016 (print) | LCC JF1501 (ebook) | DDC 352.3—dc23
LC record available at https://lccn.loc.gov/2016017500

9 8 7 6 5 4 3 2 1

Typeset in Sabon and Eurostile

Composition by Westchester Publishing Services

*To my parents*
*Foppe de Jong and Anke de Jong-Van der Graaf*

# Contents

# Preface

How can we deal effectively with bureaucratic dysfunction? This book examines the problem and develops a novel approach to solving it. Drawing from academic literature on bureaucracy and problem solving in the public sector and the clinical work of the Kafka Brigade, a social enterprise dedicated to diagnosing and remedying bureaucratic dysfunction in practice, this study reveals the shortcomings of conventional approaches to bureaucratic dysfunction. The usual methods have failed to diagnose problems, distinguish symptoms, or identify root causes in a comprehensive or satisfactory way. They have also failed to engage clients, professionals, and midlevel managers in understanding and remedying the dysfunction that plagues them. This book offers conceptual frameworks, theoretical insights, and practical lessons for dealing with the problem in practice. It sets a course for rigorous public problem solving to create governments that can be more effective, efficient, equitable, and responsive to social problems.

I argue that successfully addressing bureaucratic dysfunction depends on employing diagnostics capable of distinguishing and dissecting various kinds of dysfunction. The "Anna Karenina principle," applies here: all well-functioning bureaucracies are alike; every dysfunctional bureaucracy is dysfunctional in its own way. I also argue that the worst dysfunction occurs when multiple organizations share responsibility for a problem, but no single organization is primarily responsible for solving it. This points to a need for creating and reinforcing distributed problem-solving capacity focused on deep (cross-)organizational learning and revised accountability structures. Our best shot at dealing with dysfunction may therefore not be top-down regulatory reform, but rather relentless bottom-up and cross-boundary leadership and innovation. Using fourteen clinical cases of bureaucratic dysfunction investigated by the Kafka Brigade in the Netherlands, I demonstrate how a proper process for identifying, defining, diagnosing, and remedying the problem can produce better outcomes.

I cofounded the Kafka Brigade in the Netherlands in 2005 and helped develop its methods and action research approach to cross-organizational and cross-sectoral learning and innovation. Through our work in numerous cities and multiple countries, my colleagues and I have had the opportunity to observe bureaucratic dysfunction up close and experiment with approaches to diagnosing and remedying the problem. Hundreds of people have contributed to the work, including researchers, "bureaucracy-survivors," civil servants, clients, activists, policymakers, political executives, and sponsors—too many individuals to thank here, but I am deeply grateful to all. Special thanks go to my co-founders, Arre Zuurmond, Joeri van den Steenhoven, and Lobke van der Meulen, and to the current leaders of the Kafka Brigade, Arjan Widlak, Chris Sigaloff and Leo Smits, for their passion, curiosity, and commitment to the mission. I thank Goos Minderman and the late Caren van Egten for providing me with a space at the Free University in Amsterdam (VU) to work on the research that underlies the book. Their support has been much appreciated. In the United Kingdom and Ireland, Irwin Turbitt, Megan Mathias, and John Palmer have been exceptional partners in pioneering the approach. Harvard University's John F. Kennedy School of Government, where I first arrived as a visiting scholar in 2008 and now serve on the faculty, provided me with an intellectually stimulating environment that values problem solving in practice. Mark Moore in particular has been extraordinarily generous with his time, thoughtful and helpful in his feedback, and has generally inspired the writing and completion of this work. I could not have wished for a better mentor, colleague, and friend. The Ash Center for Democratic Governance and Innovation at Harvard Kennedy School has afforded me the opportunity to further develop the ideas about public problem solving presented here and apply them in practice through the Innovation Field Lab. This experiential learning course *cum* action research project in Massachusetts cities was made possible by the vision and generous support of Ash director Tony Saich and executive director Marty Mauzy. It allows me to continue the work that I care about so much at the intersection of academia and practice and take it to the next level.

Additionally, I am indebted to a large number of colleagues who inspired and encouraged me. Some provided me with feedback on early versions of this manuscript, others participated in the Kafka Retreats in the UK and the Netherlands or the Innovation Round Table sessions on public problem solving at Harvard, and yet others helped me think through the various dimensions of the subject of this book in one-on-one meetings. The list is probably not complete, but in addition to the people mentioned above, I would like to thank Michael Lipsky, Deborah Stone, Archon Fung, Albert-Jan Kruiter, Steven de Jong, Meike de Jong, Mark Rutte, Atzo Nicolaï, Martin Dooms, Mariënne Verhoef, Linda Bilmes, Jay Rosengard, Asim Khwaja, Harry Spence, Jack Donahue, Lant Pritchett, Matt Andrews, Malcolm Sparrow, Steve Goldsmith, Geoff Mulgan, Mark Bovens, Bob Behn, Ronnie Heifetz, Erik Gerritsen, Koos van der Steenhoven, Bertine Steenbergen, Fred Voncken, Jacqueline Rutjes, Ig Snellen, Mark van Twist, Gowher Rizvi, Linda Kaboolian, Roel in't Veld, Natasha Warikoo, Leo Huberts, Ed Vosselman, Arre Zuurmond, Jouke de Vries, Kees Mouwen, Arthur Docters van Leeuwen, Herman Tjeenk Willink, Saskia Stuiveling, Alex Brenninkmeijer, Gerard Visser, Quinton Mayne, Martijn Groenleer, Maurits Waardenburg, Christina Marchand, and Peter Kasbergen. Jessica Crew and Adam Sitterly offered invaluable research assistance and support in preparing the manuscript. Gaylen Moore has been a stellar editor who helped not only to make the book more readable, but also to make the argument more articulate. At Brookings Institution Press I could not have wished for more patient, skillful, and resourceful partners than Janet Walker and Angela Piliouras, who coordinated the project, Eileen Hughes, who edited several chapters before retiring, and was followed by Marjorie Pannell, and Rebecca Schlenoff, who provided an excellent cover.

My beautiful and strong-willed daughters, Dante (8) and Dylan (4), have taught me more about life, human behavior, and the merits and limits of "governance" than I will ever be able to articulate in a written work. As for my warm-hearted and witty wife, Sanderijn Cels, who has been my intellectual sparring partner since the start of the millennium, I thank her for everything.

This book is dedicated to my loving parents, Foppe de Jong and Anke de Jong-Van der Graaf. As front-line civil servants, they brought home the stories of people who were let down by the system, and the stories of those who were cheating the system. They instilled in me a deep sense that the potential for achieving good governance and social justice lies in our ability to treat others with humanity while we perform the complex tasks of delivering services and enforcing laws. The ambition to make government work and to make it work for everyone is a key theme in this book. I therefore dedicate it with pride and love to them.

# 1

# Introduction

*Bureaucracy has a rational character; rules, means, ends, and matter-of-factness dominate its bearing.*

MAX WEBER, *Wirtschaft und Gesellschaft*, 1922


*A bureaucratic organization is an organization that cannot correct its behavior by learning from its errors.*

MICHEL CROZIER,
*The Bureaucratic Phenomenon*, 1964


In Terry Gilliam's movie *Brazil* (1985), a low-level civil servant is confronted with a problem that is not being solved through the regular business processes of his organization. The protagonist, Sam Lowry, works at the Ministry of Information, which is responsible for processing information requests from other government agencies, archiving government documents, and keeping citizen records. The problem that Lowry tries diligently to solve is the immediate result of a technical failure of a government printer brought about by a *literal* bug: an insect falls into the printer at the moment that the printer is processing arrest warrants. The insect causes a stain on a form, changing "Mr. Tuttle" into "Mr. Buttle" by smearing the first "T." This splotch goes unnoticed by the people in charge of the printer; as a result, an innocent man, Mr. Buttle, is arrested and the (presumably) guilty Mr. Tuttle gets away. An activist on behalf of the unfortunate Buttle family attempts to bring the case to the

1

government's attention, but she is routinely stonewalled by front desk officials.

Because he has personal feelings for the activist, Lowry attempts to intercede with the relevant agencies. The initial response of the government is to deny the error because, after all, the whole system was designed to be impervious to error. To acknowledge an error would be to suggest a design flaw in the state apparatus. In addition, because the base assumption is that no mistakes are possible, no redress procedures exist. The activist helping Mrs. Buttle discovers this fact first, as she is sent from one office to the next with a dismissive "It's not our problem." Lowry goes beyond his job description in his efforts to help the activist and the Buttles—behavior that upsets his superiors—and he endangers himself by trying to remedy the dysfunction. In fact, for siding with the victims of a government mistake, Lowry himself is declared an enemy of the state.

## Bureaucracy and Bureaucratic Dysfunction

There is something about bureaucracy that is profoundly unsettling. As a type of organization, it is all around us and we are familiar with its workings. At the same time, we find bureaucracies to be alienating and frustrating institutions. We are generally quite content with the bureaucratic process and the substantive outcomes accomplished through bureaucratic organizations, yet we are quick to dismiss the entire enterprise when something goes wrong. While we encounter public sector bureaucracies primarily as clients, our expectations and standards are also informed by our roles as taxpayers, voters, employees, employers, concerned citizens, and so forth. The claims that we make about the performance of bureaucracies are often incomplete and contradictory; like the blind scholars in John Godfrey Saxe's poem "The Blind Men and the Elephant," we stumble upon the phenomenon and exercise judgment based on limited information and our personal perspective. As a public, we often are inarticulate and incoherent in expressing our values, interests, and preferences with regard to public sector bureaucracies.

For that reason, bureaucratic dysfunction in the public sector is a practical as well as a theoretical problem. If there is no clarity or con-

The Blind Men and the Elephant (John Godfrey Saxe—1816–1887)

sensus about what we expect from well-functioning bureaucracies, figuring out whether and how bureaucracies are dysfunctional will be an intellectual and a practical challenge. As it seeks to produce actionable knowledge to deal with bureaucratic dysfunction, this book addresses both of those challenges. By constructing conceptual frameworks, discussing theoretical perspectives, and conducting an empirical inquiry into the phenomenon, I develop a novel and hopefully more adequate approach to an age-old, untamed problem.[1] In so doing, I aim to make a contribution to social science as well as to public problem solving in practice.[2] But first it is necessary to take a step back and ask what the nature of the problem is and why it needs solving.

In the case of Mr. Buttle's tragically mistaken identity, one may answer that the problem was simply a matter of technical failure caused by the malfunctioning printer. After all, without the jammed printer, there would have been no further trouble. Another answer could be that because of their negligence, the individuals operating the printer were the problem. If they had exercised better quality control, the problem would have been solved right there. However, a more

1. Major studies of bureaucratic dysfunction dating back to the 1950s have argued that the problem has a tendency to persist despite efforts to eliminate it or counteract the consequences (Bozeman 2000; Merton 1952; Kaufman 1977; Albrow 1970; Blau 1956; Crozier 1964).

2. On the social science end, I aim specifically to contribute to bureaucratic theory and public value theory. How this study contributes to those theories, as well as to the concept of the practice of public problem solving, is discussed in chapter 2.

advanced analysis of the problem suggests that all organizations should anticipate some technical failures and human errors. Therefore, in Mr. Buttle's case the blame should have been placed not on the printer or its operators but on the management and oversight of the entire Ministry of Information. Better monitoring and accountability mechanisms could have prevented the tragic course of events that unfolded.

Yet another line of reasoning could be that the root cause of the incident was an overall lack of responsiveness, flexibility, and problem-solving capacity, which turned a small problem into a big problem. However, that assessment implies that the underlying problem could not have been solved with the resolution of the Buttle case alone. After all, simply fixing the printer, reprimanding individuals, or adjusting business processes would not have guaranteed against similar future problems. Instead, one would have had to investigate patterns deeply entrenched in organizational culture and dysfunctional mechanisms innate to the institution, such as a punitive accountability structure that systematically pushed blame onto low-level workers. Then again, some people may dismiss all of these answers entirely: "Don't make too much of this—it was just a bug!"

It is difficult to pinpoint where problems begin and where they end, and any decision on the matter depends very much on how far one is willing to pursue the discussion. But pinpointing is exactly what we need to do if we want to take public problem solving seriously—and if we want to get better at it. This chapter begins the book by defining the problem and offering the rationale for the research presented.

## Encounters Gone Wrong

Bureaucratic dysfunction is experienced most directly in actual encounters between clients and bureaucracies in the public sector.[3] By "public sector clients" I mean people who in one form or another engage in transactions with the government.[4] Clients take on different

3. These encounters may be actual (face-to-face) or virtual (conducted in cyberspace), and they may occur in city hall offices, on the streets, or in people's homes. I use the term "encounter" here in the broadest possible sense of the word. A conceptual framework for analyzing problematic encounters is presented in chapter 2.

4. In chapter 2 I elaborate on this definition. For an overview and discussion of the concept of "public sector client," see Alford (2009) and Hoogwout (2010).

roles because their relationships and interactions with the government vary in nature. When the government is a direct provider of services and benefits, clients encounter the state as beneficiaries or as customers—in general terms, in the role of *recipient*. When the government regulates social and economic behavior and enforces its regulations through licensing, inspections, and other means of control, clients encounter the state in a different role: they do not receive services or goods; instead they are subject to requirements with which they must comply, in the role of *obligatee* (Sparrow 1994; Moore 1995; Alford 2009).

If clients experience the consequences of bureaucratic dysfunction in their role as recipient, they may have trouble accessing services or obtaining benefits. In their role as obligatee, they may for one reason or another find it difficult or costly to comply. Problems may vary from minor misunderstandings to major conflicts between officials and clients. Waiting times might be long, procedures cumbersome, and paperwork incomprehensible. Sometimes client and government may not encounter each other at all because one could not locate the other. In addition, encounters may last too long because the parties could not effectively conclude their transaction.[5] When encounters go wrong and clients and governments cannot complete their business, losses are incurred (Howard 1994; United Nations 2008; World Bank 2009; OECD 2007, 2010). Clients may suffer material losses (opportunities, benefits, money, and time) as well as immaterial losses (energy, hope, dignity, and respect for government). If that happens infrequently and inadvertently, it may be a simple matter of bureaucratic flaws or errors. Human beings make mistakes, and since organizations are designed, managed, and populated by human beings, so do bureaucracies.

In the case of Mr. Buttle in *Brazil*, determining whether the losses are the result of simple human error or deeper bureaucratic dysfunction raises the question of whether the problem is an exceptional or a fundamental issue. In other words, is the Buttles' predicament an extraordinary case or the result of a structural problem within an organization? At first glance, it appears to be the former. After all, the chances of a bug falling into a printer and causing a smear resembling another letter in the alphabet are not very high.

---

5. Chapters 2 and 3 elaborate on the variety of things that can go wrong in theory, while chapters 5 and 6 offer numerous examples of encounters that did go wrong in practice.

Many "bugs" are not easily detected in bureaucratic organizations. In addition, it is conceivable that many small undetected problems can culminate in exceptional problems, with serious consequences. Moreover, problems may not be the only exception to the rule. The fact that the Buttles' difficulties came to the attention of a civil servant may be the exception—not the bug in the printer. When bureaucratic encounters go wrong frequently, flaws appear to be systemic, and errors seem to follow a pattern, then something more serious might be happening. When bureaucracies fail to notice and address structural problems in their encounters with clients, they enter the domain of bureaucratic dysfunction.

### Loss of Value

Bureaucratic dysfunction often is evaluated in terms of loss of value to the client. In problematic encounters, the negative consequences are experienced first and foremost by clients. Clients define government performance to a large extent in terms of the government's ability to construct productive encounters.[6] I argue, however, that the public also loses, if indirectly. By "the public," I mean the citizenry at large, which as a collective has mandated the government to act on its behalf. In liberal democracies, the public expects the government to carry out its tasks efficiently and effectively and in accordance with the rule of law. These tasks include delivering public services to clients and imposing duties on clients. But the expected results of government activities go beyond client satisfaction (Moore 1995). The public is interested in the social outcomes accomplished through encounters with clients. For example, in the case of public ser-

6. The Netherlands Institute for Social Research (Sociaal en Cultureel Planbureau, SCP) recorded that 53 percent of the population had confidence in the capacity of government agencies to perform well. In 2008 a comprehensive survey was conducted on the quality of public services as perceived by users and non-users. The data showed that on average, satisfaction with services had increased, although there was high variability across the range of services; however, citizens were considerably more satisfied with the product of the service than with the process of acquiring the product or using the service (Pommer, Van Kempen, and Eggink 2008). The SCP observed that most of the government's efforts had gone into improving product quality—for example, safer medical procedures—while the users were primarily concerned about waiting lists, lack of information, and the way in which they were treated.

vices, such as income support, health care, and education, the public hopes to achieve a fair distribution of wealth and increased public health, well-being, and economic potential. In the case of regulations, such as food safety standards, traffic laws, and rules governing business transactions, the public hopes to protect itself from harms.[7]

So if government bureaucracies become dysfunctional and fail to establish constructive and productive encounters, they do more than just dissatisfy clients: they fail to improve social outcomes. In such cases, the public has reasons for concern. It has legitimized government intervention through elections and paid for it through taxes. If the government is not delivering services adequately, the question arises of whether it is using tax money effectively and efficiently. If it is not implementing or enforcing regulations adequately, concerns arise regarding the use of law: is the government using its authority carefully and in proportion to its task? While disgruntled clients may ask these questions in their roles as recipients and obligatees, the public can ask them from a different perspective, for different reasons. If bureaucracies are dysfunctional, government fails the public in at least two ways: it is not using its authority and fiscal resources responsibly, and it is not achieving optimal social outcomes.

### Who Cares?

Does the public care whether the government uses its authority and fiscal resources responsibly and achieves optimal social outcomes? Do people care if some people or groups of people are having significant trouble with government red tape while they are not? When does red tape become a serious problem for the public? While the perspective of the individual public sector client may seem straightforward, the general public does not always articulate its preferences

---

7. Obviously, members of the public may disagree about the necessity, desirability, and specific characteristics of many public policies. The point is that the social compact in liberal democracies rests on the notion that as *a public,* people invest in collective arrangements administered by the government. The fruits of governmental efforts are enjoyed by individual clients (especially in the case of public services and benefits) and by the public at large (especially in the case of regulations).

or concerns well. It does, of course, comprise a diverse body of people who have different values, interests, positions, and opinions; moreover, competing values and contradictory positions may exist even within an individual member of the public. The public may care about optimal social outcomes but also about the responsible use of tax money. It may have concerns about easy access to services and benefits: for example, it may subscribe to the notion of employment benefits but worry about moral hazard among recipients if it is too easy to get a government handout. In fact, the public may implicitly endorse policies that make encounters cumbersome, unpleasant, or simply impossible as a means of rationing services (Lipsky 1984, p. 3; 2008, p. 137; de Jong, and Rizvi 2008). As a result, what appears to be dysfunction to a certain group of clients may be seen by the public at large as an effective way to limit access to services.[8] The public may not pressure government to improve the performance of certain government bureaucracies because it wants to protect specific interests, save money, exclude certain groups of clients, or simply sabotage the accomplishment of certain social outcomes. However, very rarely will the public articulate its values, goals, or preferences—or its views with respect to making trade-offs.[9]

In *Brazil*, Sam Lowry doesn't know at first how serious the problem is or how frequently it occurs. The case itself is not enough to motivate him to take any substantial action. Were it not for his feelings for the activist helping the Buttles, he would not go through all the trouble. The lack of a sense of urgency to act on what seem to be tragic cases and unfortunate mistakes prompts a third question: Whose problem is it, anyway?

Only when Lowry decides to get to the bottom of the matter do his superiors and colleagues at other government departments be-

---

8. While this seems contradictory, the mechanism is understandable if we keep in mind that the public embodies many different opinions and ideas about what is good, fair, and just. Governments typically are elected by a majority of voters, implying that a substantial portion of the public might not agree with some or all of a government's policies.

9. The outcome of an election—an important expression of public opinion—can be taken as an articulate endorsement or rejection of certain policies. At the same time, many people vote not for particular policies but for particular candidates; referendums, of course, are an exception.

come concerned. However, the problem that they perceive is not that Mr. Buttle has been victimized or that the government has made a mistake; they are concerned because Lowry is trying to address the incident. His superiors repeatedly ask him to drop the case. Since he does not, Lowry himself becomes a problem. This problem, however, is much more easily solved: Lowry is arrested and put away.[10]

In the end, both the innocent client, Mr. Buttle, and the well-intentioned civil servant, Sam Lowry, become casualties of a system that refuses to deal with bureaucratic dysfunction. Lowry's position and attitude are especially interesting in this regard. In the beginning his actions are dictated by the rigid accountability system of the bureaucracy, by adherence to rules and obedience to authority. The turning point comes when Lowry decides that it would be morally irresponsible to hide behind the formal accountability structure. To him, the value lost by not addressing the consequences of a serious mistake is greater than the value gained by staying on the straight and narrow. Then the pendulum swings the other way: Lowry pledges allegiance to the task at hand—resolving the Buttle issue. Consequently, Lowry's actions are no longer aligned with those desired by the Ministry of Information. Having switched sides, Lowry is now held accountable for his actions by the activist, not the ministry. Is there a better way to deal with bureaucratic dysfunction than to abandon one set of accountability standards for another? Is there a way to appreciate the value of rules, regulations, and chain of command and simultaneously create real value for clients and reduce the negative effects of inflexible bureaucracies?

I advocate an approach to problem solving that does not ignore or abandon accountability systems but transforms them and makes them more responsive to exceptions, changing circumstances, and the broader context of public organizations. Such an approach could detect and address problems so that people like Mr. Buttle could avoid a tragic fate and people like Sam Lowry could make positive changes without sacrificing their well-being.

---

10. The ending of the movie leaves Lowry's exact fate open to question. For a discussion of the movie, see *Brazil* (www.imdb.com/Brazil).

## A Problem without a Public

In *The Public and Its Problems*, the American philosopher John Dewey examines the workings of democratic societies in terms of the ability of the public to understand and act in its own interests (Dewey 1954). While the functioning or malfunctioning of the government apparatus in the implementation of public policy affects the interests of the public significantly, no public per se exists with regard to bureaucratic dysfunction.[11] In the political debate, the spotlight is typically on public policy. While public sector clients are quite perceptive regarding the consequences of bureaucratic dysfunction to the extent that it affects them or people that they know, they are less aware of the magnitude and nature of value losses caused by malfunctioning institutions.[12] For a long time the focus has been on the client, particularly on the (aggregated) loss of value to individuals (Bozeman 2000; Barzelay and Armajani 1992; OECD 2007, 2010). I argue that as a society, we lose more than the sum of all the time, money, and energy wasted in cumbersome bureaucratic encounters. We lose the ability to deliver our collective goals, uphold our values, and keep our faith in the project of building a good system of governance for a just and prosperous society. There is a lot at stake here, both in a material and an immaterial sense. But to assess the real loss—and the real opportunities for improvement—we need a more comprehensive assessment of the problem, its causes, and its consequences. Taking a step back to assess the problem helps us not only to under-

---

11. Moore and Fung has recognized Dewey's notion of "calling a public into existence" as an important part of the work of value-seeking public managers who would like to contribute to social change (Benington and Moore 2011). Chapters 2 and 3 further elaborate on this notion in the context of public problem solving applied to the issue of value loss and bureaucratic dysfunction.

12. There is, of course, ongoing public, academic, and political debate about the proper role and size of government and government performance. For a discussion, see Zuurmond and de Jong (2010), Noordegraaf (2008), de Jong and Zuurmond (2010), and Howard (2011). In such debates, which typically are very general and ideological, "bureaucracy" and government at large often are subjected to wholesale attacks. However, my focus is not on the general question of whether bureaucracy is a good system but on particular situations in which bureaucracy fails—at least from the vantage point of some major stakeholders—to produce public value.

stand why bureaucratic dysfunction has been such a persistent problem in modern societies but also to develop a more sophisticated approach to dealing with the problem.

### Red Tape as an Entry Point

If the problem of bureaucratic dysfunction is so complex and elusive, where and how do we start to investigate it? There is probably no one best way to do it; as discussed in the following chapters, each approach has advantages and disadvantages. However, an actual encounter gone wrong between bureaucracies and clients provide us with a good point of departure. The issue of red tape, understood from the perspective of the client as excessive bureaucratic requirements, can serve as a point of entry into a more comprehensive study of underlying mechanisms and how they could be remedied. Red tape is commonly understood as excessive regulation, unreasonable application of rules, cumbersome procedures, burdensome administrative requirements, unintelligible bureaucratic behavior, or any combination of those elements. It is associated with the mindboggling experience of having to deal with dysfunctional bureaucratic organizations (Merton 1952; Kaufman 1977; Howard 1994; Barzelay and Armajani 1992; Bardach and Kagan 2002; Mashaw 1983; Bozeman 2000).

The encounter gone wrong can be described as a clinical opportunity to diagnose and remedy losses of value to the individual client and to the public at large. Our attention is directed first to the interaction between client and government (not to the public's opinion of how the bureaucracy is functioning), but we simultaneously set out to discover the public dimensions of bureaucratic dysfunction by unraveling the complexities of red tape. Red tape may be an entry point, but it is certainly not the end point of the inquiry.[13]

While red tape refers to symptoms—the problems on the surface as immediately experienced by clients—bureaucratic dysfunction refers

13. The three forms of inquiry into the phenomenon of bureaucratic dysfunction undertaken in this book—conceptual, theoretical, and empirical—have this in common: the effort to uncover the multiple ways in which bureaucratic dysfunction constitutes a loss of public value and simultaneously to identify ways to counteract the problem.

to underlying mechanisms that adversely affect the performance of government bureaucracies. Since this book aims to unravel the relationships between value lost to the client and value lost to the public, it focuses on cases of red tape that best exemplify the varied and contested nature of the problem. As discussed in chapter 2, cases that are both technically and politically complicated provide the best entry points for clinical research. These cases are characterized by lack of both information and consensus among those involved about the causes and consequences of the problematic situation. Since the very definition of the problem is at stake, these cases are most likely to provide a good entry point for learning what value is lost and how it could or should be regained. Also, complex cases—think "Buttle"—are least likely to get noticed and be solved by regular problem-solving mechanisms and institutions.

### Practical and Theoretical Challenges

Bureaucratic dysfunction is both a real-life problem and a matter of academic interest. While the academic literature on the subject is rich and diverse, it has not provided much actionable knowledge on how to resolve the problems of bureaucratic dysfunction in practice. The literature that does offer "solutions" typically disregards the varied nature of the phenomenon.[14] There is a plethora of one-size-fits-all remedies for dysfunctional bureaucracies that are prescribed without proper diagnosis—for example, pleas for deregulation, smaller government, more room for the professional, adopting private sector models for customer service, and so forth. Despite their merits, these approaches ignore an important dimension of the problem: "dysfunction" is a socially constructed problem with political implications, and value trade-offs are made in addressing it. As discussed earlier, claims about bureaucracy are made from a variety of vantage points, depending on the stakeholder's perspective and interests. What some people find dysfunctional may not be that disturbing to others. The challenge is to approach the problem rigorously while remaining sen-

---

14. Examples of generic "business" solutions that have inspired public managers and policymakers over the past two decades include Kaplan and Norton (1996, 2006), Hammer (2001), and George (2003).

sitive to the intricacies and complexities of its social and political context.

## Understanding Bureaucratic Dysfunction

Because bureaucratic dysfunction is a varied and slippery phenomenon, working toward a fuller understanding requires a multi-dimensional approach. To see the problem clearly, one has to synthesize insights from the abstract world of theory and literature and bring these directly to bear on the real-world interactions, experiences, and efforts of those on both sides of bureaucratic encounters.

### *Conceptual, Theoretical, and Empirical Explorations*

How can we effectively deal with bureaucratic dysfunction? That is the question that this book intends to answer, in three different ways. First, it examines the subject *conceptually*, using ideas borrowed from bureaucracy theory and public value theory. To that end, chapter 2 elaborates on the definition of the research problem and develops conceptual distinctions to guide the ensuing theoretical and empirical explorations. It also situates the study in the academic literature. Chapter 3 explores the manifestations of the phenomenon theoretically, by discussing and organizing the academic literature from a variety of disciplines to provide a more nuanced and multidimensional understanding of the problem. It also offers a meta-framework that helps shape a diagnostic approach to dealing with the problem in practice. Chapter 4 discusses the methodological implications for further inquiry into the conclusions in the literature review. It explains how I generated and used the empirical data, and it acknowledges the merits and limits of the methodology. Chapter 5 describes in detail the operating principles and techniques that the Kafka Brigade, a diagnostic team, used and how they were developed over time in the first four case studies, while chapter 6 presents a systematic, in-depth investigation of ten additional cases of red tape. In chapters 7 and 8 I revisit the question of how to deal with bureaucratic dysfunction and answer it on the basis of the results of the conceptual, theoretical, and empirical inquiries. I discuss under what conditions a clinical approach like the one pioneered by the Kafka Brigade is most likely to resolve the problem of bureaucratic dysfunction, and I present guiding principles for a generic *process* solution to the problem. I also suggest ways in which this solution and the principles that guide it can be further tested in practice.

## Academic Research and the Kafka Brigade

My clinical work and academic study have informed each other. This book is the result of a sustained effort to seek a deeper understanding of a problem that I care about through two separate but linked avenues of inquiry. Driven by worries about the limited scope and poor results of so-called reform agendas in the public sector and inspired by new ideas and emerging practices, I collaborated with colleagues to establish a research team with a novel problem-solving methodology, the Kafka Brigade (Docters van Leeuwen and others 2003; de Jong and others 2004). The activities of the Kafka Brigade, which was first launched in the Netherlands, evolved from the cooperative efforts of many individuals, including Arre Zuurmond and Joeri van den Steenhoven. The Kafka Brigade—named after the great novelist Franz Kafka, who wrote about the hope and despair of individuals living in the alienating landscape of modern bureaucracy—was an independent team focused on organizational learning across government silos and levels of management. The brigade investigated cases in which people had fallen through the cracks and did not know where to go—cases like that of Mr. Buttle, which, while not always as grim, often were more complex and never easy to solve. The cases were examples of how value was being lost, for the individual person, for the larger category of people in similar situations, and for society at large. A final similarity in the cases was that what mechanisms caused the problems and what could be done to solve them was unclear to the clients, professionals, managers, and policymakers involved.

Using a bottom-up diagnostic approach, collaborative inquiry, creative problem-solving techniques, and a pressure-cooker environment, the Kafka Brigade has tapped into the knowledge and experience of hundreds of public officials and public sector clients. As a result, the research of the brigade presented and examined in this book involved many instances of identifying, defining, diagnosing, and attempting to remedy bureaucratic dysfunction. The data set consists of documented cases of red tape researched by the Kafka Brigade, as well as documented reflections by academic and practitioners alike regarding the cases and methods. I treat the whole Kafka Brigade enterprise, from its inception to its consolidation, as a single case. This one case, of course, consists of many small cases. Methodologically, it is important to emphasize the distinction between the research presented in this book as an academic study and the research of the Kafka Brigade, conducted by a clinical team in the field. The former uses the Kafka Brigade experience to explore bureaucratic dysfunction as a phenomenon and to make recommendations about how to deal with it in general. The latter investigates real-life cases to diagnose and remedy particular instances of bureaucratic dysfunction in practice. Both kinds of research require methodological justification, which is provided in chapter 4.

Applying the principles and criteria for validity and quality discussed in chapter 4, I reflect on the Kafka Brigade's experimental approach to problem solving in order to develop an approach to help practitioners deal with red tape in particular instances. This approach is different from the one-size-fits-all substantive remedies in that it does not prescribe a cure but suggests a diagnostic protocol. While the Kafka Brigade has been successful in facilitating the diagnosis and treatment of bureaucratic dysfunction in some cases, it has failed in others. The report on the Kafka Brigade research is therefore not a story of successful solutions but an account of probing, learning while doing, and critically reflecting on factors that may lead to failure or success.

### Advancing Knowledge on Public Problem Solving

If the state of scientific knowledge about bureaucratic dysfunction or dealing with red tape in practice had allowed it, conducting a systematic, quantitative, empirical social science study would have been the preferred method of inquiry. It would have enabled me to make more universal claims about the nature of the problem and the relationships between causes and effects. If red tape and bureaucratic dysfunction were less contested, varied, and elusive phenomena, I would have been able to construct a dependent variable ("bureaucratic dysfunction") and test hypotheses about the effectiveness of specific interventions ("ways to deal with it") in terms of their effect on the dependent variable. I would then have been able to do empirical social science research, perhaps even randomized controlled trials, on the effectiveness of these interventions in solving the problem. If the research were broad and systematic enough, significant findings might have appeared that could lead to generalizable conclusions. One of the theoretical motivations for my research has been to contribute to the possibility of a quantitative empirical research method in the future.

As of yet, there is no integrated conceptual framework that captures the phenomenon of bureaucratic dysfunction and there are no comprehensive theories that provide testable hypotheses. Any attempt that pretends otherwise is likely to lead to flawed generalizations and imperfect conclusions. To stay true to the principles of social science, I chose plan B. If we value close attention to empirical facts and methodological rigor, we need to use an appropriate method of inquiry. This must be a method that engages with the issue and with those who are involved with the issue. While it may not produce results that are universal truths, it contributes to theory and practice.

In the concluding chapter I reflect on my chosen path. My dual goal, to improve knowledge as well as practice, has informed my research strategy and methodological choices. In retrospect, they may seem unnecessarily laborious, clumsy at times, and not particularly parsimonious. Still, compared with what the literature on the subject has yielded in terms of analysis and practical guidance, this path may not be the worst. Forty years ago Herbert Kaufman, who wrote one of the first books that focused specifically on bureaucratic dysfunction, advised: "What we need is a detached clinical approach rather than heated attacks, the delicate wielding of the scalpel rather than furious flailing about with a meat ax" (Kaufman 1977). This book aims to meet that need.

# 2

# Foundational Concepts

*All life is problem solving.*
KARL POPPER, *All Life Is Problem Solving*, 1991, p. 99

While bureaucratic dysfunction is a fascinating phenomenon in its own right, it is not my main concern. The larger issue at stake is the loss of value, both to the individual and to the public at large. As discussed in the previous chapter, it is easy to focus on one set of symptoms or another but quite challenging and even disorienting to diagnose the problem thoroughly, systematically, and comprehensively. For that, we need a strong set of concepts to serve as a foundation on which to build an understanding of the general problem in its various manifestations and to help describe and examine the problem in specific, concrete situations. Developing this set of concepts is the purpose of this chapter.

I also further discuss a key variable in the central research question: the unspecified "we" in "How can we deal effectively with bureaucratic dysfunction?" Who is the agent or actor most responsible for or capable of taking on the task of dealing with bureaucratic dysfunction? If we come up with an answer to the question of how the problem can be dealt with effectively, then who should take action? A more structural version of that question is this: To what extent is the existing governmental problem-solving infrastructure capable of detecting, diagnosing, and remedying dysfunction? How well can it acknowledge and reconcile multiple vantage points and ways to assess the problem, and deal with conflicting interests?

Finally, I discuss how certain cases of red tape can be used as a point of entry into investigating bureaucratic dysfunction and its consequences. That leads to an operational definition of the term "bureaucratic dysfunction," building on the ideas already developed. This definition, applied to the variety of encounters that people have with government, helps us determine where and how encounters might go wrong. By conceptualizing the elusive phenomenon of bureaucratic dysfunction, proposing a concrete point of entry into its study, and suggesting next steps in the process of understanding the problem in real-life situations, this chapter provides the analytical foundation for the rest of the book.

## Situating the Research in Two Conceptual Traditions

The study presented in this book is practice-oriented. The goal is to inform and promote clinical research in the real world of social problem solving. As a contribution to the academic literature, while recognizing insights into bureaucratic dysfunction from a wide variety of perspectives, this book primarily refers to *bureaucratic theory*, which focuses on organizations and institutional structures, and *strategic public management*, which takes senior public managers and their interactions with those organizations and structures as its primary unit of analysis. In other words, the former focuses on organizational structures, the latter on human agency within those structures. To define bureaucratic dysfunction—which has one foot planted firmly in each of these realms of study—in a way that could light a path to remedial action, I looked to the conceptual frameworks developed in these two traditions.

### *The Value of Bureaucracy*

Since Max Weber's *Wirtschaft und Gesellschaft* (*Economy and Society*), bureaucratic theory has helped us understand the ubiquitous form of organization we have come to call "bureaucracy" (Weber 1922; Albrow 1970). Though Weber never intended to endorse bureaucracy—he merely offered analytical tools for studying it empirically and interpreting it as a cultural phenomenon in the context of modern society—the very model of bureaucracy has been subjected to wholesale attack (Osborne and Gaebler 1992; Howard 1994; Grumet 2001). It has also been praised and defended (Du Gay 2000, 2005; Goodsell 2004). However, we do not have to choose sides; most organizations that we work for or deal with every day are bureaucracies. They are bureaucracies in the sense that they fit the profile that Weber first sketched: an organization characterized by regulated continuity, standardized procedures, and formalized documentation, and in which expert workers—subjected to a hierarchical authority structure—separate their private interests and beliefs from their public function in order to fulfill their specialized tasks in a rational and efficient manner (Gerth and Mills 1946).[1] Of course, Weber's model is a pure model, an *Idealtyp* (ideal type).[2] Few organizations actually fully match the profile, though most aspire to come close. For it is not so much the exact design of the bureaucratic organization that is universally appreciated and applied as it is the underlying values. Ultimately, the principles of formalization, standardization, specialization, and so forth are rooted in values that most people would subscribe to: rational decisionmaking, integrity, effectiveness, efficiency, transparency, accountability, and fairness (Peters 2003, p. 113).[3]

## A System of Rules or a System of Values?

Frequently, however, people's encounters with bureaucracy appear to be shaped more by the rigid application of rules and principles than by the underlying values (de Jong 2011). The unwillingness to make an exception for a client in need seems "unfair," the endless paperwork

---

1. Chapter 3 discusses Weber's theory of bureaucracy in more detail.

2. *Idealtyp* is the German term used by Weber for the analytical description of a phenomenon in its most essential form. It should not be confused with "ideal" in the sense of the purest form or the best form and therefore something that should necessarily be aspired to.

3. That is to say, people would subscribe to these values from John Rawls's "veil of ignorance" perspective: if they knew that they would personally benefit from the absence of these values, principles, and rules, they might favor an alternative to bureaucracy, such as clientelism. The Rawlsian thought experiment presupposes that just institutions can be designed purely and honestly only if people do not take into account their own private interest (Rawls and Kelly 2001).

to confirm eligibility for benefits seems "inefficient," and the perceived randomness and shallowness of regulatory inspections seem "ineffective." Such experiences and perceptions have given bureaucracy a bad name (Herzfeld 1992). For many people living in modern welfare states, "bureaucracy" has become synonymous with its dysfunctional version. (Private sector bureaucracies can be equally dysfunctional, but at least one can usually switch providers.) But instead of proposing that organizations become more bureaucratic, in the Weberian sense of the term, people (including politicians and academics) dismiss bureaucracy altogether. That seems to risk throwing the baby out with the bathwater. A more nuanced take on the issue would be to acknowledge that bureaucracy, as a form of organization and the dominant model for government action, has both merits and limits. When bureaucracies cease to uphold the fundamental values on which they were founded, they become dysfunctional.[4] Since public support for bureaucracy as a suitable model for facilitating governmental administration depends on public support for its underlying values rather than on support for its externalities (for example, paperwork, wait times, complicated procedures), it is important to deal with dysfunction.

As the late Dutch professor of accounting and management control in the public sector Caren van Egten writes, "The growth of government, in combination with the modernization of society, has increased the complexity of the work that government bureaucracies are doing" (Van Egten 2011, pp. 13–14). While there is no shortage of sweeping ideas as to how government should reinvent, reshape, or redirect its bureaucracies in the future, little attention is given to the nitty-gritty details of problem solving in the present. This book's contribution to bureaucratic theory is the proposal of conceptual frameworks for interpreting bureaucratic dysfunction in general and heuristic frameworks for diagnosing it in particular instances. The hope is to improve understanding of the conditions under which bureaucracies may be able to address their own dysfunction (or allow it to be addressed) and to lay out an agenda for further clinical research.

---

4. In the previous chapter, I observed that whereas a single error or flaw does not constitute dysfunction, a persistent pattern of error that does not get addressed does constitute dysfunction. The dimension of violation of bureaucratic values that is discussed here further specifies the nature of the errors and flaws.

## The Challenge of Strategic Management

Bureaucracies are institutional structures that govern social order, human behavior, and professional cooperation. But they cannot think, feel, or learn by themselves; that is the work of human beings (Argyris and Schön 1974; Argyris 2010). When it comes to problem solving in action, we need to look at agency, not just at agencies. If insights about institutional structures cannot be combined with an understanding of how people work within or around those structures, there is no hope of producing actionable knowledge. The field of strategic public management recognizes that the interaction of a public organization with its environment routinely produces dilemmas for public managers (Mulgan 2009). As Mark Moore argues in *Creating Public Value* (1995), managers can be understood as agents of change who seek to create public value by strategically aligning the operational capacity at their disposal, the authorizing environment they rely on for legitimacy and support, and the task they see in front of them (their value-creating goal). Moore's notions of legitimacy and support, operational capacity, and public value help map the landscape for public managers who seek to make positive change. There is political work to do (obtaining legitimacy and support from the authorizing environment); there is a managerial job to do (creating operational capacity both within and outside the organization); and there is an entrepreneurial, imaginative, and philosophical dimension to the job (envisioning public value). The major challenge facing an agent of change is to reimagine the very notion of what is permissible, doable, and valuable.

## Public Managers as Value-Seeking Explorers

Over the past two decades, Moore's approach has triggered much debate among academics and practitioners, especially in the United States, Australia, the United Kingdom, and the Netherlands (Benington and Moore 2011). One of the most important contributions of *Creating Public Value* to the long tradition of scholarship on executive leadership and managerial responsibility from Woodrow Wilson to James Q. Wilson was the introduction of "public value" as a guiding if ambiguous concept for the entrepreneurial, imaginative, and value-seeking public manager. Public value does not equal the formal job description or defined performance metrics of a public manager, nor does it replace them. The public value approach emphasizes the roles and responsibilities of public managers by reimagining their task and developing analytical tools that help them understand and shape their efforts to create value. This approach has informed an increasing amount of scholarly work on public entrepreneurship (Cels et al. 2012), network management (Goldsmith and Kettle 2009; Minderman 2010), social change (Ganz 2009), innovation and improvement (Hartley 2008), law enforcement and control tasks (Sparrow 1994, 2000, 2008), and public service delivery (Kruiter and others 2008; Alford 2009). What most of those studies have in common is that they adapt or fine-tune the conceptual framework that Moore initially developed from his interactions with participants in executive education programs at Harvard University's Kennedy School of Government. An important note is that "public manager" is very broadly defined, both in Moore's work and in much of the work that followed. A public manager is defined by the nature of his or her work, not by the legal status of the employer. In other words, what makes a person a public manager is the focus on creating public value, whether in the private sector, the nonprofit sector, or—naturally, but not automatically— in the public sector.

While Moore's work has resonated well among public managers interested in innovation in operations and cross-boundary collaboration, one of its more powerful messages is more political in nature: creating public value sometimes requires public managers to help their authorizing environment (all those actors in a position to provide legitimacy and support for their enterprise) articulate a public value proposition. That alone is a departure from the conventional view of public management, in which civil servants simply carry out the mandates they have been given. But while the notion of public managers being involved in defining public value better reflects reality, it also poses a dilemma: how far can or should a public manager go in shaping the deliberative process? Moore suggests that managers have a duty as explorers: they should push the limits in order to make government more responsive, more effective, and more accountable (Moore 1995). In *Creating Public Value,* that responsibility is still primarily a diagnostic one: managers should find what Weber calls in *Politik als Beruf* "passion"—not a heightened emotional state but rather "the ability to let realities work upon [the politician, or in this case the manager] with inner concentration and calmness" (Weber [1919] 2004), p. 21). In other words, to get the right diagnosis, managers must treat the realities of the dilemmas—or strategic choices—they face with the utmost care and attention. In Benington and Moore (2011), a piece reflecting on twenty years of debate on the concept of public value, the authors highlight a much bolder implication of the responsibilities of value creators:

> The single most important contribution of public value theory in the future may be its potential to redirect attention to the critical role that democratic politics and public management can play in helping to shape a sense of community and public purpose. . . . The core question of public value theory is how . . . a public can be brought into existence—a public that can articulate the value it wants to produce through the assets it has turned over to its government.

Building on John Dewey's classic *The Public and Its Problems* (1954), Benington and Moore argue that a central task of public leadership and management is to "call into existence a public that can understand and act on its own best interests." That leaves little doubt about how political the nature of strategic public management really is—and, the authors argue, should be. The moral and practical imperative at the heart of public value theory is the appeal to *anyone* to engage and take responsibility for an inclusive process of value articulation, production, and evaluation. In that sense, public value theory is not only radically different from the classic Wilsonian formulation of the separation of politics and administration, it is also radically different from what is sometimes referred to as the New Public Management approach that appeared in the late 1980s. Conventional public administration holds that politicians formulate goals and administrators execute them (Shafritz and Hyde 1992). New public management advocates entrepreneurship among public managers, but managerial entrepreneurship, not political entrepreneurship. While managerial innovation is encouraged, political mobilization is virtually absent. Moore's contribution to the evolution of public management theory first of all has been to correct the flawed conception of public management as an apolitical realm. Dismissing values and interests is empirically wrong, and it is normatively and practically undesirable. If one really wants to understand and improve public management, Moore maintains, it is better to acknowledge and embrace the presence of politics and play a positive role in making politics more inclusive, responsive, transparent, and accountable—in other words, more democratic.

This book engages with the public value school of strategic management in government in three different ways: first, by approaching bureaucratic dysfunction from the perspective of its consequences for public value (a loss of value for the individual public sector client is a potential loss of value to the public as well); second, by examining and exploring the role of individual agents of change in dealing with bureaucratic dysfunction instead of focusing on policy or institutions alone; and third, by exploring the practical challenge of organizing forums in which values and interests can be discussed and drawing lessons for public managers through empirical research. This book proposes a process-based approach to dealing with bureaucratic dysfunction. This approach focuses on mobilizing the capacity of policymakers, managers, professionals, and public sector clients to articulate the public's interests, detect the loss of public value, diagnose the problem, and act on a reimagined sense of public purpose. It is a decidedly value-driven, democratic approach to dealing with bureaucratic dysfunction rather than a tool-driven, technocratic approach.

## Agents of Change in Bureaucratic Environments

Understanding bureaucratic dysfunction enables public managers in the broad sense of the term to do something about it. There are different ways to approach the subject. Bureaucratic dysfunction is an encompassing term that may refer to different kinds of problems, including policy failure, mismanagement of agencies, and corruption.[5]

5. Recent studies of relevance to the creation of public value, though conducted at a different level of analysis, include Engbersen (2009), Schuck and Zeckhauser (2006), Klievink (2011), and Weick and Sutcliffe (2007). Studies with a similar focus on problem solving by change agents in organizational systems but without a focus on public value per se include Kahane (2004, 2010), Bazerman and Tenbrunsel (2011), Buchanan and Badham (1999), and Gause and Weinberg (1990). Cels, de Jong, and Nauta published a study in 2012 about agents of change from a public value perspective.

There is no compelling objective criterion for determining the best way to approach bureaucratic dysfunction or where to begin. I choose to approach the problem from the perspective of those whom bureaucracies are supposed to serve: people who encounter bureaucracies as public sector clients. Even though public sector clients are not a proxy for "the public," they seem an attractive starting point. Though the public at large is diffuse and often inarticulate, the public sector client is a tangible and researchable individual. Moreover, the public sector client is a meaningful subject not only as a member of the public who can evaluate the quality of public services offered or the experience of public duties imposed but also as a co-producer of public value (Sparrow 2000; Alford 2009). Since it is clients' experiences and encounters with the government that reveal both the quality and the utility of the policies and actions that create dysfunction, they seem to constitute a suitable subject for unraveling dysfunctional practices and figuring out how to cope with them. As reflected in the problem definition (How can *we* deal effectively with bureaucratic dysfunction?), the effort to produce *actionable* knowledge about bureaucratic dysfunction presupposes a potential agent of change who can take responsibility for solving the problem. Who is meant by "we"? The entity most responsible, most capable, or best positioned to take on the task of dealing with the problem is not yet known—at least, the question cannot be answered in general until we better understand the nature of the problem and the knowledge and skills required to deal with it effectively. That is exactly why the intersection of bureaucratic theory and public value theory is conceptually fruitful: it acknowledges the particularities of bureaucratic organizations without preconceiving or presupposing an actor or institution with primary responsibility.

## Locating Responsibility and Capacity for Problem Solving

To see what actors in society are *currently* concerned with or responsible for identifying and screening problems of bureaucratic dysfunction, designating them for further diagnosis, and initiating remedial action, we will take a quick look at the institutions that can be found in most developed democracies under the rule of law.

*Ombudsmen, Elected Representatives, Auditors, and Counselors*

One might immediately think of ombudsmen and other mechanisms for handling concerns of citizens as public sector clients. There are a variety of institutionalized channels for addressing individual grievances, the best of which also make the effort to analyze patterns and advise governments on how to improve encounters with citizens (Ziegenfuss and O'Rourke 2011). While some ombudsmen are more assertive than others, their mandate rarely allows them to address matters of interorganizational conflict, policy design, or statecraft.[6] In some countries, most notably the United States, elected officials play an important role in helping people navigate the system, sort their problems, and mediate conflict with government agencies. Case workers in the offices of members of Congress are dedicated to "constituent services," using the formal and informal authority of elected representatives to cut through red tape and expedite problem solving for victims of bureaucratic dysfunction. They typically focus on resolving individual problems without addressing the root causes or structural mechanisms that resulted in the undesired outcomes for individual constituents (Lieber 2012; Petersen 2014). Other institutions, such as high-level advisory councils to national governments, are charged with providing expert advice on policy formulation and institutional design. These institutions fulfill an important role with respect to policymaking in a democratic state under the rule of law. However, they are not especially inclined to pay attention to the details of policy execution or the evaluation of outcomes from the perspective of public sector clients. Finally, one might point to audit institutions, like the Government Accountability Office in the United States, the former Audit Commission in the United Kingdom, and the Court of Audit in the Netherlands. These institutions typically focus on evaluating the government's performance. They scrutinize dysfunctional patterns of policy implementation and help the national legislature hold the executive branch accountable. Even though some supreme audit institutions have shifted their attention to investigating the links between govern-

6. For example, former Dutch national ombudsman Alex Brenninkmeijer has published reports that offer firm critiques as well as specific recommendations regarding the roles and responsibilities of policymakers, government ministers, and public managers (De Nationale Ombudsman 2007, 2008).

ment efforts and policy outcomes,[7] their core business is auditing. Their main focus is on the organization and the extent to which the organization has executed public policy effectively, efficiently, and in accordance with administrative law and accounting standards. Their primary goal is not to address problems in order to solve them.

Such institutions, although focused primarily on overseeing and advising the executive branch, can increasingly be found at many levels of government and in all functional areas. They are the official watchdogs of modern governments, having a constitutional mandate to investigate and report. However, they typically are limited by that mandate and rarely are able to intervene directly in a binding way to structurally address problems. Most ombudsmen and courts of audit have the neutrality and the stature of, say, the judiciary, but they lack real countervailing powers.

So, if the watchdogs lack the focus or the power to engage in comprehensive problem solving, should governments themselves be held responsible for doing so? Can they solve the problem of bureaucratic dysfunction? Have they? As government reform agendas around the world have demonstrated, most explicit government-initiated efforts to fix the problem *generically* (that is, by way of a one-size-fits-all solution) have not been very successful, and scholars have long suggested that hopes for generically solving the problem of bureaucratic dysfunction should be given up (Merton 1952; Kaufman 1977; Du Gay 2000, 2005; Raad voor Maatschappelijke Ontwikkeling 2008). Studies from New Zealand and the United Kingdom have found that the public management reforms of the 1980s and 1990s, which focused on privatization and customer choice, created new problems. Increased fragmentation of responsibility for public services and a general lack of accountability resulted in widespread discontent with the lack of progress in improving government performance (Gregory 2003, p. 41; Beecham 2006). On the basis of an in-depth analysis of six "wicked social problems" in the Netherlands, Maarten Arentsen and Willem Trommel concluded that failure to make progress on solving social problems has become a problem in itself for governments

---

7. The Dutch Court of Audit under President Saskia Stuiveling has initiated a strategic agenda focused on developing methods to include citizen experiences as indicators of policy outcomes (Algemene Rekenkamer 2010).

and society (Arentsen and Trommel 2005). According to some observers, bureaucratic dysfunction manifests itself in governments' unsuccessful attempts to exert control over individual lives and broad social conditions (Engbersen 2009; Schuck and Zeckhauser 2006). We may conclude, then, that failure to solve social problems is not a matter of policy failure, overregulation, underperforming organizations, flawed institutional design, or inadequate oversight; it is a matter of any or all of those factors. Bureaucratic dysfunction manifests itself in a variety of ways and thus eludes the scope of institutional mechanisms for problem identification and problem solving.

### Problem-Solving Institutions versus Problem-Solving Processes

Does the failure of institutional mechanisms for identifying and solving problems mean that it is impossible to design a foolproof system for problem solving? Perhaps. Does it mean that we as a society cannot get better at public problem solving? Not necessarily. If established *institutions* fall short in dealing with bureaucratic dysfunction, it seems important, first of all, to better understand what the *process* of dealing with bureaucratic dysfunction actually entails. If we can understand the nature of the phenomenon that we call "bureaucratic dysfunction," we can begin to imagine what a process for dealing with it would look like. Under what circumstances and through which institutions or agents can we increase the effectiveness of this process? When the losses register for both individual clients and the public at large, and (for both clients and publics) in terms of both justice and welfare, the responsibility for improving the process of comprehensive problem solving lies not necessarily with institution A, B, or C—or even with the government as a whole—but with all of us as members of bureaucratic systems, sharing in their benefits and burdens and involved in the processes that produce or reduce dysfunction from a wide variety of social positions. That is why the question at the center of this study is, again, *How can WE effectively deal with bureaucratic dysfunction?*

## Identifying the Consequences: Value Losses to Client and Public

People encounter the state in many different ways and in many different places. As *clients*, they encounter government bureaucracies in government offices and public institutions such as schools and hospitals, on the streets, in their homes, and online. Encounters typically have specific goals, and the client or the state or both have an interest in doing business with each other. As *citizens*, people encounter the state in different kinds of ways (see figure 2-1). Voters encounter the state at the polling station, where it enables them to exercise a democratic right. Randomly selected lay jurors in the United States encounter the state when they are summoned for jury duty because they are expected to share the social responsibility of exercising impartial judgment. Citizens may also participate in public decision-making processes, voicing their concerns and providing opinions on plans for the use of land or other public resources. Finally, people may answer a call of the state to voluntarily contribute to public purposes in one way or another, by recycling their trash or acting as teachers' helpers in their children's public school classrooms in a public-spirited way.

Such citizen encounters are quite different from the bureaucratic service and obligation encounters of public sector clients in the sense that neither the encounters nor the people nor the state have a specific purpose that relates to the specific individual in question. Elections are about determining the aggregate preferences of the electorate; jury duty is about getting a certain number of qualified people to exercise judgment on behalf of the larger public; participation in public deliberation forums and voluntary public-spirited actions are about acting on one's own to shape public policies or contribute to the public good. In other words, in the realm of services and obligations, people encounter the state as clients in a specific functional relationship. In the realm of participation in a democratic society under the rule of law, people encounter the state as *citizens*, driven by a desire or obligation (moral or constitutional) to participate not on behalf of their own interests alone but on behalf of the public of which they are a member. These two realms are governed by different principles, rules, customs, expectations, and attitudes.

Figure 2-1. **Roles and Responsibilities of People and the State and Examples of How They Intersect**

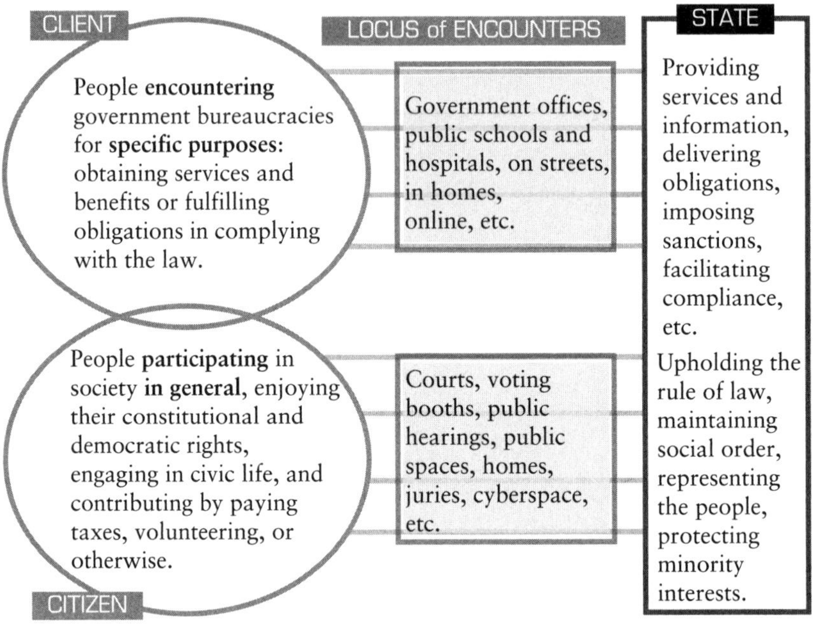

There are, however, situations in which people encounter the state in their citizen and client roles simultaneously. When they file their tax returns, for example, they encounter the tax authority principally in the role of client (obligatee). It is an administrative transaction that can be more or less cumbersome and more or less pleasant, but it is always functional and tied to the tax status of a specific individual. At the same time, the obligation to pay taxes is of a different order than most other obligations, such as getting a driver's license before driving a car on public roadways, complying with environmental laws, or getting a business license. Paying taxes makes the existence of a working state possible. Therefore, while the transaction between tax-payer and government bears a resemblance to many other client en-counters, the transaction brings out the role of citizen as well. Especially in countries where tax law is based on the honor system, each indi-vidual client has to decide how much to report or deduct. Besides the obvious risk of noncompliance with state obligations, there is a civic consideration: as a citizen, what is the right thing to do?

The overlap between the roles (or capacities) of client and citizen may seem small, and the boundaries are not necessarily very sharp. After all, even as they play one role, people do not necessarily completely disregard their other roles. Many approaches to improving government performance, especially those labeled new public management, have eliminated the notion of citizenship (in the sense described above) from the realm of services and obligations. In its place is a conception of public management informed by a purely functional transactional model borrowed from the private sector. At the same time, much literature on democratic theory has neglected the fact that people evaluate their government and develop ideas about what is just, fair, and right through their functional encounters with the state as clients.

It seems possible that the tension between the roles of clients and those of citizens vis-à-vis the roles and responsibilities of the state could be *productive tension*. This potential is of crucial importance to the subject of bureaucratic dysfunction and red tape. As I noted earlier, if the state fails to perform, evaluative claims about state performance are made from multiple perspectives, even by the same people. People can reflect on the government from the client perspective and from the citizen perspective at the same time. To use the example of paying taxes, as a client one might dread paying a particular tax bill, but as a citizen one might agree with the tax code. Or one might fully support strict enforcement of speed limits, until one is stopped for speeding by the police. That is not to say that people always or necessarily have double standards but that we simply think about public value in different ways in different situations and view it from multiple perspectives, both as members of the public and as individuals. The key to understanding why the notion of bureaucratic dysfunction is so elusive is acknowledging that we are often not very clear or explicit about what vantage point we are speaking from when we evaluate government performance. To get a better grip on the problem, it seems important to distinguish these perspectives and identify evaluative criteria with respect to what the state does or does not do that are most relevant to people in their different roles.

### The Client Perspective

Evaluative claims about red tape are typically made from the perspective of those on the receiving end of encounters: public sector clients. In their immediate encounter with red tape, they develop feelings and opinions about it and attach meanings to it (Herzfeld 1992). Only when one encounters an organization as a client does one become aware of the full extent of the administrative burdens that red tape puts on people. "Why does it have to take so long?" "Why so much paperwork?" "Why do I have to answer these questions all over again?" Red tape may sometimes replace human judgment and action. When rules are applied in a cold and rigid way, without regard for individual cases or specific contexts, they can be demoralizing. On the other hand, if administrative decisions are completely left to individuals, one can expect a certain amount of dysfunction to arise through corruption, incompetence, bias, or human error of many kinds (Merton 1940, p. 101; Lipsky 1980; Rose-Ackerman 1999; OECD 2010).

A discontented client reasons that the bureaucracy has failed her, which is undesirable from her personal perspective. She may have lost time, money, benefits, or opportunities, or suffered other material losses. We call this the *welfare loss* to the client. But the welfare loss is not the only loss at stake. The client may also have suffered in immaterial ways: one can imagine all kinds of situations in which a person feels maltreated, discriminated against, humiliated, insulted. We may call that the *justice loss* to the client. From the perspective of the client, these losses are not only undesirable but also often incomprehensible.

If bureaucracy is understood as a rational and efficient form of organization, as described by Max Weber (Gerth and Mills 1946), red tape problems are hard to reconcile with a well-functioning bureaucracy. This logic does not recognize, however, that red tape may actually serve a goal. The goal may not be clear, understood, or accepted by the client, but it is nevertheless an intentional use of red tape. For example, rigorous checks on eligibility for services may be desirable to prevent fraud and to increase accountability. Not all red tape is necessarily dysfunctional. And the opposite also is true: the absence of red tape does not necessarily imply that the organization is creating more net value for the public. For example, if there are too few checks on eligibility for services, fraud may be encouraged, and if an organization's performance is not monitored, resources may be wasted.

Every government bureaucracy dealing with clients makes trade-offs: how can encounters with clients be made easier while ensuring accountability? Or conversely, how can accountability be maximized while keeping encounters easy for clients? From a client's perspective, reducing red tape is of more immediate interest than maximizing accountability. As a citizen or taxpayer, a person might be interested in maximizing accountability, but as a client, a person typically focuses on maximizing utility and minimizing transaction costs.

Many recent public sector reform initiatives have centered on making service delivery more customer-focused, user-friendly, and so forth. The client perspective on government bureaucracy has become an important factor in public management (Hood 1991, p. 3; Pollitt and Bouckaert 2000; Hoogwout 2010).[8] This approach, mentioned earlier in this chapter, has been labeled "new public management" or "reinventing government." Its proponents have promoted a complete indictment of red tape, mainly because it does not serve the interests of public sector clients (Osborne and Gaebler 1992; Barzelay and Armajani 1992). In the customer-focused paradigm, far more attention has been paid to welfare losses than to justice losses to clients. Many governments have developed and implemented policies to reduce administrative burdens, using indicators of the average amount of money and time lost by clients as a result of red tape. Organizations like the Organization for Economic Cooperation and Development and the World Bank have developed measuring and monitoring mechanisms that help move such policies forward (OECD 2007, 2010; World Bank 2009).

### The Public Perspective

As I noted in chapter 1, evaluative claims about red tape can also be made from a *public* perspective. This perspective is more nuanced, partly because there are many different ways to define what "the

---

8. Only recently has more attention been paid to other values, interests, and capacities that public sector clients might represent. John Alford, for example, has argued that the client perspective on public services is no longer that of a recipient; public sector clients have become increasingly involved in co-producing government services, such as welfare-to-work programs, heath care policy, and public education. That means that values other than maximizing utility and minimizing transaction costs might come into play (Alford 2009).

public" is and what it wants (Stone 2008; Sen 1992, 1999; von Hayek 1994; Roemer 1996, 1998; Walzer 1983, 2004). The public is not simply the sum of all people; it is a collection of people who take on many different roles vis-à-vis the state and each other. Sometimes they are united on and articulate about certain interests, but most of the time they are not. People may find contradictions in their own set of beliefs, perceived interests, and preferences. Therefore, it would be a conceptual mistake to define "the public" as the aggregate of public sector clients. That, however, is roughly the claim that new public management has made to reduce bureaucracy in the public interest: reducing red tape is in the public interest because each client will benefit individually and all clients will benefit as a whole.[9]

Another way to define a public perspective on red tape would be to focus on the value of accountability, checks, and balances (Behn 2001). An evaluative claim made from that perspective would focus on the public's interest in minimizing fraud, abuse, corruption, free-riding, and so forth. This idea of "the public" finds its roots in social contract theory, especially in the Hobbesian view of the role of government in society: people do not trust each other and cannot be trusted with common properties and resources; therefore government fulfills the role of the sovereign force that disciplines society on behalf of the collective. Another public perspective might evaluate red tape in terms of its capacity to protect the collective's resources, such as taxpayer money and public goods, and make sure that they are distributed or allocated appropriately and responsibly. Red tape in this view is a defense against cheats and frauds; therefore, it is not necessarily a bad thing. However, the concept of accountability in this view of the public interest is defined very narrowly. It emphasizes accountability for public expenditures—for example, the use of fiscal resources to pro-

9. This depiction of new public management's tenets might be slightly exaggerated. However, David Osborne and Ted Gaebler, who have almost become synonymous with the movement, write in their classic *Reinventing Government* about "the bankruptcy of bureaucracy" on the basis of the claim that it has not been able to serve clients in a cost-effective way (Osborne and Gaebler 1992). The problem with this line of reasoning is that it does not differentiate between the collective of public sector clients and the collective of people who benefit from public services and the enforcement of regulations because they enjoy the social outcomes of these government interventions. Conflating the two categories makes it very hard, if not impossible, to understand why problems occur and persist.

vide services. It places government in the role of gatekeeper and book-keeper and deemphasizes the relevance of the social outcomes that public expenditures are supposed to ensure. What is lacking from this view is the notion of accountability for *performance*: governments are expected not only to manage the public's money responsibly by carrying out policies and procedures to the letter but also to achieve the desired results that animated the design of the policies and procedures. In other words, a public perspective on red tape can never be defined by a focus on accountability for public expenditures alone. That would limit our ability to understand why bureaucracies are perceived to be dysfunctional. After all, a discussion of means without a clear sense of ends is bound to be confused. Nevertheless, this accountability perspective does play a role in the public evaluation of red tape.

Yet another way to think about what a public perspective on red tape might entail builds on the idea of collective action,[10] by which I mean the pursuit of social goals by groups of people. In that view government is essentially a mechanism for producing social outcomes that societies collectively decide are worth investing in. These outcomes include public goods—from which everybody benefits and no one can be excluded—such as national security and clean air. Two other forms of collective action that involve government are the redistribution of wealth through taxation and the administration of justice through the criminal justice system. In developed societies, the most visible and tangible form in which government acts on behalf of the public is through the provision of public services, such as education, social security, affordable housing, and health care. Government, on behalf of the public, provides a variety of services that benefit individuals. It does so because the public, through democratic elections, has authorized the government to do so because it believes that the government can provide those services best or because it fears that if the government does not provide them no one will, an outcome that would be undesirable.

---

10. There are multiple definitions of "collective action" in the social sciences, referring to various dimensions of the phenomenon or disciplinary contexts: economics, sociology, philosophy, and political science. I do not go into specific definitions here because my purpose is to apply the term in my own context and develop a specific idea about what a public perspective on red tape might mean.

The delivery of public services almost always involves encounters between the government bureaucracy and public sector clients. Individuals reap specific individual benefits from the existence of a public service. As discussed, these individuals typically evaluate their encounters with the government from their personal perspective. Because public sector clients are the primary and direct beneficiaries of a public service, they experience the most immediate impact of bureaucratic dysfunction and red tape. As instruments of collective action, government bureaucracies also serve the public. Through client encounters, they produce social outcomes on behalf of the public at large. If a child goes to a public school, he or she benefits from public services directly, but the public at large also expects to benefit from that investment, if indirectly, by paying to increase the employability of graduates, improve the social behavior of citizens, and promote economic growth through innovation and entrepreneurship. To that end, governments have created public school systems to educate students. If the delivery system does not work optimally, it fails both the individual client and the invested public.

That is where the public perspective on red tape becomes more interesting and more intricate. Society invests in social services such as unemployment benefits because society believes that it serves a social goal—for example, avoiding poverty, reinforcing social solidarity, or controlling economic damage. If the encounters between the welfare client and the government bureaucracy are characterized by a lot of red tape, it has an immediate impact on the client, who will probably evaluate red tape negatively. But how should society evaluate red tape from a public perspective? Should people imagine that they too could one day become a welfare client and therefore sympathize with the affected client? Should they be glad that the system does not make it too easy for welfare clients to access public resources? Or should people consider what social outcomes the employment benefits program is supposed to improve?

## The Difficulty in Defining the Public Perspective

The myriad perspectives composing a public make developing a comprehensive, well-balanced, and articulate public perspective on red tape extremely difficult. We can measure client satisfaction, and we can gauge public opinion about accountability and fraud control. However, it seems very difficult to bring these perspectives together while simultaneously introducing the issue of improving social outcomes through public service encounters into the equation.

We may take as an example the government's task of licensing restaurants. If "the public" favors maximal client satisfaction, it would want to reduce red tape in the licensing process as much as possible. However, the public is also wary of entrepreneurs who do not comply with tax laws or who violate public health and safety regulations, so it does not want to make it too easy for entrepreneurs to get a license. Because the public also has a stake in economic growth, urban development, job creation, and other spinoffs of private entrepreneurship, the government licensing system also functions as a gatekeeper that excludes unfit businesses even as it enables business development. From this perspective, the public wants to have the ideal amount of red tape: not so much that it would limit the positive effects of commercial enterprise but enough to prevent the negative effects.

The ambiguity inherent in the public perspective on red tape is exactly the reason why it is so important to address the issue. If we want to better understand red tape in order to minimize its dysfunctional elements, we need to acknowledge the ambivalence of the public's preferences and positions. More important, we need to develop a way to assess the loss of value to the public because of red tape. Like the client perspective, the public perspective has a material component and an immaterial component. Material losses include wasted tax money spent on ineffective and inefficient government operations as well as missed opportunities to improve social outcomes and generate economic growth. Immaterial losses—losses measured in terms of justice and fairness—could entail the exclusion of certain demographics from public services or systemic corruption. It is clear that in either dimension, calculating lost value would require more than simple math.

### Summary: Losses in Welfare and Justice at Individual and Collective Levels

Though red tape is typically defined and evaluated from the perspective of a client who claims to suffer a loss of welfare, a loss of justice, or

Table 2-1. **Perspectives on the Loss of Value Caused by Red Tape**

| Perspective →  ↓ | Welfare (Material goods) | Justice (Immaterial goods) |
|---|---|---|
| **Private** (People as clients) | Loss of: Time, money, entitlements, and opportunities | Loss of: Rights, human dignity, and hope |
| **Public** (People as citizens) | Loss of: Effectiveness and efficiency of public services | Loss of: Equity and social equality |

both, it is also possible to evaluate red tape from a public perspective. The public may also suffer a loss of value as a result of red tape (as fiscally responsible taxpayers, as voters, and as supporters of certain kinds of collective action needed to achieve social outcomes). However, that perspective is less straightforward. In all of those capacities, the public may suffer material or immaterial losses from red tape. The combination of the public and client perspectives of red tape leads to the matrix shown in table 2-1, which supports the following propositions:[11]

- It is hard to define red tape in objective terms because ultimately it is a normative concept that carries a pejorative connotation.
- At the same time, red tape is a real phenomenon with real impacts in practice, and it can cause a loss of value in numerous ways to many different people.
- The better we get at dissecting the red tape conundrum, the better we can assess what values are being lost, protected, or created, and for whom.

11. These two perspectives are not intended to be exhaustive: there are others, such as those of the professional meeting clients at the service end of the organization, the regulator, the pressure group, and so forth. The evaluative perspectives are also arbitrary to some extent; however, for the purposes of this study (contributions to bureaucratic theory, public value theory, and the practice of problem solving), I have found these analytical distinctions most helpful. To keep the conceptual complexity of the research problem within manageable limits, I try to confine the discussion to the client and public perspectives and the welfare and justice perspectives.

With this review of where the problematic encounters occur, where and how the losses register, and the shortcomings of the existing institutional infrastructure for remediating those losses, the next step is to zoom in on the particular kind of encounters between government bureaucracies and clients that seem to produce ream upon ream of red tape.

## Defining Bureaucratic Dysfunction as a Mismatch

To define bureaucratic dysfunction in a way that allows us to deal with it, we must closely examine the specific interactions between clients and public agencies that produce the experience and the aggravation of "red tape." In what specific roles do individuals and the state encounter one another? When and how do their goals align, and when and why do they so often fail to do so? And how many flavors does bureaucratic dysfunction come in?

### Roles and Relationships in Client-State Encounters

What does it mean for bureaucracies to be dysfunctional? We have already established that the definition of the problem depends on normative perspectives. But in order to proceed we need a more generalized, neutral working definition. At the outset of the chapter, bureaucratic dysfunction was described as a "mismatch" between the state and the public it is trying to serve. To get a better working definition of dysfunction, it is useful to assess what specifically happens to relationships between the state and its citizens when bureaucracies are (or are perceived to be) dysfunctional.

Figure 2-2 illustrates the various roles in which people encounter the state, the various roles in which the state encounters people as citizens or clients, and the nature of their encounters. In the figure, there is a match between the roles of clients and the roles of the state with regard to clients. Service encounters enable the recipient to obtain services and the state to deliver them; obligation encounters enable the state to impose obligations and the client to comply with them. Bureaucracies are imagined as government-sponsored productive enterprises that deliver services and enforce regulations through encounters

Figure 2-2. **The Nature of Encounters: Roles and Relationships of People and the State**

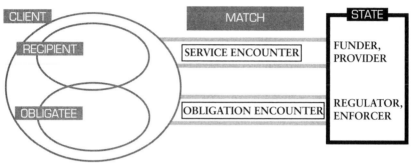

with clients. Though the goal is not only to serve clients but also to improve social outcomes through those encounters, performance with respect to both goals depends on establishing effective, efficient, equitable, and responsible encounters with clients. Therefore, dysfunction can be defined as the failure to do so.

### Bureaucratic Dysfunction as a Mismatch

I propose the following definition of bureaucratic dysfunction:

> Bureaucratic dysfunction is the mismatch between state capacity to deliver services and enforce regulation and people's capacity to benefit from public services and the enforcement of rules and regulations as individual clients or citizens in general or both.

It is important to note that this definition simply focuses on the mismatch without presupposing or alluding to causes and consequences. It does not assume that the government bureaucracy or the client is at fault or that the public is confused or conflicted in its expectations or preferences; it just observes that for some reason, encounters have not occurred or resulted in services delivered and obligations fulfilled. This definition serves the purpose of my inquiry because it does not come with a preconceived idea about who or what causes the mismatch. It simply states that something is preventing certain interactions from occurring, thereby straining some relationship between

Figure 2-3. **Mismatch between Client and State in Various Capacities**

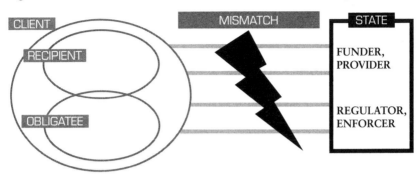

state and society, between government and people. If we want to really understand what is going on in problematic situations, we need to keep an open mind with regard to all possible causes and avoid a priori exclusion of causes. My focus on the mismatch between government and citizen rather than on either side of the equation is intended to guarantee that agnostic point of view. Figure 2-3 illustrates the basic conceptual model associated with the definition, which is informed by all previous conceptual considerations; however, it does contain a number of terms that need to be explained. To that end the arguments related to each element of the definition are briefly summarized below.

### Why Service Delivery *and* Enforcement of Regulations?

Fundamentally, bureaucratic dysfunction is a problem of mutual access (Lipsky 1980, 1984, p. 3; 2008, p. 137; de Jong and Rizvi 2008). On one side are clients who are trying to receive government services or to fulfill their obligations. Some of them have a right to services (eligible clients), some do not (potential frauds). Some comply with regulations that apply to them (lawful citizens); others may comply even if they are not legally obliged to do so and do not even want to do so (potentially misinformed or misdirected citizens). On the other side are governments trying to get access to clients in order to deliver services (even to those who may prefer not to receive them, such as drug addicts, school dropouts, and some victims of domestic abuse) or impose duties (especially on those who attempt to evade enforcement, such as tax evaders, deadbeat parents, and unlicensed merchants). My definition allows us to look at mixed or hybrid encounters as well: in many instances, clients who try to access a public service are required to comply with some kind of regulation in order to do so. For example, an entrepreneur trying to license her business may want to obtain information, advice, or even assistance from the government; at the same time, she has to comply with regulations to get the required license. The definition of bureaucratic dysfunction given above allows us to look at the multiplicity of relations and interactions that the state has with clients, even in a single encounter.

## Why *People's* Capacity?

People benefit from the state either directly and individually as clients or indirectly, as citizens who reap the general benefits of a well-functioning state that provides effective, efficient, and equitable public services and enforcement of rules and regulations. In this study I choose to zoom in on the client encounter because each encounter provides a concrete data point. The examination of red tape in client encounters can be and is evaluated from client and public perspectives, as well as from welfare and justice perspectives. To develop a good understanding of the context of a specific client encounter, it is important to look not only at what the state is doing (or not doing) but also at what the client is doing (or not doing) to obtain services or comply with regulations. It takes two to tango. Clients are often, perhaps always, co-producers of an encounter, and as such they help create a successful encounter. To do so requires more than just showing up, collecting their benefits, or fulfilling their obligations. For people bring some or all of their values and perspectives as citizens to the service or obligation encounter. It is important to understand to what extent and with what frequency those values and perspectives enter into and influence what happens in these encounters. As governments deliver services and enforce laws on behalf of the people, it is important to know to what extent clients are capable of doing and willing to do their part of the work.

## Why *State* Capacity?

Governments have a variety of ways to shape their encounters with clients through bureaucracies. They develop rules, regulations, procedures, forms, channels of communication, and places to meet. Through their offices, staff, and online presence, governments construct encounters of various kinds. The question is whether those encounters are shaped and constructed in the best way possible to achieve the desired results. From a public perspective, the question is whether the state is capable of achieving the intended social outcomes through service delivery and regulatory encounters. The encounter is where *outputs* of government activity appear, but the outcomes and impacts appear later. Whether delivering services such as education, social benefits, and health care or imposing obligations such as traffic stops and tax audits, government encounters with individual clients serve social goals. When talking about state capacity, it is important to think about both the capacity to deliver services and enforce laws and the capacity to accomplish social outcomes or public goals through those means (Moore 1995; Sparrow 2000; Alford 2009; Schuck and Zeckhauser 2006).

## Why a Mismatch?

When I define bureaucratic dysfunction as a mismatch, I do not intend to suggest that a perfect match is possible. Even the best-performing governments cannot fully understand or accommodate the complexity and volatility of modern societies, and even well-informed and capable people make mistakes that make their encounters with government difficult or unpleasant. There will always be some sort of trouble. However, understanding the nature of the mismatch helps identify actions that might counteract its undesired consequences.

### False Positives and False Negatives

Building on the earlier distinction between service recipients and obligatees, we can distinguish four roles that result from a mismatch:

- Eligible nonrecipients: people who are entitled to benefits or services but do not receive them.
- Ineligible recipients: people who are not entitled to the benefits or services that they receive.
- Noncompliant obligatees: people who legally should comply with regulations but fail to do so.

Figure 2-4. **Client Roles, State Roles, and Types of Mismatches in Encounters**

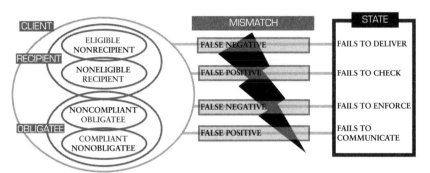

- Compliant nonobligatees: people who legally do not have to comply with a regulation but unknowingly or unwillingly do so because they think they have to or they simply cannot find a way to get out of a bureaucratic predicament.

These roles are based on two fundamental ways in which a mismatch can occur: false negatives and false positives (see figure 2-4). I borrow these terms from statistics. Statisticians designate as a false negative the rejection of a hypothesis that is true; acceptance of a hypothesis that is not true constitutes a false positive. A similar logic applies to service delivery and the enforcement of rules and regulations—"law enforcement" in the broadest sense. Services can be denied when a client is eligible, resulting in a false negative, or they can be delivered when a client is not entitled to them, resulting in a false positive. If the government fails to impose an obligation on someone who is legally bound to comply with a regulation, there is a false negative; if a person complies with a regulation even if he or she does not have to, there is a false positive.

   If there is a mismatch, the first question is what kind of a mismatch it is, false positive or false negative? If it is a false negative in service delivery, the person could be actively trying to access services or actively avoiding services. If it is a false negative in law enforcement, someone may be actively trying to resist compliance, but it is also possible that he or she is willing to comply but is not aware of the regulation or is incapable of fulfilling the obligation to comply.

Table 2-2. How Certain Types of Mismatches Affect People
in Their Capacity as Client and Obligatee

|  | Service delivery | Law enforcement |
| --- | --- | --- |
| **Match** | Recipient | Obligatee |
| **Mismatch—false negative** | Eligible nonrecipients *(For example, a disabled person does not receive disability benefits)* | Noncompliant obligatees *(For example, an entrepreneur evades sales taxes)* |
| **Mismatch—false positive** | Noneligible recipients *(For example, an employed person receives welfare)* | Compliant nonobligatees *(For example, an elderly person pays more taxes than needed)* |

The same is true for false positives in service delivery: people may not know that they are ineligible for services, but people also may commit fraud. Finally, false positives in law enforcement may include cases of people who are not aware that they are paying too much tax to the government or are incorrect in thinking that they are not allowed to do certain things, such as use certain funds for certain purposes (see table 2-2). Certainly, ineligible recipients would be a target for law enforcement. And compliant nonobligatees should probably be eligible for help (compliance assistance).

All of this leads to the conclusion that there are many ways in which encounters can become complicated. The situation will differ depending on whether the case involves a false negative or positive, in service delivery or in law enforcement. It can be difficult for clients and officials who are closely involved to figure out what exactly the case is in particular situations. Understanding bureaucratic dysfunction in terms of false positives and false negatives in service encounters as well as obligation encounters helps widen the assessment to include the broader losses to individual clients and the general public.

While perfect encounters between governments and clients may not be possible, a perfectly pleasant encounter may not be too much to hope for. It is conceivable, for example, that obtaining a passport may be a very pleasant experience. It is harder to imagine an encounter between a department of child protective services and a broken family as perfectly pleasant. And as the empirical part of the research shows, there are a great many shades in between. But the fact that encounters between government and citizens are designed to improve social outcomes rather than please clients can make a pleasant encounter less than ideal and an ideal encounter less than pleasant. When it comes to bureaucratic dysfunction, the opposite of a mismatch is not a match but an acceptable level of not-matching. That, of course, reinforces two points—first, that addressing bureaucratic dysfunction is a matter of values and norms, and second, that red tape is a symptom of underlying complex issues that are both technical and political in nature.

## Determining the Entry Point: Complex Cases of Red Tape

Red tape comes in many shapes and sizes. The label may refer to a variety of phenomena, including the mere existence of regulations, the application of rules by officials, and procedural requirements and paperwork. Red tape is difficult to define objectively because it is a normative concept. A preliminary question, therefore, is what kind of instances of red tape would constitute good points of entry into the investigation of bureaucratic dysfunction.

### *Simple, Complicated, and Complex Cases*

An example here is a government agency that is made aware that citizens find its procedures confusing and cumbersome. If the agency acknowledges the problem and if it has sufficient knowledge to rectify it, this can be considered a *simple* case. The agency and the citizens may not agree on a solution, but at least there is consensus about the definition of the problem and there is sufficient knowledge about the problem. If for some reason they do not have sufficient information to define the problem, the case becomes *technically complicated*. This may happen when there is more than one agency involved in the procedure. If a client has to obtain documents or permission from multiple sources, he or she might run into rules that contradict each other or multiple procedures that are poorly aligned. In that situation, neither the client nor the government may have sufficient knowledge about the nature of the problem, even if they agree that there is an undesirable amount of red tape. If, on the other hand, sufficient information is available but client and government disagree about the nature or severity of the problem, the case becomes *politically complicated*. For example, a procedure may have been designed to maximize accountability to prevent abuse and encourage diligent keeping of records and receipts by government employees. A citizen, however, may not like the stringent procedures for personal reasons (for example, time and energy spent), even though from the public perspective there are reasons to keep the situation as it is (risk reduction). There are now two competing values at stake: the value of a client-friendly system that does not waste citizens' time and energy and the value of a rigorous reimbursement procedure that maximizes accountability for public expenditures. This case is politically complicated because the matter cannot be solved by technical means alone; values, interests, and consequences have to be considered and a decision must be made regardless of whether the status quo strikes the right balance between the competing values.

Finally, we can imagine a case of red tape in which it is not clear what or who is creating an administrative burden and the agencies involved do not feel that they need to find out. This is what makes cases *complex*: a lack of consensus about what values the status quo supports or violates, paired with a lack of knowledge about the exact shape and scope of the problem. If not enough is known about the problem—such as the number of people involved and how and to what extent they are affected—it is hard to weigh their material and immaterial value losses against the value of accountability that the bureaucratic system is supposed to uphold. Conversely, if there is no consensus about a possible lack of balance of values, there may be no incentive to engage in further inquiry and action. Technically complicated cases require technical responses, and politically complicated cases require political responses. But what kind of response is required when cases are complex? And when can we legitimately claim that a case is complex or that it deserves anyone's attention in the first place?

### *Technical and Political Dimensions of a Problem*

Table 2-3 helps distinguish cases on the basis of the two dimensions, consensus and knowledge, discussed above.[12] It is loosely adapted from theorists on "wicked" social problems (Rittel and Webber 1973, p. 155; Hoppe and Van de Graaf 2007; Grint 2005, p. 1467; 2008) and theorists on adaptive leadership (Heifetz, Grashow, and Linsky 2009; Kahane 2010) The concepts and analytical frameworks of these scholars differ, but they have in common a close attention to the factors that make problems hard to solve: the interrelatedness of technical and political complexity.

Let us return to the question with which we began this discussion: exactly what cases of red tape should this study focus on, given its stated goals? What kind of "encounter gone wrong" provides us with the best possible entry point for investigating underlying bureaucratic dysfunction? In the effort to develop an understanding of bureaucratic dysfunction and the phenomena we call red tape, this study focuses on losses of value—in terms of both welfare and justice—as they register with individual clients as well as the public at large (the four options in table 2-3 may or may not fit that profile). To get at the knottier questions of value and where trade-offs may lie, this study also looks at complex cases, which I think constitute uncharted waters in dealing with bureaucratic dysfunction. These cases seem to offer the possibility of leveraging research resources most productively and making the largest possible contribution to knowledge and practice.

But there is a catch with complex cases: one does not yet know the causes of a problem and the full extent of the consequences. A case may come across as complex simply because it is confusing. The problem seems to be that we do not really know to whom and to what extent red tape is detrimental until we investigate it. *Precisely because*

---

12. It is important to note that the very notion of a "problem" is problematic in the matrix in table 2-3. What is a problem? Situations are problematic only to stakeholders who experience them as a problem. For our purposes, table 2-3 suffices to make analytical distinctions because it helps us dissect the concept analytically. In theoretical and empirical explorations it is important to keep in mind that in practice, problems are defined in a social and political context and are never an objective "given." The definition of a problem is informed by normative ideas about what is good and just, the responsibilities of citizens, the role of the state, and so forth.

Table 2-3. Simple, Complicated, and Complex Cases of Red Tape

| Dimensions of the problem: Amount of knowledge and consensus | Sufficient knowledge about nature of the problem and potential solutions | Insufficient knowledge about nature of the problem and potential solutions |
|---|---|---|
| Consensus about causes and consequences of the problem | Simple case | Technically complicated case |
| No consensus about causes and consequences of the problem | Politically complicated case | Complex case |

*there is lack of knowledge and lack of consensus about the problem, it is highly probable that at the heart of these cases lie unresolved issues that affect the value-creating process of government in practice.* Clients may experience losses in terms of their personal welfare or their sense of being treated justly in accordance with their rights, and the public at large also may suffer welfare and justice losses. The clients, bureaucracies, and officials involved may or may not be aware of the losses. Therefore it is important to find out how and to what extent there is a mismatch between government's capacity to create and people's capacity to contribute to productive encounters. Complex cases of red tape can serve as red flags—warning signs of potential bureaucratic hazard.

## Actionable Knowledge

While many academics have studied red tape in one way or another, very few have produced actionable knowledge about effective ways to deal with it (Kaufman 1977; Bozeman 2000). As discussed in in chapter 3, much of the academic literature focuses on description, measurement, interpretation, or explanation of the phenomenon. There is a huge amount of literature on possible solutions to bureaucratic dysfunction in general and at a high level of abstraction—books on business process redesign, total quality management, human resource management, customer focus, public management reform, regulation reform, and reduction of administrative burdens, to name just a few areas of investigation. These works are undoubtedly useful, and certainly may improve the performance of government, but are not much help when it comes to dealing with a particular problem at a particular time and place.

The goal of this study, again, is to develop a better understanding of bureaucratic dysfunction and an effective approach to dealing with it in specific instances. The concepts explored and explained in this chapter should help serve this goal in the following ways:

- Placing the study in the conceptual traditions of bureaucratic theory and public value theory implies a focus on the value-seeking change agent who wrestles with the constraints of his or her bureaucratic environment.
- Distinguishing between problem solving as a responsibility of designated institutions (such as ombudsmen and auditors) and problem solving as a process that can be driven by any actor taking responsibility helps shift the focus away from the established institutional infrastructure and toward a more open-minded approach to public problem solving.
- Further exploring the notion of value loss from the perspectives of the client and the public helps define the consequences of the problem more sharply. That in turn helps us to better understand how and why bureaucratic dysfunction is difficult to deal with. The fact that the public often is not articulate about its values, not coherent and consistent in its preferences, and not organized to act on its interests makes it both harder and more important to look at bureaucratic dysfunction from a public perspective.
- Elaborating on the multiple roles and responsibilities that the people and the state have vis-à-vis each other leads to the construction of an analytical framework for distinguishing a variety of government-client encounters.
- The formal working definition of "bureaucratic dysfunction" as a mismatch leads to the creation of a more specialized analytical framework identifying potential problems in the various relation-

ships between clients and government. Using the logical notions of false positives and false negatives, various client roles emerge: eligible nonrecipients, ineligible recipients, noncompliant obligatees, and compliant nonobligatees. While any of these roles may all result from encounters ridden with red tape, both the root causes and the consequences of the problem are very different in each case.

Taken together, these fundamental ideas and frameworks provide a language and a conceptual scaffold from which we may work simultaneously on the technical, political, and normative dimensions of the collective problem we call red tape.

# 3

# Theories of Bureaucratic Dysfunction

*Once a plan gets too complex, everything can go wrong.*
WALTER SOBCHAK, in *The Big Lebowski*, 1998

Scholars and practitioners alike—from various eras, countries, and disciplinary fields and with very different perspectives and motivations—have written much about the phenomenon of bureaucratic dysfunction.[1] This has resulted in a wealth of descriptions, distinctions, interpretations, and explanations. It also has resulted in an extremely fragmented field of study.[2] In this chapter, I present an overview of the most relevant literature on the subject. My goal is not to attempt to reconcile conceptual approaches or to synthesize particular theories; that would be too much of a stretch, given the current state of theory. Instead, I am looking for conceptual guidance to explore bureaucratic dysfunction in practice while remaining sensitive to its multidimensionality and keeping in mind the scientific knowledge on the problem. The idea is to build on the existing body of knowledge

1. This chapter features contributions from sociologists, anthropologists, economists (both orthodox and heterodox), political scientists, philosophers, lawyers, management theorists, organization theorists, medical doctors, former civil servants, and ombudsmen.

2. Some have said there is not yet even a field of study because of lack of coherence on the conceptual, theoretical, and methodological levels (Merton 1952; Albrow 1970). Note that Robert Merton concluded this in 1952, Martin Albrow repeated it in 1970, and in 1989 James Q. Wilson claimed that there still had not been much development toward convergence.

and push the boundaries when it comes to its relevance and applicability for real-world problem solving. In other words, I use existing theories to help develop an adequate approach to investigating bureaucratic dysfunction in practice.[3]

I have selected those works that are most likely to have diagnostic value for empirical research. For example, some contributions help us understand what bureaucracy is about, as a system of rules, values, and design principles. Others make helpful analytical distinctions about organizational behavior in bureaucratic organizations. Still others identify mechanisms that apparently cause dysfunction. Some focus on the consequences of bureaucratic dysfunction in terms of political gains and losses for stakeholders. Individually, these theories and analyses all help to clarify some dimensions of the phenomenon. Very few, however, present scientific knowledge in the form of empirically tested theories about bureaucratic dysfunction.[4] This means that for the most part we will be looking for meaning, not for proven causality between variables. In addition, there is high variability with regard to the normative neutrality of authors.[5] So, individually, these theories simply present different perspectives on a problem. In this chapter I attempt to organize those perspectives and gauge their heuristic potential for the purposes of my inquiry.

The current state of knowledge is an important determinant of any research design (King, Keohane, and Verba 1994). In this case,

---

3. Chapters 4 and 5 deal extensively with the rationale for methodology and research design.

4. Most of the books and articles about bureaucracy and bureaucratic dysfunction use literature review, case studies, and logical reasoning to develop analytical frameworks or to generate hypotheses. Only a few contributions have used empirical data to test hypotheses (Zuurmond 1994; Bardach 1998; Huber and Shipan 2002). Even the contributions by economists are mostly qualitative and interpretive in nature. About one-third of the approximately 100 books and articles that I reviewed to write this chapter can arguably be labeled works in the study of humanities and about two-thirds as works of qualitative social science.

5. Some authors declare themselves enemies of bureaucracy from the outset (Howard 1994; Grumet 2001), while others adamantly propose a detached, clinical, and objective approach toward the subject (Downs 1967; Kaufman 1977; Wilson 1989). Some authors explicitly work on the assumption that bureaucracy is an institution of the past (Goldsmith and Eggers 2004; Meier and Hill 2005, p. 51) while others are confident that bureaucracy will prevail in the twenty-first century (Du Gay 2000, 2005; Goodsell 2004).

the literature review helps us to consider more carefully what kind of operational inquiry the current state of knowledge allows researchers to pursue and what methods they have at their disposal to do so.

I first examine the concept of bureaucracy before turning to the key concept of dysfunction. I then organize the discussion of theories of bureaucratic dysfunction in categories based on the perspective of various stakeholders in a democratic welfare state: the people in their role as clients (as service recipients or obligatees), the public sector professional (including but not limited to frontline workers), the public manager (mid- to top level), and the policymaker (legislators and top aides of the executive branch of government). I define these perspectives in more detail and explain why they seem to be especially relevant for my purposes. I ask the question "Dysfunction how?" from the perspective of each of the four immediate stakeholders. Who suffers or benefits from dysfunction? Who contributes consciously or unconsciously to the problem? Some very interesting answers to these questions are suggested by a variety of scholars.[6]

The chapter continues with a summary of the most salient points derived from the literature. It concludes by applying the lessons to a real-life case, identifying the most important implications of the state of knowledge for dealing with bureaucratic dysfunction in practice. After all, it is important to keep in mind the central question of this study: How can we deal effectively with bureaucratic dysfunction?

## Dysfunction of What?

Most analysts take Max Weber as the originator of the theoretical concept of bureaucracy and his work as a point of departure for theirs.

---

6. Some of the authors may not see themselves as scholars of bureaucratic dysfunction per se. The selection was made based on two criteria: Does the author address dysfunction, failure, or problems in the functioning of government or organizations working for the government? Does the author offer an original perspective on the description of dysfunction or contribute to knowledge about its nature in any other way? The order of discussion is not entirely arbitrary. I did take questions of readability and logical sequencing into account. It seemed to me that some sections followed each other more naturally and fluently than others. To some extent, that has to do with the way I have conceptualized bureaucratic dysfunction in my own mind. No conception beats another, but some conceptions emerge from others. Yet all conceptions remain present at the same time.

However, before Weber's work, at least three important theorists paid considerable attention to bureaucratic systems: Karl Marx, Robert Michels, and Gaetano Mosca (Etzioni-Halevy 1983). Weber's distinctly ideal-typical (*Idealtyp*) approach toward bureaucracy may break with the scholarship of these three thinkers, but he did build on their precedent.

## Power Relations

The early theorists, while taking different perspectives, all focused on power relations in society and the role of bureaucracy as an instrument in and of the state. Karl Marx includes bureaucracy in his larger economic theory about the state and the ruling class, arguing that the ruling class uses the state, specifically the bureaucracy, as an instrument to exploit the lower classes. In his essay "Critique of Hegel's Philosophy of Right" (1843), Marx argues:

> The bureaucracy has the being of the state . . . in its possession; it is its private property. The general spirit of the bureaucracy is the secret, the mystery, preserved inwardly by means of the hierarchy and externally as a closed corporation. . . . But at the very heart of the bureaucracy this spiritualism turns into a crass materialism.[7]

For Marx, domination is bureaucracy's purpose; to that end, it manifests itself through a range of symbols and cultural codes meant to distance bureaucracy from ordinary people. Thus, the mannerisms of bureaucracy are inherently exclusive. Gaetano Mosca shares Marx's view that bureaucracy is a tool to consolidate power in the hands of a ruling elite. Mosca distinguishes two kinds of government, feudal and bureaucratic. In both types, there is an elite class ruling the masses. In a feudal society, a simple system of power allows the elite to exercise direct economic, judicial, administrative, and personal authority over the ruled classes. However, in bureaucratic societies, these state functions become sharply separated from one another, leading to a specialization of roles within the elite. For Mosca, an Italian political scientist, journalist, and civil servant in the early twentieth

---

7. Marx (1977, p. 47).

century, bureaucratization is also the inevitable result of the modernization of society, with its larger, more diverse, populations and greater social problems. Modernization demands more sophisticated state responses.

Marx offers an economic theory of bureaucracy; Mosca offers a political theory. Robert Michels is the first to present an organizational model, which focuses on the distribution and consolidation of power *within a group*. In 1911, summarizing his analysis of organizations, he wrote, "Who says organization says oligarchy" (Michels [1911] 1962, p. 365), suggesting that in every organization the top will find ways to exercise and consolidate power over the rest. Michels extends and refines Mosca's ideas to develop a more precise formulation of the distribution of authority in bureaucratic systems. According to Michels, the salaried official is the inevitable element of organization in modern society and the emergence of a career bureaucracy leads inevitably to the formation of oligarchies as a means of consolidating power within and between organizations.

## Rational Organization

Now let us turn to Max Weber himself. While Robert Michels was the first to look inside organizations to distinguish processes that appear in certain bureaucracies, Weber was the first scholar to take bureaucracy itself as an object of study. Weber's taxonomy provides a model for organization based on a synthesis of imperfect versions of bureaucracy that Weber had observed in reality. As a form of legal and rational domination—rather than the form of domination present in feudal and traditional societies—bureaucracy is itself an expression of the process of modernization of society. Bureaucracies have recognizable features that distinguish their offices and how they are organized, its officials and how they work, and its tasks and how they are distributed. These organizational features can be observed not only in the public but also in the private sector and even in churches.

Following Albrow (1970) and Etzioni-Halevy (1983), I cluster the principles of Weber's ideal type of bureaucracy into six categories:

- Principle 1: *Regulated continuity.* The bureaucratic office is organized in such a way as to ensure the continuity of its tasks through regulation. Work is not dependent on individuals; it is perpetual in nature.

- Principle 2: *Functional specialization.* The tasks of bureaucracy are divided in a manner that appears rational. With every task come specific authorities, resources, and sanctions.
- Principle 3: *Hierarchical organization.* An elaborate, hierarchical authority system within each bureaucracy assigns duties to every official, so that the means of control depends on obedience to higher levels of authority.
- Principle 4: *Expert officialdom.* Because bureaucratic work is structured through regulation and functional specialization, officials must be experts in applying rules technically and legally. This requires expertise on the part of employees that demands targeted recruitment, selection, and training.
- Principle 5: *Distinction between public and private spheres.* The resources of an organization and of the particular office that a bureaucrat holds may never be appropriated for personal use. An official must maintain a strong distinction between the private and public spheres and avoid bringing his or her individual interests or opinions to the job.
- Principle 6: *Formalized documentation.* Administration depends on written documents and formal communication. This emphasis on documentation explains why the office (or bureau) is the hub of the modern organization.

Weber viewed bureaucracy first and foremost as an inevitable phenomenon closely related to the rationalization of society. In this respect, his formulation does not differ drastically from those of Mosca and Michels. Though Weber saw the particular form of organization that the bureaucracy offers as the most efficient way for organizations to achieve particular purposes, he saw the dangers associated with this particular form of organization.

## An Emerging Field of Study

In 1952 the American sociologist Robert Merton put together a reader on bureaucracy with the sole purpose of generating discussion and interaction in a field of study that had yet to become a field. Merton concluded that many scholars had written on bureaucracy in the wake of Weber but that they all wrote on specific elements of bureaucracy from a range of perspectives and applying different methodologies. He argued:

It would be premature to refer to "the theory of bureaucracy" as though there existed a single well-defined conceptual scheme adequate for describing this form of organization. Nevertheless, categories for description and analysis and empirical generalizations connecting these categories have been developed, and these prove useful in analyzing the structure of bureaucracy, the conditions of its growth and decline and the sources of intrabureaucratic conflict, the relations of bureaucracy with its social and political environment, and the connection between bureaucratic structure and the social and personal characteristics of the bureaucrat.

Though many contributions in the field had uncovered the need for a more elaborate conceptualization of bureaucracy as a form of organization, Weber's conceptual framework remained dominant. The preeminence of Weber's ideal type gave the impression of theoretical unity where, in fact, there was none. In 1970 Martin Albrow made another admirable attempt to synthesize an ever-growing field of study. Concluding that it was not possible to develop a new concept of bureaucracy, Albrow instead chose to survey the variety of theories of bureaucracy available, investigate their relations, and explain their development. Albrow rejected the development of a new conceptualization of bureaucracy because it is a moving target: it develops and changes even as it is being studied.

Bureaucracy is also difficult to conceptualize because it inspires such diverse and conflicting feelings in people. The term "bureaucracy" is not at all neutral; it attaches to pejorative connotations or to partial explorations of the concept. In addition, scholars have studied popular perceptions of bureaucracy as a phenomenon in itself, adding to the confusion. At the conclusion of his essay Albrow proposes abandoning the term "bureaucracy" altogether, to increase the conceptual clarity of the field. At the same time, he acknowledges that the idea of bureaucracy has a major information function in that it links a variety of topics logically, historically, and even culturally. As a unit of analysis, perhaps, "bureaucracy" is not productive, but if we use the term to denote a multitude of phenomena that includes a variety of units and levels of analysis, it does have important meaning for both academics and citizens alike (Albrow 1970).

## From Theoretical to Empirical Orientation

One of the most important scholars of bureaucracy in recent decades is James Q. Wilson, whose book *Bureaucracy* (1989) has become one of the most highly regarded accounts of Western bureaucracy and a standard textbook all over the world. He takes on the challenge articulated by Albrow: How does one discuss a concept that refers to such a wide range of phenomena? From the outset, he makes it clear that his goal is not to reconcile the many different perspectives and theories that bureaucracy has given rise to or to propose a theory of his own. Instead, he chooses to describe what is known with some certainty about what is referred to as "bureaucracy," using empirical examples. In the preface to the 1989 edition of *Bureaucracy*, Wilson admits that he had tried his hand at producing a more consolidated theory of bureaucracy, a task at which he had failed. This failure to consolidate theories extends not only to bureaucracy but also to organizations at large:

> I have come to have grave doubts that anything worth calling "organization theory" will ever exist. Theories will exist, but they will usually be so abstract or general as to explain rather little. Interesting explanations will exist, some even supported by facts, but these will be partial, place- and time-bound insights. . . . I think it might be helpful to public discourse and to college students if someone were to set forth what we now know about government agencies in all (or at least most) of their complexity, and to do so by sticking as close as possible to what actually happens in real bureaucracies.

Wilson proceeds to describe bureaucracy in terms of the people who work there. He distinguishes three main categories of bureaucratic officials, each with their particular tasks, responsibilities, challenges, and dilemmas. Wilson's first category is *operators*, those who perform their tasks at the front line of bureaucracy, such as teachers, police officers, and city hall clerks. Wilson describes their work in terms of the circumstances under which they do their job, the beliefs that they hold about their profession, their interests as a member of their organization, and the organizational culture that arises from the preceding three. The second category of bureaucratic official that Wilson identifies is the *manager*, by which he means those in middle management. The job of these managers is to direct workflow, allocate resources, and ensure that the goals of the organization are accomplished. Wilson discusses their work in terms of the constraints that they experience vis-à-vis the constraints of managers in private firms; the relationships that they share with subordinates and executives; the compliance that they need to enforce their organizational rules; and the difficulties that they experience managing people. Wilson's third category is the *executive*, the head of bureaucratic agencies. Wilson characterizes their work first of all as maintenance of the autonomy of their organization in the larger institutional arrangement. Executives must develop strategies to protect their agencies and accomplish their goals; they also handle problems in the organizational environment by, for example, developing innovative organizational procedures.

Wilson's concept of bureaucracy differs from Weber's in terms of the focus that Wilson places on public sector bureaucracies. He confines his description to organizations such as armies, prisons, and schools. Wilson claims that these organizations differ from others in terms of the particular constraints that they share as public bureaucracies. They have limited ability to control their resources and manage their processes because they are bound by laws and political masters. Operators, managers, and executives display behavior that may seem "bureaucratic" and "irrational" to outsiders but that is in fact rational within the context of their institutional environment and its constraints. These bounds on rationality (going back to Herbert Simon's 1946 book, *Administrative Behavior*) lead to a variety of coping strategies. Thus, Wilson concludes, "it is foolish to speak about bureaucracy as if it were a single phenomenon" (p. 48).

## Returning to Values

In a 2003 essay, "Dismantling the Weberian State," B. Guy Peters, another distinguished scholar of public administration, reflects on the contributions that scholars of bureaucracy have made over the past eighty years. Peters claims that a set of values underlies Weber's principles of organization, including legality, probity, predictability, and impartiality. Many scholars who address Weber confine their analysis to his ideal type and its set of characteristics, without analyzing the principles that structure his work. For Weber, bureaucracy was more than a form of organization. Peters makes the helpful observation that there are at least four interpretations of Weber's theory of bureaucracy:

- First, it is a description of the development of bureaucracy in Prussia in the late nineteenth century.
- Second, it is grounded in capitalism and state legitimacy and as such provides a form of rational, legal authority.
- Third, it is based on a process of change rooted in a particular moment in history characterized by a tendency to move toward a more rational, efficient state.
- Fourth, it is an ideal type, a conceptual framework in its purest form, making it neither a theory nor a description but a methodological tool.

Peters argues that some modernizers, particularly those who advocated administrative change in the 1980s and 1990s, set Weber up as a straw man. The dismantling of the Weberian state that Peters has observed in many Western bureaucracies, especially in the United States and United Kingdom, involves the introduction of more businesslike methods into public administration. Peters claims that these reform efforts have not led to the revolutionary effects that reformers imagined; nonetheless, they have done damage to the underlying values of the Weberian state:

> The bad news is that those values of concern for legality, probity, and predictability of outcomes were threatened rather severely by the reforms implemented during the 1980s and 1990s. . . . The good news, however, is that there has been some reassertion of the importance of the values that had been threatened. . . . This is not to argue that the Weberian State is necessarily the only, or even best, solution for the problems of governing. (pp. 113–14, 128)

In other words, Peters emphasizes an ethical framework, claiming that the Weberian conception of bureaucracy has more value in terms of the principles that it embodies than as an ideal type for a given bureaucratic organization.

### Bureaucracy and Infocracy

Arre Zuurmond takes up similar questions about the values of the Weberian state in his 1994 book on infocracy, *De Infocratie*. He reconsiders Weber's bureaucracy in the context of the information age, using empirical research on the way that social benefits offices in the Netherlands manage their tasks to develop a new concept of bureaucracy that builds on the underlying values and norms articulated by Weber. Zuurmond characterizes the development of the welfare state as a process of bureaucratization, which he defines as a process of increasing emphasis on Weberian principles. The problem with increasing bureaucratization is that, theoretically, it should ensure a more impartial and accountable delivery of services. However, in practice, the ability of bureaucracy to honor the values on which it was built decreases as an organization grows more formal. While increasing bureaucratization brings with it specialization and rigid hierarchies, the application of values requires judgment based on particular cases. The gradual elimination of the use of individual discretion may serve the ideal type of an organization, but it does not necessarily support the value system from which that ideal type developed.

Zuurmond argues that a new ideal type of bureaucracy is required in the information age. Without a reformulation of the bureaucratic model, the Weberian system of organization will fail to deliver on its promises and will create dire tensions in the execution of policy. Zuurmond coins the term "infocracy" to describe this new organizational form, which will retain its Weberian principles but include additional values. Through the smart deployment of information technology, the infocracy will introduce

- an integrated approach to replace today's fragmented bureaucratic organization,
- virtual replacement of traditional documentation methods,
- mass customization for an increasingly diverse population,
- reduced procedural complexity through continuous business improvement, and
- the speed to serve a more demanding client base.

Technology itself will not bring about these changes; only a complete reconsideration of the bureaucratic organization in terms of its values, organizational principles, and structure will permit the introduction of a new ideal type for the information age bureaucracy (Zuurmond 1994).

## New Governance Paradigm

Zuurmond claims that Weberian principles can remain in place and become even more sophisticated with the assistance of new technology. For Zuurmond, it is not the structure but the values of organizations that need greater development. Lester M. Salamon and Odus V. Elliott, authors of *The Tools of Government* (2002), propose an opposing view: they write that government has developed numerous innovative forms of organization, which they refer to as tools from among which the government can choose to achieve particular public goals, such as service delivery or law enforcement. Examples of such tools include the use of economic regulation, the provision of public information, contracting out service delivery, issuing grants and vouchers, and social regulation. These instruments differ from traditional concepts of bureaucracy in that they are not organizations or even programs; they are particular means of governance.

By conceptualizing bureaucracy as one tool in a toolbox, Salamon and Elliott propose that the manner in which governments do business does not have to be limited by a particular form of organization. Government can look at the problems it wants to solve and evaluate which tool would be the most effective and efficient in achieving a particular purpose. Thus, the uniform bureaucratic organization has, in effect, been replaced by a multitude of methods. Salamon and Elliott argue that bureaucracy's Weberian values have remained the same but that new forms of organization have emerged to realize those values, which they identify as efficiency, equity, effectiveness, manageability, legitimacy, and political feasibility. They make the sweeping claim that a new era of government problem solving has dawned in the Western world, involving a completely different manner of doing business. In a sense, Salamon and Elliott believe that both the conventional concept and structures associated with bureaucracy have disappeared in light of the new governance paradigm (Salamon and Elliott 2002). Table 3-1 shows the characteristics of this paradigm.

Table 3-1. **Comparison of Classic Public Administration and the New Governance Paradigm**

| Classic public administration | New governance paradigm |
| --- | --- |
| Program or agency | Tool |
| Hierarchy | Network |
| Public versus private | Public and private |
| Command and control | Negotiation and persuasion |
| Management skills | Enablement skills |

*Source:* Salamon and Elliott (2002).

So it seems, at least according to Salamon and Elliott, that bureaucracy as a form of organization—and as a way of thinking about organization—has become obsolete. However, if we look at their argument critically, we may still ask ourselves how—and by whom—these tools are to be managed. In other words, even in Salamon and Elliott's new governance paradigm, bureaucracy as a form of organization may still play a role at the superior level, where the tools are designed, chosen, contracted, managed, and evaluated. The tools of government may indeed be tools of bureaucracy instead of its replacement. In terms of a Wilsonian concept of bureaucracy, we must still have operators, managers, and executives dedicated to the deployment of given tools.

Nonetheless, Salamon and Elliott's governance toolbox does force us to redefine the inheritance of the Weberian form of modern organization. Whether we think that tools have replaced or merely supplemented state bureaucracies, we must acknowledge that in both the real world and in theorization about the real world, bureaucracies have become more complex. From an academic perspective, we have new iterations of organization theory to respond to increasing real-world complexity, making this field of study increasingly comprehensive and rife with variables and relationships between variables.

## The Future of Bureaucracy

In their contributions to *The Oxford Handbook of Public Management* (2005), Kenneth Meier and Gregory Hill ask how sustainable Weberian bureaucracy is in the twenty-first century. They define bureaucracy narrowly—that is, they take Weber's bureaucracy as an instrument of rationality and propose six new challenges to it. The first is politics, meaning both the influence of politicians on bureaucracies and the populist call for streamlining, curbing, or even doing away with bureaucracy. Political interference can obstruct expert administrations' pursuit of rational goals. This threat is especially sharp because bureaucracy remains enduringly unpopular with the electorate. However, even politicians must eventually acknowledge that they need competent bureaucracies to deliver on their campaign promises and to achieve their goals, so politics is not such a great threat.

Second, Meier and Hill identify New Public Management (NPM) as a movement that both challenges and reinforces bureaucracy. The tenets of NPM include more businesslike government and replacement of bureaucratic procedures with market-oriented tools of governance. At the same time, despite its gestures toward the market, NPM reinforces bureaucracy by emphasizing performance management, which requires accountable governance and strictly defined targets. NPM also calls for increased deliberation by managers, and it could give bureaucrats more discretion to achieve their goals. Thus, NPM could actually be a blessing in disguise to bureaucracy. Third, there is the postmodern challenge, a basically academic view opposed to ideals of positivism and rationality. Postmodern critiques of bureaucracy reject rigid, formal structures, which they find unhelpful in terms of both organizing governance and understanding reality. According to Meier and Hill, postmodernists have created a straw man of bureaucracy and do not do justice to its infinite variety of forms. They also claim that the postmodern challenge also lacks any empirical basis, which entirely neutralizes its threat to bureaucracy.

The fourth challenge comes from the principal-agent model, which presumes that public bureaucracies are agents acting on behalf of their principal, the political executive, who in turn is expected to act on behalf of the public. This challenge arises from the opposite perspective of the postmodern school. In order to explain and even predict behaviors within agencies that are conducive to political management, economic empiricists have developed an extensive theoretical base for modeling various aspects of bureaucracy in relation to political actors. The primary challenge that this model presents is the claim that bureaucracy as an organizational form does not matter and that all relationships can be reduced to contractual obligations between agents and principals. While Meier and Hill are more sympathetic to this view of bureaucracy than to that of the postmodernists, they claim that it still fails to grasp the full complexity of bureaucracies. The empiricists can explain only what they model, which presents a simplified version of reality.

Returning to the new governance paradigm of Salamon and Elliott, the fifth challenge to Weberian notions of bureaucracy is the rise of networks. Many new forms of organization and cooperation have emerged, meaning that numerous activities no longer come under the direct jurisdiction of public bureaucracies. Networks of organizations present a practical challenge to organizational bureaucracy in that their inherent lack of hierarchy can generate a broader inability to compel performance. Meier and Hill provide a counterargument to this challenge, pointing out that networks can actually deliver better services more effectively if they imitate the organizational principles of bureaucracies.

The sixth challenge to bureaucracies is complexity. It has been argued that the increasing complexity of society, in terms of its diversity and the nature of its problems, presents difficulties to bureaucracies because they are inherently inflexible and incapable of adapting to environmental changes (Ferlie, Lynn, and Pollitt 2005). This inverse relationship between system complexity and outputs can lead to pressures that provoke major, catastrophic change. Meier and Hill nevertheless claim that despite the possibility of bureaucracy being a complex organization, it is built to last. Increasing environmental complexity will not necessarily interrupt bureaucracy. Of course, the issue that the authors do not address in their answer to these challenges is this: while bureaucracy certainly may survive, to what extent does its survival necessarily serve society? Their analysis of the architectural complexity problem appears theoretical and one-sided.

Meier and Hill conclude that bureaucracy is here to stay: the six most significant real world and theoretical challenges that they identify do not present any significant threat, either to bureaucratic forms of organization or bureaucracy as a theoretical paradigm. They write:

> In short, bureaucracy will continue to flourish in the twenty-first century for many of the same reasons that it has flourished in the last century, it facilitates the governance process in ways that other organizational forms do not. Challenges to bureaucracy will always be challenges at the margin, moving tasks from a public sector bureaucracy to a private sector one, for example. Underneath these cosmetic responses to reforms, however, one will still see Weberian bureaucracies continue to perform a myriad of tasks. (p. 51)

## Bureaucracy: Semantic and Conceptual Issues

What can we make of this discussion and what does the scholarship on bureaucracy mean for the effort to develop actionable knowledge about bureaucratic dysfunction? First, one has to conclude that bureaucracy has come to mean many different things and its definition only grows in complexity as it becomes applicable to an increasing number of phenomena. At the same time, its meaning has remained remarkably constant: bureaucracy's most frequent definition remains the ideal type of organization that Weber theorized in 1922. This simultaneous diversity and consistency of meaning requires us to be careful in using the word "bureaucracy" if we want to refer to one particular phenomenon. For some people, the word remains synonymous with rational organization; they see it as a standard of efficiency and a beacon of reliability and accountability. However, for others, "bureaucracy" has become the equivalent of dysfunction—a symbol of inefficiency, arbitrariness, ignorance, and even catastrophe.

In this book, I use primarily the adjectival form, "bureaucratic," to indicate a range of phenomena, the relations between them, and the meaning that people give to them. Using the adjectival form puts more emphasis on the noun that often follows it in this book: "dysfunction." As I said in the introduction, my primary interest is not in bureaucracies but in the loss of value to the individual public sector client and to the public at large. In other words, I am not interested in dysfunctional bureaucracy as much as in bureaucratic dysfunction. The working definition of "bureaucratic" that I use is this: "potentially pertaining to all phenomena that are labeled 'bureaucracy' as well as to certain characteristics of these phenomena."

A second conclusion one can draw from the discussions of eminent scholars over the course of the past eighty years is that it is not possible to arrive at a consolidated analytical framework that does justice to all the meanings that bureaucracy might have. Moreover—and partly because of this diversity of meaning—it is not possible to develop a single theory of bureaucracy because to do so would require conceptual clarity and a coherent set of propositions. On the contrary, as we have observed, the field of study on bureaucracy is diverse and heterogeneous. To recap the discussion in terms of Peters's typology:

- *Bureaucracy as a descriptive concept:* Weber used the concept in the first place to describe an emerging and fast-growing form of organization in nineteenth-century Prussian society. Nowadays the term "bureaucracy" is applied to a wide variety of organizational forms around the world (Albrow 1970; Wilson 1989). For some the concept is reserved to denote public sector organizations, for others it includes organizations in any sector (Meier and Hill 2005, p. 51; Salamon and Elliott 2002). For some the term implies a normative connotation (varying from very positive to very negative); for others it is a neutral term that merely describes reality and carries no normative connotation (Albrow 1970; Peters 2003, p. 113).
- *Bureaucracy as theory of organization:* Since Weber, some of the literature on bureaucracy has focused specifically on identifying and measuring variables and relationships between variables within and in the immediate external environment of organizations that are labeled bureaucracies (Wilson 1989; Zuurmond 1994). From these studies, a theory of bureaucracy has emerged that may have explanatory power for phenomena in a larger population of bureaucratic organizations.
- *Bureaucracy as a social process:* Early theorists including Marx, Mosca, Michels, and Weber examined bureaucracy in the first place as an element of broader economic and political developments. While their normative analyses vary largely, they all suggest that bureaucracy, in various forms and ways, is both an expression of and a driving force in the societal process of modernization and

rationalization. Michels and Weber offered the first studies of bureaucracy as a phenomenon in its own right.

■ *Bureaucracy as methodological tool:* The principles of bureaucratic
organization constitute a conceptual standard with which to com-
pare real-life phenomena. According to Peters, most studies citing
Weber take the construct of the bureaucratic ideal type as a *pars pro
toto* from his work. That certainly is true for Meier and Hill (2005,
p. 51), who test the sustainability of Weber's principles for the future,
but it certainly is not for Wilson (1989), who describes bureaucracy
in terms of the kinds of people who work there and the kinds of
challenges that they face.

## Dysfunction How? Dimensions of Bureaucratic Dysfunction

Bureaucracy is an important concept for heuristic purposes, but it is
not bureaucracy per se that we need to care about but the values that
it embodies and is supposed to uphold. When we talk about bureaucratic dysfunction, we are talking about bureaucracy gone wrong,
meaning that the actual manifestation seems to be in conflict with a
generally held belief about what it should stand for.

Table 3-2 lists the Weberian characteristics of bureaucracy alongside the values they are rooted in (left column) and the concrete rules
and procedures they result in (right column). If one looks only at the
right column, one might get the feeling that bureaucracy consists primarily of or produces mostly rules and procedures. When one looks
at the left column, one might get the impression that bureaucracy is
all about upholding shared values of democratic governance.

Let us consider a real-life example of bureaucratic dysfunction that
can illustrate how bureaucracy becomes "dysfunctional" in a concrete situation, one characterized by red tape that was both technically and politically complicated. The case concerns Tamer Akgün, a
Dutch entrepreneur of Turkish descent who tried to start a sandwich
shop in a deteriorating neighborhood in the western part of Amsterdam.[8] For two years after he first decided to start the shop, his quest

8. This example is based on the research I did with Noor Huijboom for chapter 5 of
*Belgen doen het beter* (Belgians do it better) (Huijboom and de Jong 2005). The case

Table 3-2. Weberian Bureaucracy: Underlying Values, Characteristics, and Resulting Rules

| Underlying value | Weberian characteristic of bureaucracy | Resulting rules and procedures |
|---|---|---|
| Stability, robustness, trustworthiness | Regulated continuity | Rules about documentation and archiving, formal paperwork, professional standards, hours, formats, and other clerical standards |
| Efficiency; rationality | Functional specialization | Rules about jurisdiction, business process design, and professional authority |
| Accountability (democratic) | Hierarchical organization | Rules about chain of command, accountability mechanisms, and professional relationships |
| Effectiveness, professionalism, absence of nepotism | Expert officials | Rules about job qualifications, recruitment, promotion, and performance reviews |
| Integrity, accountability | Distinction between public and private spheres | Rules about procurement, conflict of interests, behavior, and dress |
| Due diligence, accountability, transparency | Formalized documentation | Rules about paperwork, informational requirements, evidence of eligibility, and other reporting standards |

was largely unsuccessful. Although the shop was ready to welcome customers, the doors remained closed. To apply for commercial licenses and building licenses for his location, Akgün had to register with his municipal chamber of commerce. To register, he had to rent a location without knowing whether he could actually use it. Once he rented the building and started paying rent, he registered and applied for the licenses, only to find out that he first needed to apply for a license for reconstruction because he wanted to add a door to his premises. This small alteration incurred extra costs and three additional months of waiting because the door had to conform to the appearance of the neighborhood and comply with fire department regulations.

These complications were by no means the last: the sandwich shop was treated as a retail store for the purposes of the building license, but because it was to sell food, it became subject to numerous environmental laws and regulations that the owner found almost impossible to comply with. "I had to deal with ten, fifteen, maybe twenty different agencies," he said. "I stopped counting." While awaiting official permission to open his shop, he had to pay the rent without being able to make money, which drained his bank accounts. He found that no agency in Amsterdam, not even the city district's self-declared one-stop shops for entrepreneurs, could provide a would-be entrepreneur with all the information needed, let alone guidance to help him sort out his situation. "I think I know more about the rules now than the government itself," Akgün said. "They don't know their own rules, but they have the power. It's very complicated." The ordinances were indeed so complex that even the desk manager at the local district business desk was advising entrepreneurs (off the record) to start their businesses directly, without going through all the legal hoops, and see what happened. "If I believe in an entrepreneur, if I really have confidence that he is going to make it," he said, "I usually tell him to go rogue and deal with licensing later. After all, law enforcement rarely even notices or cares." The number of rules, the length of the procedures, and the nontransparent enforcement of regulations

---

of the sandwich shop was later the subject of further research by the Kafka Brigade (see chapter 5 in this book) and has been used at Harvard Kennedy School as a teaching case.

have frustrated not only entrepreneurs but also the civil servants dealing with them. Asked why the situation had not improved even though
the local business desk was aware of the problems, the manager answered bitterly, "We have long talked about a *real* one-stop shop, but
it's just not going to happen. I don't know why. Talking about it seems
the highest achievement possible in this organization." The ultimate
burden, however, seemed to fall on Tamer Akgün, who had to close
his shop, though he still dreams of opening one. At the end of one
of the interviews, he desperately sighed, "The rules are killing me."

This example, which we will revisit and examine more closely later
in this book, shows that the concrete rules and procedures, while
traceable back to the Weberian characteristics, have become detached
from the values that they are supposed to serve, at least in the perception of the client. To him, the bureaucracy seemed anything but
reliable, efficient, accountable, and transparent. What seems to be
the problem here?

First of all, from the limited information provided above, we
could establish that the owner of the shop was dealing with more
than one organization. Second, these organizations represent multiple sectors: the government agencies are in the public sector, the bank
and his landlord are in the private sector, and the chamber of commerce and some of the one-stop shops are hybrid organizations.
Akgün was also dealing with organizations at multiple levels of government (the City of Amsterdam and the district offices). In short, he
was dealing not with one but with many bureaucracies. All of these
organizations have different responsibilities. Some deliver services,
like information or advice. Others impose obligations, like compliance
with fire and food safety requirements. From the entrepreneur's perspective, these organizations do not coordinate well. In some instances
their respective rules cause conflicts; in other instances the operational
procedures are not aligned well and do not seem to communicate or
share information. The burden of the integrative work falls on the
entrepreneur.

The entrepreneur, in this case, was willing to comply with any
regulations that applied, but he was advised to just get started and
wait for law enforcement to come by. Technically, the business desk
manager told him to break the law. His comments suggest that this
particular employee of the local government had no confidence in the

licensing system (because it would take forever) or in the enforcement system (because the chances of inspection were low and nothing bad would happen if one got caught). Instead of initiating change in his own organization, the government employee advised entrepreneurs to just get started. The civil servant lacked confidence in his organization's ability to deal with dysfunction or in his own ability to make improvements.

This brings us to an important point in the diagnosis of red tape: it is not a problem from the client's perspective alone. There are many other perspectives to be considered: the perspective of the frontline worker (or operator, in Wilson's terms), of the manager or executive officer, and of the policymaker. All of them are in some way engaged in the functioning or malfunctioning of the bureaucratic organization. All of them may have their own point of view, interest, and explanation for what is going on. All of them may to some extent be part of the problem and, perhaps, part of the solution. It is therefore important to develop diagnostics that help triage the problem of dysfunction (Caiden 1991). In the literature on bureaucratic dysfunction, contributions can be roughly organized into categories associated with these perspectives.

## Red Tape: The Perspective of the Public Sector Client

Perhaps the most obvious or visible manifestation of bureaucratic dysfunction appears at the level of client encounters with the government. Individuals who experience difficulties in attempting to deal with government typically characterize their experience as "red tape." The client of public services is, fundamentally, a person who encounters the government at its business end through individual encounters and transactions (Moore 1995; De Jong 2009; Bjorkman and others 2011). However, the client is not a customer in the business sense, given that government not only provides services to clients but also imposes obligations. Government organizations that deal with obligatees meet their individual clients not in the role of service provider but as "representatives of the state obliging clients to absorb laws on behalf of society at large" (Moore 1995). On the subject of the multiple roles of clients in relation to government, John Alford writes, "A client is either a paying customer, a beneficiary, or an obligatee, and all of these terms describe roles rather than categories. Any person can have a mixture of these roles together with that of citizen" (Alford 2009). The involved parties include the collective citizenry and individual clients, who include not only paying customers, like those in the private market, but also beneficiaries and obligatees. Government organizations simultaneously create public and private values affecting both the citizenry and individual clients. Those clients may embody one or more of the roles of paying customer, beneficiary, or obligatee (Alford 2009).

From this, it follows that people may be affected by bureaucratic dysfunction in many ways and in many capacities. The sandwich shop owner experiences frustration both as an obligatee, trying to comply with business regulations, and as a client, trying to obtain information and assistance in setting up a shop. The recipient of social benefits suffers from bureaucratic dysfunction if his monthly payment does not arrive in time or if the application procedures are prohibitively complicated. But the broader public may, in fact, have an interest in not paying too much of the taxpayers' money to people on welfare. Michael Lipsky coined the term "bureaucratic disentitlement" for the rationing strategies that underfunded agencies employ to deter clients. Public expenditure is kept within limits not by narrowing the eligibility criteria but by deliberately creating bureaucratic hurdles, like difficult application procedures or long waiting lists (Lipsky 1980). However, if a police department is not functioning properly, criminals may not be arrested as they should be. Such noncompliant obligatees benefit from bureaucratic dysfunction while society at large is harmed. Finally, we should be mindful of the eligible nonclients: individuals entitled to public services who are either unaware of how to access their benefits or afraid to use them. Although bureaucratic dysfunction can manifest itself in failure to reach target groups, such dysfunction may go unnoticed because those people, who are entitled to benefits but do not receive them, are less likely to report their lack of access. Government agencies may never know why they have not applied.

Making analytical distinctions between individual and social experiences of bureaucratic dysfunction not only helps to identify where and how dysfunction can occur but also helps us understand why some dysfunctions persist, go unnoticed, or are not reported. However, the literature on red tape almost exclusively focuses on the discontented client who is negatively affected by red tape.

### Bureaucratic Dysfunction as a Breach of Common Sense

The most infuriating way in which bureaucratic dysfunction can manifest itself is when rules imposed on us are in direct conflict with our sense of justice and reason. Almost everyone who has written about bureaucratic dysfunction gives anecdotes featuring a breach of common sense in one way or another. There is frequent mention of Franz Kafka, whose novels feature protagonists who are routinely treated unreasonably and inhumanely (Kafka 1954, [1925] 1998; Kafka and Harman 1998). A Kafkaesque breach of common sense suggests a bureaucracy's total lack of respect for a person's individuality, a lack of discernible motivation for the actions bureaucracies take, and inexplicable situations in which nobody knows what to do (de Jong, and Rizvi 2008).

A more particular form of breach of common sense is found in Joseph Heller's 1961 novel *Catch-22,* in which the protagonist describes a military rule governing the deployment of pilots flying fighter planes. This rule, the titular catch-22, states that a pilot cannot fly a plane if he is insane and that if he is insane, he should ask to be relieved of flight duty. However, flying a plane during wartime is arguably insane. Ironically, by this logic, if a pilot asks not to fly a plane, he proves his sanity and therefore cannot be relieved of duty. Catch-22 demonstrates a logical contradiction.

Many authors have taken up the issue of lack of common sense in bureaucracies. For example, Philip Howard, author of *The Death of Common Sense* (1994), speaks of Mother Theresa, who came to New York to build a homeless shelter for drug addicts. She planned to cover all of the shelter's costs and had acquired a perfect building for the symbolic amount of one dollar. However, if a building is used as a shelter, it must comply with city regulations, including one requiring multistory buildings to have elevators. Installing this elevator would have cost so much that Mother Theresa had to abandon the plan, and no homeless shelter was built. Howard's point, in relation to this anecdote and to Western bureaucracy in general, is that law has become too detailed and too ubiquitous. Western societies have grown to desire certainty. Howard claims that what societies have tried to do is to create government by law rather than by men, so that all cases will be treated alike and dangers will be controlled. His concern is shared by many other legal scholars (Bardach and others

1982; Bardach and Kagan 2002; Tamanaha 2004, 2007; Conley and O'Barr 1990; Kagan 2001; Ayres and Braithwaite 1992; DiIulio 1994). Howard argues that the effort to control has defeated its purpose because it has replaced human judgment with rules and regulations:

> We would revolt if government tried to prohibit us from standing on a chair to reach something on a high shelf, or tried to restrict the number of cups of coffee we drink, or told us how to clean our house, but that is the level of detail of modern regulatory law. We suffer it as individuals mainly through institutions like schools, hospitals, and places of work, but these institutions are a large part of our lives and wrap closely around us. The thin separation only mutes each indignity, causing an overall ache and making it hard to pinpoint the cause. We don't revolt mainly because we don't understand. (p. 52)

Bardach and Kagan take up the issue of regulatory unreasonableness, especially in law enforcement. In providing explanations for what can be perceived as breaches of common sense, they conclude that what seems unreasonable from a civilian perspective is actually reasonable from the perspective of the official or the law. To be successful, regulations must be inclusive, detailed, and strictly enforced; they must reduce the occurrence of harm; and they must be accountable for sanctioning or not sanctioning noncompliance. However, the more ambitious that lawmakers and regulatory agencies are, the more overly inclusive, excessively detailed, and inordinately rigid they become in enforcing laws and regulations. For example, they may ignore actual social problems in favor of focusing on violations of rules. Instead of concentrating on reducing the probability of harm, they may attempt to prevent harm from occurring at all. In an attempt to remain accountable, they produce a lot of paperwork thought to rationalize the intervention. As Bardach and Kagan write,

> Regulation implies standardization, for without standardization we cannot hope to honor the values of due process and equal treatment before the law. But the standardization that is necessary to make officialdom effective and accountable is ill-suited to the diversity, complexity, and fluidity of the real world.

Hence, regulation in some sense cannot help but be somewhat unreasonable. (2002, p. 92)

## Symbolic Interaction

Going back to the case of the sandwich shop, we see that people's perceptions of bureaucracy are shaped by their encounters—especially by encounters gone wrong. Red tape can break a person's spirit, un-reasonableness can drive a person to behave unreasonably, and lack of clarity can create a deep sense of insecurity and resentment. The failure of encounters and the responses they provoke, however, are the fault not only of bureaucracy but also of the client. An approach to this phenomenon that puts more emphasis on the responsibility of clients themselves in creating the red tape experience comes from Michael Herzfeld, who in *The Social Production of Indifference* (1992) describes bureaucracy as the ideology and practice of accountability. He finds bureaucracy to be a symbolic system growing out of the culture of Western societies. Despite claims of universal rationality, its meaning is always culturally specific; it cannot break free of its social context. According to Herzfeld, bureaucratic dysfunction is not an exception in a well-functioning bureaucracy but its defining characteristic: through mismanagement and in particular through people's reactions to mismanagement, bureaucracy accrues its specific cultural meaning. Bureaucratic dysfunction is a primarily a system of our own making, designed to produce indifference. Yet, we have little consciousness of either its origins or its consequences. That paradox may cause our frustration with bureaucracy, but it is a defining characteristic: for Herzfeld, bureaucracy's function is its dysfunction. He writes:

The symbolic roots of Western bureaucracy are not to be sought, in the first instance, in the official forms of bureaucracy itself. . . . They subsist above all in popular reactions to bureaucracy—in the ways in which ordinary people actually manage and conceptualize bureaucratic relations.

In Herzfeld's view, it is important not to take clients' vituperation about bureaucracy at face value. Without putting the blame on clients themselves, it is important to consider their own contributions to how encounters with government occur and how they are perceived.

*Cultural Problem: The Perspective of the Public Sector Professional*

On the government side of the encounter, we immediately find the public sector professional. In James Wilson's distinction, these would be the "operators." Frontline operators can be either bureaucrats responsible for transactions and administrative actions or conventional professionals, such as teachers, police officers, and nurses. According to frontline operators themselves, the line between bureaucrat and professional is growing thinner as a result of bureaucratic dysfunction (Freidson 2001; Zuurmond and de Jong 2010). Numerous police officers and medical professionals complain that they must fill out a lot of paperwork and submit to multiple managerial regimes to account for their every decision, which impinges on their room to maneuver and exercise judgment. At the same time, city hall clerks are confronted more and more often with problems that result from failing public services. Desperate clients come to city hall to demand services that clerks are not equipped to provide, which can lead to confrontation and aggression. Even though these frontline officers are clerks, they become involved, often against their will, in bureaucratic dysfunctions that occur elsewhere. What civil service professionals at the front line have in common is that they are closest to the outcome of bureaucratic dysfunction as it affects clients' lives. Yet because they are bound by specific rules, standard procedures, and the bureaucratic culture in general, they cannot always act as they like (Hofstede and Hofstede 2005; Gerritsen and de Lange 2007).

### Bureaucrats as a Product of Their Environment

As mentioned earlier in this chapter, Robert Merton was the first thinker to reflect on how bounded rationality manifests itself as bureaucratic dysfunction. He sought behavioral explanations for bureaucratic unreasonableness; according to his thinking, perceived unreasonable behavior is the result of constraints that limit rationality for those working in bureaucracies. Merton builds on Weber's argument that modern culture has given rise to bureaucracy as a form of organization and that bureaucracy has had its own cultural impact on society in turn. Bureaucratic structure shapes the personality of its workers and the social relationships that they maintain among themselves and with clients. The chief merit of bureaucracy is its technical efficiency, with a premium placed on precision, speed, expert control, continuity, discretion, and optimal return on input. At the same time, bureaucracy tries to eliminate personalized relationships and nonrational behaviors—for example, hostility, anxiety, and affective involvement—to reduce interference with the rule orientation that is considered a guarantee of impartiality and efficiency. However, Merton argues that disciplined conformity to rules leads to a lack of adaptation to new or special circumstances and therefore to inefficiency: "The very elements which conduce toward efficiency in general produce inefficiency in specific instances" (Merton 1940, p. 101).

Thus bureaucratic dysfunction manifests as trained incapacity. Bureaucracies effectively incapacitate people to be fully aware, alert, mindful, or thoughtful, in Merton's analysis. Actions based on training and skills that have proved successful in the past may nonetheless result in inappropriate responses under changed conditions. Bureaucrats' trained incapacity combines with strong discipline to generate goal displacement: the means—rules—become ends in themselves. Underlying this trained incapacity is a set of social mechanisms that influence the behavior of bureaucrats: their careers and the approval of their peers depend on maintaining the norms, symbols, and raison d'être of the bureaucracy. To demonstrate their loyalty to their in-group, they become even more indifferent, rigid, and domineering to clients. Merton writes, "By reaffirming the formality of relationships they serve the group, even when, in individual instances, a more personal treatment would have served the client better, not in the material sense but in terms of formal appropriateness" (p. 101).

### Cognitive Limitations

In 1945, Herbert Simon published a groundbreaking study on administrative behavior that focused particularly on decisionmaking among policymakers and higher officials. For Simon, the limits on rationality for this particular group were caused by inevitable cognitive problems arising from the work of bureaucrats. He observes that the behavior of humans in general and decisionmakers in particular can be explained by two extremes in the social sciences: economists, who view the individual as a rational decisionmaker, and social psychologists, following Freud, who are mainly driven by affects (Simon [1945] 1997). Simon suggests that it is useful to look more specifically at the nature of the task of making decisions. Those who are charged with this task have two general problems: first, fully rational decision making requires complete prior knowledge of consequences, which is almost never possible because we cannot look into the future to see what happens. Second, because decisions have an impact on the future, imagination must supply the social responses to the decisions made. Social values can be only imperfectly anticipated, he says. Finally, Simon concludes that dysfunction may occur as a result of these constraints on rational behavior, aggravated by the fact that people work in a social environment whose dynamics reinforce the constraints through group pressure and socialization. He writes, "Social institutions may be viewed as regularizations of the behavior of individuals through subjection of their behavior to stimulus-patterns socially imposed on them" (p. 117). For Simon, those patterns have to be studied to understand the functions—or lack thereof—of an organization.

## Obsessive-Compulsive Disorder

Picking up where Merton and Simon left off, Gerald Grumet, a psychiatrist, goes beyond a descriptive typology of personality and behavior. In his 2001 study/manifesto, *Taming the Bureaucrat*, he writes: "After studying bureaucracies and bureaucrats for a while, I have come to believe that the nucleus of the problem resides in the rigid, obsessional, orderly (or structured) personalities that form the functional core of advanced societies" (p. 9). Grumet claims, as both a psychiatrist and a scholar of bureaucracy, that the root cause of bureaucratic dysfunction is the obsessive-compulsive personality of bureaucrats (we must note that he uses this term in a pathological rather than pejorative sense). Grumet explains the commonplace of bureaucratic dysfunction in an increasingly complex society as the natural result of placing people obsessed with structuring their environments in high positions in government institutions. Individuals with this type of personality become obsessed with consolidating their grip on modern life; therefore, Grumet suggests, bureaucrats should be treated as patients and bureaucracy as a disease. He also concludes that if bureaucracy is treated as a disease, "it fits quite comfortably into the medical model: it can be readily diagnosed and its pathological signs and symptoms far more easily described than cured"

(p. 390). Although Grumet claims that he has found the root cause of bureaucracy, at the end of his study he implies that a real diagnosis would lead to an infinite regression. He writes: "If the root cause of bureaucracy is the structured personality, its pathogenesis can be found in the corporate mechanics designed by structured thinkers" (p. 394). But as Merton—and Weber before him—knew, those mechanics are rooted in the broader process of modernization. In other words, Grumet's contention that bureaucratic dysfunction should be located and diagnosed as a personality disorder eventually brings us back to the analysis of bureaucracy as a cultural phenomenon.

### Organizational Behavior as De Facto Policy

Michael Lipsky developed a completely different take on the relation between organizational behavior and bureaucratic dysfunction in his seminal study, *Street-Level Bureaucracy* (1980), in which he focuses on the frontline operators who must juggle limited resources, ambiguities in interpretation of policy, complex lives of clients and obligatees, and demands for accountability on a daily basis. Studying the patterns of practice among frontline operators, Lipsky observes that to deal with the constraints on their performance, street-level bureaucrats develop coping strategies. The more discretion that frontline operators have, the more their decisions may be based on their own biases, beliefs and subjective assessments. If a clerk at a welfare office needs to assess the credibility of a claim and the rules allow the clerk some degree of latitude, personal beliefs and suspicions may strongly influence his or her decision. Discretion at the level of the street-level encounter with clients adds up to de facto agency behavior; discretion at the agency level, in turn, amounts to de facto public policy. Therefore, Lipsky concludes, public policy is influenced not only by its designers but also by its implementers. For an analysis of bureaucratic dysfunction, it is important to take into account not only policy and organizational design but also the de facto policy as it takes shape in practice.

Going back to the sandwich shop, we can ask this question: What de factor policy is being created here? If the entrepreneur followed the advice of the civil servant ("Start your shop and worry about licenses later"), he would be running an illegal shop and would run the (marginal) risk of being caught and fined, his customers would not be assured of fire safety and food safety, and the neighborhood would not be assured of the aesthetic value of the shop front. If on the other hand the entrepreneur abandoned his plans, other downsides could be imagined. There are economic losses; first, for the entrepreneur, who would lose his investment, and second, in terms of jobs not created and taxes not levied. In terms of social loss, we can think of the missed opportunity to have a new public venue with a social function, and also the missed opportunity to allow a member of an ethnic minority group to earn a living and be his own boss.

The way that frontline professionals (operators) interpret and apply rules and procedures is a very important factor in shaping organizational performance and policy outcomes. Developing hypotheses as to why certain behaviors exist and persist is an important part of the work of uncovering the root causes of bureaucratic dysfunction.

### Structural Problem: The Perspective of the Public Manager

From a managerial perspective, bureaucratic dysfunction often appears as balancing act gone wrong. While managers may be blamed for creating bureaucratic dysfunction by improperly balancing the conflicting demands of their agencies, we can also see them as sufferers from bureaucratic dysfunction (Noordegraaf 2000, 2008; DeHart-Davis and Pandey 2005).

Weber long ago predicted the difficulties of higher-level managers with the proliferation of bureaucracy. In principle, bureaucracy prevents arbitrariness, inefficiency, and corruption, but it can also lead to tensions with democracy, because the rule-based system prevails over the deliberation-based system. As managers are not expected to engage in deliberation (yet their task, inevitably, is to rethink the rules), this creates structural tensions. Dysfunction that originates at the managerial level is, according to Weber, a threat to bureaucratic and democratic functions and ultimately to humanity (Gerth and Mills 1946).

Managers therefore have an important responsibility to uphold the values of both bureaucratic and democratic systems (Etzioni-Halevy 1983; Burke 1986). However, managers are sometimes perceived as simple rational actors who want to maximize their budgets and protect their turf, thereby losing perspective on the role that they play in the bigger picture—delivering public value (Niskanen 1971). Others perceive managers as individuals who must cope with the double bind between accountability and service delivery created by constraints on public sector organizations. In Wilson's typology, executive managers are the heads of agencies; as such, they are responsible for the performance of their organizations and compliance to applicable material or administrative laws. Wilson claims that executives have a key role in innovating or initiating innovation to solve problems. Mark Harrison Moore (1995) envisions a role as innovator not just for the executives but for any manager who aspires to be an agent of change. As managers become aware of the constraints to delivering public value, they can begin to assume a more political role. Using the public value proposition as a lever, they can inform and influence their authorizing environment in order to reshape their mandate and maximize legitimacy and support for changes in both means and the ends of their operations. Managers can abandon their roles as victims of the system and become proactive in solving problems. While this may be a hopeful and inspiring view, reality often disappoints.

### Failure to Adjust and Adapt

In Michel Crozier's work *The Bureaucratic Phenomenon* (1964), he asks why bureaucracies stick to unproductive procedures. Why does the system not collapse? According to Crozier, the bureaucratic system of organization is characterized by the existence of relatively stable vicious circles that stem from centralization and impersonality. The rigidity of task definition, institutional structure, and structure of professional relations and human interaction result in a lack of communication. Consequently, people fail to really understand each other, the nature of their collective task, and the environment surrounding them. But instead of readjusting the model, individuals and groups use the resulting difficulties to improve their positions in power struggles within the organization. The lack of an alternative to the bureaucratic structure drives people to reinforce the suboptimal status quo— it's all they have to hold on to. That creates permanent pressure to maintain impersonality and increase centralization. Alienation from the original task ensues, and professionals and managers resort to coping mechanisms. The existing structure, which was the cause of the trouble, has now become a survival tool and the justification for certain behaviors (Crozier 1964).

As a cultural phenomenon, bureaucracy is a model that reflects two dearly held social objectives: first, the need for a stable social equilibrium to protect individuals from each other and the state, and second, the need for a device for collective action to bring about necessary change and innovation on behalf of the collective. Organizational theory helps us explore how the control mechanisms to maintain the necessary equilibrium and to introduce equally necessary changes work out in practice. And according to Crozier, it fails in either function. He does not have high hopes for bureaucracy as an organizational form nor as a social coordination mechanism. He is the first author on the subject to define bureaucracy in terms of its dysfunctional aspects: "a bureaucratic organization is an organization that cannot correct its behavior by learning from its errors" (Crozier 1964).

From the perspective of the professional public managers, bureaucracy is both a system that structurally inhibits their ability to solve problems in order to create more public value and a mechanism that helps them to cope, survive, be accountable, and prevail over others. It stimulates everything but learning—the reason that Crozier ends up defining bureaucracy in terms of its inability to learn from errors.

### Institutional Impediments to Learning

Organizational inability to learn is a structural problem that managers routinely struggle with but cannot solve. The Dutch Scientific Council for Government Policy, Wetenschappelijke Raad voor het Regeringsbeleid, or WRR, an independent think tank, has launched a comprehensive study, The Learning Government, that focuses on the problem-solving capacity of society. The study begins at the point where there is discontent on the part of both state and society about the lack of capacity for curing intractable social ills. The WRR defines an intractable problem as one that has neither a cognitive strategy (that is, sufficient information to describe the problem) nor a normative consensus (general agreement about its causes and remedies). If you have arrived at both cognitive certainty and normative consensus regarding a problem, you are in an excellent position to find technical solutions. However, if you have neither, you face a challenge that requires problem-solving capacity beyond that of standard operational management. At this stage, the problem is no longer an operational issue but a political challenge; it has become a problem of values, which requires more information from a wider range of stakeholders to address its ramifications. With this definition of intractable problems in hand, we can proceed to the WRR's question: why is there such a lack of problem-solving capacity in the Netherlands? The answer, according to the authors, lies in the fact that the government has come to assume that it has the dominant role in solving social problems and sees society itself as an extension of its organization. Also, government problem solving focuses on improving service delivery rather than on revisiting the nature of the challenge itself and asking what kinds of efforts, by whom, might help make a real difference. In doing so, the government tends to avoid political and moral dilemmas, preferring to frame issues in less sensitive terms and thereby avoiding the work needed to create genuine consensus. Instead, government bureaucratizes experience, translating individual and real-world experiences into numbers and graphs that obscure challenges as client stakeholders perceive them. Finally, there is a tendency to politicize the use of information, meaning that any available data are usually used to optimize processes within existing institutions rather than to reimagine the role that these institutions play or the value that they add. All of these elements impede the government's ability to learn. In other words, resistance to learning causes bureaucratic dysfunction, and bureaucratic dysfunction also manifests itself as resistance to learning

## Merits and Limits of Performance Management

In light of its difficulties, it is not surprising that the public sector has shown a lot of interest in the performance management approaches taken by the private sector. If governments have structural learning disabilities that limit their performance, surely one should find ways to teach them and *make* them perform better. Many of these ideas became the foundations of New Public Management. Looking back on two decades, Christopher Hood (2004) has identified seven basic features of NPM: hands-on professional management, explicit standards and measures of performance, a greater emphasis on output controls, a shift to the disaggregation of organizational units, a shift to greater competition in the public sector, stress on private sector management practices, and an emphasis on greater discipline and parsimony in using resources. Underlying these features are a consistent desire for greater accountability, more results-oriented organizational forms and procedures, and more effective management tools.

Even within the NPM's paradigm of performance, which imports biases from the private sector, variations must be taken into account. A 2004 study by William Gormley and Steven Balla on accountability and performance in the United States has attempted to account for the variability of performance in a large sample of federal agencies. The authors acknowledge up front that performance is a multifaceted concept; consequently, they develop a rating scheme for evaluating agencies on thirty-four criteria in five crosscutting areas: financial management, capital management, human resources, information technology, and results-oriented management. Their primary question was why some bureaucracies are better than others. Gormley and Balla found that variability could be explained by the nature of an organization's designated tasks, the quality of organizational relationships, the level of political support that they enjoy, and their overall exercise of leadership. For example, they found that agencies whose primary task is to distribute money to individuals tend to perform well, whereas agencies whose main goal is to collect money perform poorly. Agencies with ambiguous or conflicting missions perform less well than those with clearer mandates. Agencies with both internal and external communication and coordination mechanisms in place perform well. Agencies that are subject to the pressures of constituencies or other external controls perform well, and agencies with leaders who make credible commitments perform well (Gormley and Balla 2004).

NPM as a framework for measuring organizational performance is still alive and well, and it produces useful knowledge about bureaucracies despite its narrow focus on performance. Although it has received much criticism, this school of thought can still help us discover how dysfunction shows up as a lack of overall performance when benchmarked against the performance of other organizations. At the same time, it cannot tell us how dysfunction manifests as a violation of sets of values other than performance (for example, in terms of fairness, justice, or resilience).

### Challenging Assumptions of the Performance Movement

Others have taken a different approach to addressing the learning disabilities of bureaucratic government. Beryl Radin, for example, has written a comprehensive study on NPM, which she calls *the perfor-*

*mance movement* (Radin 2006). Radin argues that because of its initial assumptions, the performance movement has dangerously overlooked organizational and political realities; to Radin, bureaucratic dysfunction results from simplification through the imposition of a performance measurement framework that assumes, in effect, that one size fits all. Radin cites negative effects of performance evaluation, including the demeaning of professionals, masking or ignoring of value conflicts, and provision of incentives for fragmentation or insulation. Her criticism is that performance evaluators cannot reliably define performance success and failure in part because it is often difficult to ascribe effects observed in the world (social outcomes) to particular government actions. Also, public managers do not enjoy immunity from politics and political pressures and are therefore subject to less "objective" forces. Radin also questions the notions that top-down managerial control of public sector professionals is the best way to improve performance and that budgetary efficiency and cost-effectiveness would be the most important value of public sector organizations. An alternative approach would be to acknowledge that public sector organizations must balance multiple values. For public managers, that means that a narrow focus on performance management can actually exacerbate the learning disabilities of government rather than address them. To truly measure performance, managers must first go back to unresolved value conflicts and define how real performance should look.

## The Problem of the Many Hands

The challenge, of course, is that for reasons discussed earlier, no single public manager is tasked to take all the different values into consideration and bear responsibility for the production of an integrated value proposition. Since one of the principles of public bureaucracies is functional specialization, it is no surprise that when the number of tasks increases, the number of specialized bureaucratic units (or institutions) increases. Fragmentation of the institutional capacity to deliver services and impose obligations is inherent in the development of the modern welfare state. In the 1980s and 1990s, public management reform was proposed and implemented to control increasing public expenditures. To avoid fiscal crisis, governments, especially in Western countries, dramatically changed the way that services were delivered and obligations imposed. A large part of the revamping of the public sector involved privatization—contracting out government services to the private sector or to nonprofits—and the introduction of a more businesslike management framework for institutions that remained public bureaucracies.

This drive may or may not have resulted in better performance—a definitive conclusion is still disputed by both practitioners and scholars (see Pollitt and Bouckaert 2000). However, one undisputed point is that public management reform has increased fragmentation across sectors. Where previously there was only fragmentation within the government sector as a result of functional specialization, public tasks have now been dispersed across the public, private, and nonprofit sectors (Donahue and Zeckhauser 2011; Smith and Lipsky 1993; Klievink 2011). Public services such as welfare-to-work programs, waste management, and health care have all been contracted out to the private sector or to nonprofits whose main obligation is to fulfill the terms of the contracts they have with the government. These organizations do not have particular incentives to do anything beyond the task for which they are paid; they are principally responsive to the government as a client and not to the immediate environment in which they work (unless they have been specifically charged to respond to their environment by the state).

In addition to this decentralization, the devolution of tasks to lower levels of government has contributed to even more fragmentation. In many countries, there has been a concerted effort to bring governments closer to the people by transferring policy and executive responsibility to municipalities or provincial governments; yet the trend toward devolution has not been true for all public services and regulatory tasks. Consequently, some tasks remain with the central government, some with the regional government, and some with the municipal government, leading to fragmentation.

Complaints about fragmentation as a cause of bureaucratic dysfunction generally arise from lack of coordination between organizations that are responsible for specific tasks but lack the incentive to perform those tasks with awareness of the bigger picture of public service delivery and enforcement of laws and regulations. When a client's or a community's problem involves many different policy areas, individual agencies bear only partial responsibility for solving the problem; no single organization can be found to approach the challenge from an integrated or a holistic perspective.

Another common complaint about fragmentation is that the dispersion of responsibilities leads to lack of accountability and, more important, to a lack of individual and organizational responsibility. That is the problem for which Mark Bovens has coined the term "problem of the many hands" (Bovens 1998). Although the government or the state is ultimately responsible for the functioning of public services and regulation in general, it is the executive agencies that must respond to particular problems in practice, and those agencies can always hide behind their limited responsibility. If problems in practice emerge as a result of lack of coordination between individual organizations, it becomes especially difficult to find a single administrative body or individual that can effectively be held accountable or even confronted.

Some proposed remedies to the problem of institutional fragmentation focus on reorganization and restructuring of the public sector, while others acknowledge existing institutional diversity and emphasize collaboration between government silos. These efforts go by different names, including governing by network (Goldsmith and Eggers 2004); interagency collaborative capacity, or ICC (Bardach 1998); joined-up government (Bogdanor 2005); and defragmentation (Raad voor Maatschappelijke Ontwikkeling 2008). All of these approaches stress overcoming the difficulties of managing across organizational boundaries and jurisdictions, building legitimacy and support, establishing horizontal connections, streamlining business processes, sharing information, and resolving conflicts of interest and values. But in the end there will likely always be some degree of fragmentation and misalignment between govern structures and public tasks to be executed. There may not be a sustainable way to organize government in a most efficient way, as circumstances, challenges, and volitions keep changing. As a result, there will always be silos of some sort, and silos will always determine to some extent what parts of the larger task people will pay attention to.

### *Flawed Statecraft: The Perspective of the Policymaker*

Policymakers, who are responsible for drafting the legislation that determines what kinds of services and obligations the government delivers and imposes, play an important role in both preventing and causing bureaucratic dysfunction. A point of concern about the role of policymakers in bureaucratic dysfunction is that they often have top-down views on public policy and believe that anything written into legislation will be implemented according to both design and intent. Pressman and Wildavsky (1984) have shown that this ideal is an illusion and that many things happen between the moment that a law is drafted and the point that it is implemented. Whether acting as legislators or elected or appointed public executives, politicians are seemingly in a position to identify and remedy bureaucratic dysfunction. On behalf of their constituents, politicians articulate preferences and concerns for society. In the nomination, selection, and approval of policies, politicians make choices about what and who are to be regulated and sometimes even about how. However, they are not always aware of the consequences of their initial decision to intervene or not to intervene (Bovens and 't Hart 1996; Glazer and Rothenberg 2001). If interventions fail and bureaucratic dysfunction occurs, politicians will usually be informed by members of the public, their constituents, special interest groups, the media, or civil servants and professionals. These groups will either press their politicians to do something to remedy the dysfunction or to leave things as they are.

Public policy is the most common exercise of statecraft in the modern welfare state; it can include programs, rules, fiscal regulation, and any other government efforts to deliver services or address problems through the use of its authority and resources. The complete or partial failure of public policy has been the study of many authors in several disciplines, including economics, political science, sociology, and public administration. Much analysis of policy failure has focused on the unintended consequences of public policy. At this point and for the purposes of this study, I focus only on those contributions to policy analysis and statecraft that help us understand bureaucratic dysfunction as I have understood it in formulating my research questions. Political scientists through the ages have examined the relationship between state and society with regard to the occurrence of bureaucratic dysfunction (Kruiter 2010). It has been argued that the first state to employ a bureaucracy to achieve its purposes emerged in China some 10,000 years ago (Balazs 1964). The combination of state and bureaucracy in Europe is of a more recent date, having appeared around 500 years ago (Fukuyama 2004). Francis Fukuyama has pointed out that most of the debate about the state has focused on its appropriate size, strength, and scope. By government size, analysts usually mean the number of employees and the size of the budget, but strength and scope are more difficult to define. For example, the strength of the American state is the subject of substantial debate. Some argue—as Weber would and many present-day Republicans do—that the American government is strong because of its ability to levy taxes and impose regulations. On the other hand, one could claim that the American state is weak because it is based on the principle of checks and balances, so that each branch of government can impede the efforts of the two other branches (Lipset and Lakin 2004).

Fukuyama suggests that government strength can be measured in terms of "the ability to formulate and carry out policies and enact laws; to administrate efficiently and with a minimum of bureaucracy; to control graft, corruption, and bribery; to maintain a high level of transparency and accountability in government institutions; and most importantly, to enforce laws" (2004, p. 9). However, even if we agree with Fukuyama's definition, it is highly debatable how strength can and should be measured. With regard to the scope of the state, Fukuyama distinguishes minimal functions such as providing pure public goods—including defense, law and order, and property rights—from activist policies such as industrial policy and wealth redistribution. Between those poles are intermediary functions such as education, economic regulation, and social services. These roles and functions refer to what the state may do and in fact does. On the other hand, statecraft refers to how the state performs the tasks that it has set for itself. Thus, statecraft can be defined as the art of governing, referring to the exercise of authority, allocation of resources, and the extraction of revenues. Statecraft differs from the management of public organizations in that statecraft refers to the basic assumptions and principles of governance—in other words, to the design of state institutions.

## Governmentalization of the State

The design of institutions of modern Western welfare states has changed over time. Michel Foucault has examined the development of modern statecraft in his famous essay, "Governmentality." Foucault argues that the modern state has been steadily "governmentalizing" since the Middle Ages, by which he means that the state has increasingly defined its roles and responsibilities in terms of institutions, procedures, knowledge, and expertise. It has become increasingly occupied with its own competencies to impose order, exercise control, collect taxes, deliver services, and regulate society. A characteristic of this process is that the state has come to define social problems increasingly in terms of the techniques of government—"How can the state take this issue on?"—thereby limiting the real space for political struggle and contestation, "What is the real issue, and what do we think about it?" The governmentalized state shrinks the space for political debate about issues and values to an instrumental discussion about ways and means. An explanation for this process can be found in the need of states to survive: as long as public debate and political contestation takes place within the bandwidth of what the government can realistically control, the state is not in danger of being criticized at a fundamental level (Foucault and Faubion 2002). However, by limiting the debate to topics related to "governmentality" itself, the political discourse becomes increasingly self-referential and disconnected from the real world, the public and its problems. States may actually harm rather than help their chances of survival by attempting to limit the focus of discussion to its own instruments of statecraft rather than the conditions in the outside world.

### Legibility versus *Metis*

Building on the same basic set of ideas about statecraft but focusing on how the governmentalized state can fail, James C. Scott has developed an argument about what he sees as the most important tactic of government: the imposition of the concept of legibility. In *Seeing Like a State* (1998), Scott examines four major social engineering programs by modern states that have failed utterly: the collectivization in Russia, the compulsory Ujamaa villages in Tanzania, scientific foresting, and the city planning of Brasília. He argues that these planning disasters can be explained by the state's tendency to classify society and its problems in terms of administratively convenient categories. In so doing, the state makes society more "legible" for its own social engineering purposes. However, by using its coercive authority, it imposes its categories on reality, thereby forcing people, communities, and their problems to fit a predetermined model. Scott writes:

> The legibility of a society provides the capacity for large-scale social engineering, high modernist ideology provides the desire, the authoritarian state provides the determination to act on that desire, and an incapacitated civil society provides the leveled social terrain on which to build. (p. 89)

The effect of this particular form of statecraft is to destroy diversity because such standardization does not allow for deviance. Moreover, such a state loses its connection with social reality because it becomes blind to any phenomena not predicted by its own models. The state can "read" only what it has placed in its administrative categories. As a result, administrative dysfunction appears both as a disconnect between what really happens and what the state is capable of seeing and as a missed opportunity to use local, practical knowledge within the state's top-down problem-solving architecture.

One term for this local, practical knowledge is the ancient Greek term *metis*, often contrasted with *epistémê* (scientific knowledge) and *technê* (technical knowledge). *Metis*—which can be called experience, or common sense—can be acquired by living and staying in touch with one's environment. Scott defines *metis* as follows: "Broadly understood, metis represents a wide array of practical skills and acquired intelligence in responding to a constantly changing natural and human environment" (Scott 1998, p. 314). Acknowledging *metis* means recognizing that scientific knowledge and technology, while useful, have limited abilities to describe particular, concrete situations. *Metis* recognizes that those closest to a given situation may have the ability and experience necessary to influence outcomes or improve the odds of success for government intervention. To conclude, Scott explains bureaucratic dysfunction as flawed statecraft in terms of the friction between top-down, structured challenges and responses and the local capacity to provide knowledge and experience to help solve particular problems.

### Ideology of the Welfare State

Paul Frissen has introduced Scott's line of argument to the Netherlands with direct reference to the Dutch welfare state. He reflects on the efforts of the state to engage in social engineering *and* to fix the problems that it incurred in doing so. An unconscious ideology of statecraft underlies this dynamic, according to Frissen. The egalitarian values and desire to respect equal treatment under the rule of law in the Netherlands have become embedded in most policies and operations of the Dutch welfare state. However, these implicit values and attitudes are no longer recognized as ideologically motivated and therefore subject to political debate. Frissen argues that in many situations it would be more responsible and democratic to reopen the debate about value-tradeoffs between equality and other values, rather than automatically assuming that equal treatment is always the most desirable policy. He claims that some values of the welfare state have become so institutionalized that an open debate about what would be most beneficial to society has become difficult. The state as such is no longer neutral but value laden and severely biased to the value of equality at the expense of other values, such as freedom of choice, effective and efficient spending of public money, and individual or community responsibility. The danger of an overzealous state, according to Frissen, lies in its coercive power to destroy diversity, freedom, and individual liberty. Bureaucratic dysfunction, then, arises not just as a result from the inherent flaws of bureaucracy, but also from the ideological programs it is expected to execute. Through the institutionalization of political ideals in the organizations and policies of the welfare state, the original social values on which they are based have lost their meaning These principles are now expressed through the abstract legal values of bureaucracy: "The synthesis of the democratic Rechtsstaat and the welfare state connects the bureaucratic ethos of the former with the paternalistic ethos of the latter" (Frissen 2007, p. 125).

### Administrative Categorization and Path Dependency

One of the most insightful works illustrating this dynamic is *The Disabled State* (1984), by Deborah Stone. Her study of disability benefits policy in the United States analyzes how the design, implementation, and execution of disability benefits policies created a situation in which the state itself became disabled. Stone calls the state's inflexibility toward itself, its clients, and its suppliers "symptoms of the state's own disability." As the state attempted to provide services to the disabled through categorical policies and bureaucratic organization, it created a lack of capacity to solve any emerging problems. Stone finds the primary explanation for this lack of capacity in the use of administrative categories.

Stone begins with two questions: first, why would the state create an administrative category for disability in the first place; second, how did the state design this particular policy? First, the state must deal with distributive dilemmas. Creation of a disability category was intended to solve the dilemma created by the collision between a distributive system based on work and a distributive system based on need. This administrative category defines the conditions under which certain individuals are allowed to receive public benefits.

How, then, does the state design its administrative category for disability once it has decided that one is required? By establishing eligibility requirements for certain benefits, services can be delivered in a manner that regulates the redistribution of public funds, ensuring accountability to the larger public. However, once a clinical concept becomes a policy area, new tensions arise. Now, people with certain medical conditions qualify for benefits, and incentives are created for them to meet state criteria. On the other hand, this administrative category gives underfunded public agencies an incentive to reduce the number of people on their rolls who fill those criteria so that they can guard their scarce resources. This creates an automatic tug-of-war between patients and government agencies; in this political economy the doctor becomes not only a professional exercising his or her judgment regarding treatment but also an arbiter of public benefit eligibility. The creation of a new administrative category for disability changes the dynamics of supply and demand through the imposition of institutional logic by the state. The resolution of an institutional problem creates a host of new challenges in the implementation and execution of new policies.

One challenge that Stone observes in her case study is that, with administrative categories, a client can be either disabled or not disabled and will receive or not receive benefits as a result. To fine-tune the distribution of benefits, administrators created more precise subcategories. This additional refinement meant that clients with less severe disabilities could still receive some money; at the same time, with differentiation and fine-tuning of the rules, reformers also increased administrative complexity, and the incentive system became even more sophisticated and harder to grasp. The more the state tried to reduce the negative effects of its statecraft, the more it contributed to the deterioration of service delivery to disabled people. On the demand side, the result of the state's new disability benefits policy was a situation in which numerous people's lives depended on qualifying for as many categories of disability as they could. On the supply side, lots of administrators' jobs were structured in terms of the particular subcategory they served. The design of entire organizations was based on those categorizations. Consequently, it became increasingly difficult for the state to change any of its policies, because any alteration of design would upset the equilibrium that the state itself had achieved, leading to resistance and unforeseen consequences.

What we can take away from this analysis of the nature of bureaucratic dysfunction is that once government has chosen certain kinds of statecraft, it has set itself on a path that it becomes increasingly unable to change. The more the state alters initially, the less it will be able to change further down the line. This phenomenon explains the persistence of bureaucratic dysfunction despite the discontent of all parties involved and honest efforts to resolve the dysfunction.

### Intractable Problems, Institutionalized Policies

Maarten Arentsen and Willem Trommel have investigated six policy areas in the Netherlands that are stigmatized as intractable social problems: disability, higher education, health care, welfare-to-work programs, security, and immigration. They asked why, despite long histories of policy intervention, challenges persisted in these areas and to what extent public policy and its implementation had caused this predicament. Although from a distance, these policy areas look as if they have a lot in common (for example, significant social problems, significant government efforts, and significant lack of progress), on closer inspection the authors found that the causes of bureaucratic dysfunction in each area were quite different. In all cases, it appeared that there was always more than one cause; there was also generally no consensus on what the causes in a given policy area were.

Arentsen and Trommel concluded that policy problems do not necessarily persist because the challenges themselves are so complex; rather, the way that the government has designed and executed policy has influenced the nature of the problem, rendering it intractable. A second conclusion is that even though policies are often perceived by the media and society at large as failed policies, evidence does not always exist to prove that a policy is in fact not working. Expectations change, and popular perceptions are not always based on policy analysis. However, the belief that policies are failing contributes to the public feeling that given social problems are intractable. Finally, the authors note that not only governments have trouble interpreting social problems; social science also fails to account for the dynamic social and institutional developments that cause the perception of intractability (Arentsen and Trommel 2005). In order to better understand the lack of progress that governments have made in addressing social problems, social scientists should take into account a phenomenon that Arentsen and Trommel dub "the institutionalization of policy."

Institutionalization of policy is rooted in the preoccupation of governments with developing public policy to meet any and all social problems. Challenges in understanding and keeping pace with complex social realities cause disappointment and anxiety, on one hand, and the incentive to do more and better on the other. The institutionalization of policy has two faces: one might be called an autistic face, in which a government retreats into itself to develop policy that is self-referential and focuses on its own persistence as an institution. Such policies lose connection with the problem that the government is attempting to solve, legitimizing the government not in terms of the progress that it makes against social ills but in terms of its own existence. Government thinks if it has a policy for something, that in itself (the existence of said policy) constitutes a legitimate response to that thing, regardless of the effectiveness of that response. The second face is that of the glutton: governments lose themselves in their ambition to take on more problems and make more policy. In this case, the government may remain focused on social problems, but it has lost sight of its own capacity to make change. The first face demonstrates a lack of reflection on social problems, the second a lack of reflection on government itself.

From the perspective of a policymaker, we can see the multiple challenges of exercising sound statecraft. We can conclude that policy failure can sometimes be understood as bureaucratic dysfunction, and bureaucratic dysfunction may in some cases be a product of policy failure. More generally, these problems and their root causes are unlikely to be understood in their entirety if we employ only a partial framework of analysis. In the discussion above I have of course been selective—many more authors and theories could have been discussed. I simply want to demonstrate how each of these frameworks presents a uniquely helpful hypothesis to explain certain patterns of dysfunction. Also, depending the perspective that one chooses to adopt, different units of analysis and levels of analysis emerge, giving way to different sorts of diagnostic opportunities.

### Conclusion

The literature on bureaucratic dysfunction is extremely wide-ranging and varied. It includes the fields of management theory, organization science, sociology, political science, anthropology, economics, public administration, law, and philosophy. In this chapter I start my review with works that zoom in on the narrow bureaucratic encounters between client and government and expand from that in the directions that seem most helpful for the purposes of this study. In other words, I first consult the literature that focuses on the symptoms (red tape) and offers a diagnosis, and I follow up by consulting some of the literature that offers more insight into the perspectives of higher-level stakeholders in and associated with government bureaucracies: professionals, managers, and policymakers.

The four dimensions that emerge from this examination are red tape, structure, culture, and statecraft. The perspectives are not mutually exclusive or exhaustive. I focus on bureaucratic dysfunction from the perspective of actors who may or may not be mobilized to act on problems on behalf of the public. What the literature reveals is that bureaucratic dysfunction is a multifaceted, multilayered problem and that, depending on the theoretical lens one uses, different elements, causes, or consequences of the problem may come to light. Since I am not interested in partial theoretical explanations but in an understanding of the problem that helps us deal with it in practice, I bring together some of the most articulate and seminal work from different disciplines or schools of thought. Together they provide a comprehensive framework for analysis of the phenomenon, both theoretically and empirically. The framework helps one know what to look for, where to look for it, and how to look at it. It is a heuristic device that can help generate diagnostic questions in practice. Table 3-3 demonstrates how certain theoretical perspectives emphasize dimensions of bureaucratic dysfunction as a social phenomenon.

Table 3-3. Theoretical Perspectives on Dimensions of Bureaucratic Dysfunction as a Social Phenomenon

| Problem dimension | Dominant perspective | Objects of inquiry, units and levels of analysis, and major concepts | Bureaucratic dysfunction—presumptions about its nature | Contribution to knowledge and practice |
|---|---|---|---|---|
| Red tape | Client (recipient or obligatee) | Regulatory unreasonableness, administrative burdens, long and unclear procedures, arbitrary use of discretion | Unnecessary violation of common sense and citizens' rights and a waste of taxpayers' money | Pathologies, awareness, advocacy |
| Culture | Public sector professional | Values, personalities, attitudes, and behavior of individuals and groups | Organizational behavior resulting from the binding constraints of bureaucracy | Vision for human resources and organizational development |
| Structure | Public manager | Organizations, business processes, accountability mechanisms, institutional arrangements | Failure of rational, democratic institutional design or management | Organizational reform, institutional alternatives |
| Statecraft | Policymaker | Philosophies of governance, state-society relations, policy dynamics | Expression of misguided attempts to control or change society | Reflections, critiques, predictions, warnings |

*Investigating Cases of Bureaucratic Dysfunction*

The sandwich shop case has been discussed at several points in this chapter. But how do we know whether this case is worth investigating? After all, we do not know whether—and if so, to what extent—this case is an exception. We could take the case at face value and argue that it would be highly unlikely that many more entrepreneurs would find themselves in exactly the same situation, facing the same problems as the owner of the sandwich shop. But that would mean that we presuppose that the particular problems in this case have particular causes—in other words, that the circumstances that led to the occurrence of these problems are not likely to cause problems in other cases. That may be true, but it may also be false. The only thing we know is that we *do not know* to what extent this type of bureaucratic dysfunction has affected—or will affect—other people or to what extent it amounts to loss of private or public value. The question is whether we can determine the scope of the problem at hand—and if so, how. The case of the sandwich shop may be a unique problem, but is it also a symptom of a deeper and more serious form of dysfunction that we could discern and address?

*What Does "Dealing with It" Mean in Practice? Identifying, Defining, Diagnosing, and Remedying Bureaucratic Dysfunction*

Even if we cannot objectively establish whether—and if so, to what extent—the sandwich shop case represents a deeper and broader problem (and even if we cannot determine up front who would be responsible for dealing with it), we can begin to examine the potential response. What does "dealing with" bureaucratic dysfunction" mean? In applying the research question to this concrete case, I have learned that dealing with cases of bureaucratic dysfunction requires a careful approach, one that is sensitive to the complexity of a problem and respectful of the subjective experiences of those involved. Through practical and speculative reasoning I have operationalized the concept of "dealing with" dysfunction as a four-part process.[9] Each element of the process raises new questions to consider.

---

9. To formulate the definitions of these four elements, I have adopted and combined elements of definitions provided by the *Oxford Dictionary Online*, the *Merriam-Webster Dictionary Online*, and Dictionary.com.

The first step might be to figure out what it is that one is supposed to be dealing with. In the case of the sandwich shop, it is clear that no organization or individual is aware of the full extent of the problem. The entrepreneur is perhaps the person who knows most about its practical aspects and its immediate consequences for her personal situation. But she would not be able to tell what the underlying mechanisms and root causes of the dysfunction are or how those causes affect other cases or the community at large. The civil servant at the business desk, who advises clients to "just get started," may have a better understanding of what is going on inside his organization, but he does not know enough to do something about it. For some reason, problems of bureaucratic dysfunction get noticed sometimes by some people but do not get nominated for discussion and action. That brings us to a first element of dealing with bureaucratic dysfunction: *the process of identifying a problem.*

### *Identification* Is the Process of Recognizing or Establishing Something as Being a Particular Thing

What is it that we are trying to understand and solve? How do we find out if there is a problem? What mechanism do we need to detect problems? How do we know where to look? Where should we start, and when should we stop? How much data and what kinds of data do we need to acknowledge a situation as a problem? Who is entitled to nominate problems for further investigation? What method is used for the entire process of identification? How do we know whether this method is effective? How do we deal with differences in judgment?

Once a problem is identified as bureaucratic dysfunction and nominated for discussion and action, we have a new issue: what exactly *is* the problem that we have to deal with? It would be very difficult to come up with a solution for a problem that we have not yet defined. As we have seen in the sandwich shop case, there are many different ways to define the problem: first, as a frustrating experience with bureaucracy for the entrepreneur. But we could also define the problem in terms of the consequences: as an economic and social loss, for an individual and perhaps for a community. These are problems in their own right, with their own consequences. Alternatively, we could define the problem in terms of organizational performance and point to the poorly coordinated government licensing system; we could focus on the rules, as the entrepreneur does, and blame their existence for all the trouble. The problem can be defined at many levels and in many ways, and no definition would necessarily exclude another one. People define issues in different ways, depending on where they stand, what they know, and how they view reality. Establishing some sort of consensus on what the problem is would be an important part of dealing with dysfunction. Therefore, the second element of dealing with dysfunction involves *the process of defining a problem.*

### A *Definition* Is a Statement or Description of the Exact Nature, Scope, or Meaning of a Particular Thing

How can we establish the nature of a particular instance of bureaucratic dysfunction? How do we find out the scope of the problem? How do we adequately demarcate the problem to make it containable without oversimplifying it? How do we find out what the problem means to different stakeholders? How do we deal with incommensurable or conflicting definitions of the problems by different stakeholders?

If a problem is identified as bureaucratic dysfunction and a certain amount of agreement has been reached concerning its definition, the search for causes can begin. The important task here is to separate symptoms from causes and, in turn, causes from root causes. Much of this depends on the outcomes of the process of defining the problem. Let us imagine, for example, that the sandwich shop problem was defined as a flawed design in the city's licensing process. Before any immediate solution is offered, we would first want to know why the processes were designed as they were in the first place. Why did the city of Amsterdam organize licensing in this particular way? We would also want to make sure that we have sufficient understanding of the consequences of this problem. Why and how did flawed process design cause problems for the entrepreneur? Did it cause problems for other entrepreneurs or other people in general? We would also want to know whether flawed business process design explains *all* the problems of the sandwich shop. If it does, we may have adequately grasped the problem. If not, we may need to look further for causes and effects.

For example, the contradictory rules for the construction of a door did not have anything to do with the licensing process per se. Even if there were no waiting times and very little paperwork, the rules would still contradict each other. But it is conceivable that the occurrence of contradictory rules was caused by the same siloed organizational reality that explains the lack of alignment of business processes across government departments. The effort to separate symptoms from causes—and causes from root causes—is important to prevent us from fighting symptoms or recommending a treatment that will have adverse effects. The third element of effectively dealing with dysfunction is therefore *the process of diagnosing a problem.*

### A *Diagnosis* Is the Determination of the Nature of a Problem by Examination of Its Symptoms

What are the symptoms we are looking for? How do we recognize symptoms and tell them apart? What does the process of determination look like? What expertise do we need to make a good diagnosis? What are the risks and pitfalls in diagnosing bureaucratic dysfunction? How would we know if we misdiagnosed a problem?

When a problem is sufficiently identified, defined, and diagnosed, we can begin to think about actual solutions. However, just as it is not immediately clear what constitutes bureaucratic dysfunction, it is not clear what would constitute a good remedy. Straightforward solutions may not always be readily available or even conceivable. Imagine, for example, that the problem of the sandwich shop was identified and defined as a serious *regulatory* problem. Then imagine that the diagnostic process determined that the existing regulation, including the contradictory rules, was the result of hard-fought political battles between political parties, interest groups, and regulatory agencies. Finally, imagine that the suboptimal outcome of the process (poor, cumbersome, or contradictory regulations) was the price of political compromise. In that case, it would be very difficult to remove the causes of bureaucratic dysfunction since that would mean altering an institutionalized political history. In that case, it is more likely that a solution would be sought in terms of coping with an undesirable situation than in terms of removing its causes.

Alternatively, one could imagine that the problem was defined as an *informational* problem: both the entrepreneur and the government needed more information than they actually had. To get his business licensed, the entrepreneur needed information about rules and procedures and the government needed information about different aspects of the entrepreneur's situation. Diagnosis could reveal that all the required information was available somewhere, just not in one place. If the problem is diagnosed as an information management problem, remedies would probably be sought in terms of technological solutions and information flow redesign. Which diagnosis or remedy would be most accurate or appropriate does not matter for here. The point is that remedies depend on many different factors. First of all, the nature of the diagnosis will have an impact on the search for solutions. Second, the availability, affordability, technical possibility, and political feasibility of a solution all play a role in the process. And then there is the issue of perceived efficacy: Will the solution work? Is the remedy proportional to the problem? Will it have harmful side effects? Is it sustainable? In short, an important fourth element of dealing with bureaucratic dysfunction is *the process of remedying a problem*.

### A *Remedy* Is Something Applied to Counteract Something Undesirable

What are the conceivable treatments for bureaucratic dysfunction? How can those treatments be administered, and by whom? What happens if incompatible or conflicting remedies are suggested? What happens if remedies are available for only a small part of the problem? What happens if no remedy is available, conceivable, or affordable? Who monitors and evaluates progress of the remedial process? How do we know to what extent remedies have had an effect?

With these four elements established, the next chapter elaborates on the methodological challenges of investigating particular instances of bureaucratic dysfunction in practice in order to produce more general knowledge on how bureaucratic dysfunction might be identified, defined, diagnosed and remedied more generally.

# 4

# Inquiry and Action: The Kafka
# Brigade Method

*If you want truly to understand
something, try to change it.*

KURT LEWIN, quoted in *Problems of Theoretical
Psychology* by Charles Tolman, 1996

This chapter discusses the rationale for the methodological choices
that shaped the research on bureaucratic dysfunction conducted by
myself and the Kafka Brigade. The goal of this chapter is to explain
these choices. It is important in this regard to note that the study reported here incorporated three kinds of research: first, a conceptual
exploration, based on an examination of the problem from a bureaucratic theory and public value perspective; second, a theoretical exploration of bureaucratic dysfunction, based on study of the existing
literature; and third, an empirical exploration, based on an ongoing evaluation of action research in practice. These three kinds
of research were conducted concurrently over a period of six years
(2003–09). The chapter explains the rationale for this mixed-
method approach, elaborates on the specific methods used, and describes the measures that were taken to ensure validity. It also discusses
the limitations of the chosen path and their implications for the research outcomes.

## Research Paradigm and Methods

The social sciences and humanities have no shortage of methodological options. The vast literature on methods and methodology shows more debate (and even conflict) than consensus on what constitutes sound scientific inquiry.[1] Some scholars have attempted to reconcile the claims of, for example, the proponents of quantitative research and the proponents of qualitative research (for example, King, Keohane, and Verba 1994), the advocates of objectivist social inquiry and the advocates of interpretive social inquiry (Laitin 2003, p. 163), or the believers in methodological purity and those who favor methodological pluralism (Jackson 2006, p. 86). It has been interesting to see that these very attempts at reconciliation have sparked new, even more heated disputes. The "science wars," as these disputes have sometimes been called, are fought between those who uphold the ideal of emulating the exact sciences and those who urge social scientists to define and pursue their own path. While the wars have not resulted in winners or losers, or in constructively resolving the disputes, they have been helpful in a perhaps unintended way. Fighting over method may not be very illuminating, but the fight itself, and the intensity with which it is fought, prompts the question of what science is really about. What is the purpose of academic research? What is the goal of producing knowledge? What are the criteria of success in the social sciences? It seems difficult to agree on the means if there is no consensus on the goals. Any choice of methodology seems arbitrary if researchers are not explicit about their goals, and indeed values. As Gibson Burrell and Gareth Morgan pointed out in their seminal book on research paradigms, *Sociological Paradigms and Organisational Analysis* (1979), researchers have opinions about the nature of science as well as beliefs about the (desired) nature of society. If one is not clear about where one stands on these issues,

---

1. See, for example, King, Keohane, and Verba (1994), George and Bennett (2005), and Flyvbjerg (2001). The literature on methods in the social sciences and humanities, consisting of handbooks, textbooks, critical studies, and manifestos, is quite diverse in its form and content, in its scope and ambitions. Few contributions to the literature on method and methodology come without ideological or epistemological agendas. Indeed, some of the contributions are highly provocative or defensive in nature, valorizing some kinds of inquiry while derogating others.

methodological confusion can easily occur. To avoid such confusion, it helps to make one's presuppositions as explicit as possible.

### The Nature of the Research Goals

I have taken the position that research should benefit practice. By that I mean two things: first I would like to contribute to improving conditions in the world in the present (by engaging in current practice), and second, I would like to contribute to the development of an approach that will help others improve conditions in the world in the future (by applying our pioneering tools and methods, for example).

The problem statement—How can we effectively deal with bureaucratic dysfunction?—leaves little doubt as to how actionable the knowledge to be produced will have to be. The problem statement implies that at least theoretically, it should be possible to manage bureaucratic dysfunction, and it is worth finding out how. This position has had implications for the design of all three kinds of research presented here. The conceptual exploration was grounded in the normative frameworks of public value theory. Bureaucratic dysfunction was conceptualized from the perspectives of people who are affected by it and of people who might be able to do something about it. To learn about root causes of the problem in the broadest possible way, I have drawn from a number of disciplines and subdisciplines.

The design of the empirical research was also influenced by the overall goal of the study. The choice of action research as a research paradigm, and collaborative inquiry as one of the main methods, reflected my belief that both the quality and the relevance of the research would increase if the research was conducted in close collaboration with practitioners. Along with my collaborators, I carefully crafted a process of inquiry that generated unique empirical data as well as actionable ideas for improvement. More important, it afforded a continuous process of action and reflection. Even though the empirical research was always a work in progress, and we could not always provide practitioners with authoritative advice on how to deal with their particular challenges, we added value by making them part of the process of inquiry, diagnosis, and problem solving. In the upcoming chapters on the empirical research I will explain in detail how we structured and managed the research process. For the purposes of the discussion at this point, it suffices to say that I deliberately committed to a research paradigm (action research) and a research methodology (mixed methods of qualitative research) that were compatible with the overall research goals and strategy.

### The Nature of the Research Topic

The other important determinant of research design is the nature of the phenomenon one is studying. Though it may not be possible to attain the highest level of certainty regarding the causes of bureaucratic dysfunction, it is at least worth attempting, through careful application of available methods, to approximate the standards of research in the natural sciences. After all, I am interested in understanding how bureaucratic dysfunction can be dealt with effectively, not merely in how we interpret its meaning. This follows from my goal of producing actionable knowledge: I am looking for effective ways to deal with bureaucratic dysfunction, and any proposition that comes out of the research should therefore carry empirical weight rooted in observable fact—in other words, scientific validity. Since the exact sciences have set the gold standard for scientific research, it would be desirable to strive for knowledge about bureaucratic dysfunction that meets that standard.

However, from the theoretical exploration, we know that the object of study has two important characteristics: it is a highly varied phenomenon and it is a contested phenomenon. These characteristics have important consequences for research design. First of all, bureaucratic dysfunction manifests in many different ways in many different contexts. There is a large number of variables at multiple levels of analysis (for example, client-government encounters, organizational culture, institutional structure, statecraft), and the field of study is still immature. A corroborated and conceptually coherent theory of bureaucratic dysfunction is not yet available.[2] That means that it is too early to employ the standardized methods customary in the social sciences. It would be pointless and (with respect to our commitment to actionable knowledge for practice) irresponsible to conduct large

---

2. That is to say, there is no single theory that clarifies the character of bureaucratic dysfunction, understands its causes, and offers empirically tested solutions to remedy the problem.

quantitative studies, run regression analyses, and make causal inferences based on insufficiently theorized variables. Such a course of action would create the illusion of scientific validity, but it would not result in a very constructive contribution to knowledge—or action, for that matter. A more useful contribution would be to do the groundwork first, by developing a better understanding of the most relevant variables and the relationships between these variables and the pioneering methods of inquiry that pave the way for future research. When Weber developed his theory of bureaucracy, he invented categories, concepts, and analytical tools that helped structure the thinking and scientific research of future generations. He did not use statistics to prove significant cause-and-effect relations between the modernization of society and the bureaucratic paradigm, but through his *Verstehen* and his conceptual contributions, others could. In that respect, this study might be considered a small footnote to Weber's work. The conceptual analysis and empirical exploration of bureaucratic dysfunction in contemporary contexts are intended to bring the field of research one step closer to conventional "positive" social sciences.

Second, that bureaucratic dysfunction is a normative construct means that the research design should allow for the interpretation of meaning and acknowledge the subjectivity of those involved in the research. This is true for the researchers, but also for those who are interviewed or are otherwise involved in the research community. As we established early on, there is no consensus on what (an acceptable level of) dysfunction is because evaluative claims about bureaucracy are made from a variety of ideological positions, stakeholder interests, and levels of expertise or proximity to the problem. Conducting normal social science research, which assumes a normative consensus about units of analysis, variables, and indicators, would have defeated the purpose of the study. Further, it is my specific interest to uncover more about effectively dealing with the normative dimensions of the problem.

Were it not for these defining characteristics of the phenomenon, I would have chosen a research methodology that would have allowed me to draw more definitive and more universal conclusions about causes. But to remain true to some of the more fundamental principles of doing research in the social sciences—using an informed and appropriate research design, applying the method rigorously and accurately, paying close attention to empirical facts, refraining from inferring unsubstantiated claims—I had to take a step back. For this reason, the methods I chose to use and present in this book including an independent literature study and conceptual analysis for the theoretical part, case studies and collaborative inquiry undertaken with the Kafka Brigade for the empirical part, were explorative and qualitative. This does not mean that I subscribe to the view that approximation of science is not useful at all, and therefore we should give up hope of achieving more certain knowledge about our topic. In fact, I hope this enterprise brings the possibility of such research one step closer.

## Basic Research versus Applied Research

A closer look at the research question ("How can we effectively deal with bureaucratic dysfunction?") reminds us that there are in fact two methodological issues to be addressed:

- How can we generate scientific knowledge about the nature and causes of bureaucratic dysfunction?
- How can we generate scientific knowledge about remedies for bureaucratic dysfunction?

The former question refers to the nature of a more or less defined phenomenon in social reality, while the latter refers to the capacity of human efforts to change this phenomenon. This difference is sometimes characterized as the difference between basic and applied research. Basic research tends to search for causes of a phenomenon, while applied research examines the consequences of specifically designed human interventions to alter the phenomenon.[3] Both approaches, however, are similar in the sense that they force one to ponder the way relationships between variables can be explored. Let us first consider what a basic research approach to the problem would look like.

3. This distinction may make sense in terms of the short-term orientation of researchers. However, both exact scientists and social scientists agree that in the long term, basic research could have a powerful impact on applied results, and the results of applied research may generate important hypotheses for basic research (King, Keohane, and Verba 1994).

## Studying Bureaucratic Dysfunction

If one imagines "bureaucratic dysfunction" as a dependent variable, basic research would be concerned with what independent variables might correlate so strongly with the dependent variable that a causal relationship might be hypothesized. For example, one might want to find out to what extent the occurrence of bureaucratic dysfunction correlates with the level of centralization of an administrative system, or with the number of external control mechanisms, or with the demographic composition of an organization. In light of the current state of research on bureaucratic dysfunction, basic research has a long way to go. Hundreds of variables have been suggested in the literature, and many more are conceivable. At this point we have few clues as to which variables are most worthy of further inquiry. It is a genuine challenge for scholars of bureaucratic dysfunction to zero in on the relationships between the variables that matter most in terms of the impact they have on bureaucratic dysfunction. The first and foremost challenge, however, would not be to identify and define the *independent* variables but to define and operationalize the *dependent* variable. In other words, it is first necessary to establish what the phenomenon is, how it can be observed, described, and measured in a meaningful way, before relationships, perhaps causal, with other phenomena can be explored. In that sense, basic research on bureaucratic dysfunction is in its infancy and will need substantial and comprehensive exploration before it can make any attempt at describing or explaining the phenomenon of bureaucratic dysfunction.

## Studying Remedies for Bureaucratic Dysfunction

As Charles Lindblom argues in his landmark study *Inquiry and Change* (1990), to make progress on pressing social issues, social scientists should tap into a larger arsenal of methods of inquiry. Our conceptions of what science is, what it is for, and how it should be done have to be broadened, according to Lindblom. Acknowledging that systematic, scientific knowledge is the most reliable but also the most difficult, expensive, and time-consuming kind of knowledge to obtain, social scientists should also consider other forms of inquiry. Particularly when objects of study are not yet in the stage of conceptualization that allows for generating and empirical testing of hypotheses through quantitative research, scientists should remain open to a variety of methods that help further our understanding and thus make social and scientific progress possible. Finally, if the object of inquiry is an important social problem, it would be unwise of researchers to rely on conventional social science. To fully come to grips with a problem, less conventional methods of probing are indispensable (Lindblom 1990).

Thus, perhaps a better way to approach bureaucratic dysfunction is to follow the path of applied research. Those conducting applied research are mainly concerned with exploring the relationships between very specific independent variables and the dependent variable. These very specific variables in social science could be labeled "human interventions." Social scientists who conduct applied research are interested in the causal relationships between human interventions and the phenomenon these interventions are designed to have an impact on. To what extent does increasing or reducing classroom size have an influence on test results in primary education? Does participatory policymaking as a government practice have a positive impact on clients' acceptance of unfavorable decisions? Do shared service centers in government bureaucracies increase organizational efficiency? Applied research is about the efficacy or effectiveness of engineered independent variables (human interventions) with respect to the dependent variable. For a study of bureaucratic dysfunction, examples of applied research questions might include the following: Does deregulation help reduce bureaucratic dysfunction? Under what conditions does HR approach X or performance management system Y eliminate bureaucratic dysfunction, or does deliberately ignoring bureaucratic dysfunction have any consequences at all? The interventions that are the object of applied research may be designed by the researchers themselves, in experimental settings, or by practitioners who are charged with finding solutions to social problems. They may also be designed by researchers and practitioners together. Examples of the latter can be found in education research or policing research.

In many areas of study, including agriculture, medicine, policing, and education, much innovation originates in the successful collaboration of scientists and practitioners. Collaborative social inquiry of this kind naturally requires careful methodological consideration

(Bray 2000). It also requires learning while doing through trial and error, since the research itself is an experiment. This approach to science as an instrument of social problem solving brings researchers closer to their object of study and makes the results more useful to practice (Moore 1994). Pursuing this line of inquiry does not mean that more conventional methods of social science research have become redundant. It means that, as long as the conceptual and methodological requirements for conventional research methods have not been met, the more responsible, meaningful, and productive way to proceed is to broaden our research repertoire.

The core purpose of applied social science research is to evaluate the effect of certain interventions. Accordingly, the study reported here focused on interventions that can effectively deal with bureaucratic dysfunction. As mentioned, this phenomenon has not been sufficiently defined, conceptualized, and operationalized. This presents a difficulty for standard applied research in the social sciences. Another pressing issue is that standards of intervention do not yet exist. In this book, I am not evaluating the effectiveness of an existing way to deal with bureaucratic dysfunction; I am asking what an effective intervention would look like. In other words, although the research goals the Kafka Brigade and I zeroed in on through our respective forms of inquiry resembled those of standard applied research, at least two important elements were lacking: a clearly defined dependent variable and a clearly defined independent variable.

### Learning While Doing

The absence of those elements, however, does not have to be a problem. It would be a problem for conventional social science research, but the research topic, bureaucratic dysfunction, is not (yet) eligible for the standardized methods of social science research. The action research paradigm allows more bricolage in terms of research methodology. It emphasizes the importance of emerging research design. This "learning while doing" model can be contrasted with what Moore (1994) has called the "social research and development model" (see table 4-1).

The kind of problem our study tackled, and the kind of question I am asking here, point in the direction of the second model. The empirical part of the study was developed based on the principles of

Table 4-1. Comparison of the Social Research and Development Model and the Learning-While-Doing Model

| Characteristics of model | Social research and development model | Learning-while-doing model |
|---|---|---|
| Goal | Evidence-based policy: generalized propositions about what works and what doesn't | Better understanding of the nature of a problem and potential remedies |
| Method | Randomized trials and controlled variables | Probing through a multiplicity of methods |
| Assumptions | We know what the problem is, we're looking for solutions | We don't know exactly what the problem is, but we can't wait for solutions either |
| Requirements | Solid research design, accessible data, effective controls | Responsive research design, accessible people, continuous reflection |
| Disadvantages | Risk of simplification in case of immature field of study | Risk of lower certainty and less generalizability in case of specific context |
| Advantages | Generalized answers with high perceived validity | Richer lessons, more direct impact, more options for people to try out |

Source: Author

learning while doing (Argyris and Schön 1974; Argyris 1993; Reason and Bradbury 2008; Moore 1994). As a research method, learning while doing resembles the clinical process of trial and error because the nature of the research is much more like engineering than like physics, and much more like medicine than like biology. Obviously, more clinical methods of research demand more responsibility (both in an academic sense and in a social sense).

From an academic perspective, the generalization of the findings derived using this approach may be problematic. The knowledge derived from research in a particular local context may produce interesting hypotheses, but not propositions that would be valid in other contexts. From a professional perspective, interventions are in fact changing realities and interacting with social systems in which individuals have become subject to bureaucratic dysfunction. These interventions may not be as dangerous as medical research, but this work could still make people's lives better or worse, and caution must be observed.

## Action Research: Method and Tradition

Action research can be described as a family of methodologies that pursue action (or change) and research (or understanding) at the same time (Dick 1999). In most of its forms it does so by using a cyclical or spiral process that alternates between action and critical reflection, with, in the later cycles, a continuous refining of research and intervention methods as new data are interpreted in light of the understanding developed in the earlier cycles. It is thus an emergent process that takes shape as understanding increases; it is an iterative process that converges toward a better understanding of what happens. In most of its forms it is also participative (among other reasons, change is usually easier to achieve when those affected by the change are involved) and qualitative. Scholars of the philosophy of science in general and the methodology of action research in particular have paid considerable attention to developing standards for rigor and quality. These standards relate to some of the challenges that action research inherently presents to the researcher: how to deal with observer bias and remain objective about your own thought, how to improve observations and measurements, and how to develop ways to test ideas and substantiate claims. While these challenges are universal for social science, action researchers have wrestled with them a bit more.

## Rigor and Relevance

The tradition of action research goes back to Kurt Lewin, who pioneered new approaches to organizational analysis in the 1940s. Instead of studying a (social) system from a distance, he advocated engaging with the system and trying to fix any dysfunction directly: that way, he said, you stand a better chance of seeing its internal machinations, its causes and effects. "In periods of change, social systems reveal their true nature because they are being challenged," he wrote (in Stringer 2007). In Lewin's formulation of action research, there is a clear focus on instituting change—on taking actions, carefully collecting information on their effects, and then evaluating them—rather than on formulating hypotheses to be tested, although the eventual development of theory was important. This approach, which departed from the dominant forms of educational research at the time, emphasized Lewin's concern with resolving issues, not merely collecting information and writing about it. The theory that developed as a result was theory about change, not about the problem or the topic itself (Feldman 1994).

Others hold that the real founder of the tradition was John Dewey, the American philosopher whose pragmatist philosophy put engagement in a democratic process of inquiry and education at the center of human and social development. In *The Public and Its Problems*, he wrote, "It is enough for present purposes if the problem has been clarified:—if we have seen that the outstanding problem of the Public is discovery and identification of itself, and if we have succeeded, in however groping a manner, in apprehending the conditions upon which the resolution of the problem depends" (Dewey 1954, p. 185).

Among other fellow travelers, Karl Marx famously wrote, "Philosophers have interpreted the world in various ways, the point however is to change it." And many of the action researchers in developing countries have taken their cues from Paolo Freire, the Marxist-influenced Brazilian educator and activist who combined research, teaching, and social change in collaborative action, working with oppressed farmers in rural areas. His *Pedagogy of the Oppressed*

(2000) has inspired many widespread institutionalized practices in developing countries, such as participatory rural appraisals. Freire's work blurred the lines between research, teaching, and social action. Dialogue, mutual respect, and humanity are at the center of his approach to collaborative process. The learning that occurs benefits everyone involved, creates a better understanding of social conditions, and mobilizes individuals to act on behalf of the collective (Freire 1998).

Another line of development for the action research school of social science has been spearheaded by Donald Schön and Chris Argyris. Their work on the reflective practitioner and organizational learning has had a major influence on executive education, consultancy, and organizational research. Their approach, usually referred to as "action learning," involves organizing and facilitating reflection-in-action by professionals. This process results in increased awareness by professionals of their actual behaviors, as well as important information for the organization as a whole; making tacit knowledge within individuals explicit helps diagnose problems more effectively and identify and utilize the untapped potential for change (Argyris and Schön 1974; Schön 1987). The most recent publication by Argyris has specific relevance for our study because it deals with diagnosing dysfunctional patterns in organizations, which Argyris calls "organizational traps" (Argyris 2010).

As a long and rich tradition of social research, the action research paradigm can be characterized by the following principles:

- *Action research is rigorously empirical:* It does not reduce complex practices to simplified data but tries to capture the richness and multidimensionality of social phenomena through a variety of qualitative methods.
- *Action research is deliberately democratic:* It does not pretend that scientific research is a neutral process or that social phenomena can be interpreted without bias. It acknowledges the diversity of values, interests, and opinions of those involved in a social system and uses it as data to better understand the phenomenon.
- *Action research is necessarily (quasi-)experimental:* It does not impose a prestructured research design on a phenomenon. It is responsive to practice and engages the social system it studies in the process of inquiry. Through rigorous and transparent procedures

of action and reflection, action research actively seeks disconfirming evidence for findings in earlier cycles of research while fine-tuning the research design for later cycles of research.

Finally, action research emphasizes the benefits of proximity to the phenomenon and deemphasizes the value and the possibility of complete objectivity. It abides by the principles of social science in the sense that it pays close attention to the facts, and it is careful not to make invalid or careless generalizations.

As Stringer writes, "Action research . . . is based on the proposition that generalized solutions may not fit particular contexts or groups of people and that the purpose of inquiry is to find an appropriate solution for the particular dynamics at work in a local situation" (Stringer 2007, p. 6). Most conventional research methods gain their rigor through control, standardization, objectivity, and the use of numerical and statistical procedures. This sacrifices flexibility during a given experiment—if you change the procedure in midstream you don't know what you are doing to the odds that your results occurred by chance (Dick 1999). In action research, standardization defeats the purpose. The virtue of action research is its responsiveness. It is what allows you to turn unpromising beginnings into effective endings. It is what allows you to improve both action and research outcomes through a process of iteration.

*Criteria for Quality and Positionality*

In their handbook *The Action Research Dissertation* (2005), Kathryn Herr and Gary L. Anderson provide particularly useful guidelines for quality control and securing validity in action research projects such as ours. They emphasize there are two important issues to be clarified that help determine the criteria: positionality and research goals. Positionality refers to the position a researcher takes on a continuum from "outsider" to "insider" with respect to the social system that is being investigated. Traditionally, action researchers were seen as intervening from outside, working with professionals within organizations (Greenwood and Levin 2007; Bray 2000). But in recent decades more and more professionals have written master's and doctoral theses for mid-career programs, and this has raised questions about the desired level of objectivity or distance from the object of inquiry (Herr and Anderson 2005). This is part of the reason why Herr and Anderson developed a matrix outlining the positionality, goals, and validity criteria for various situations. For example, an insider studying her own practice would have as her primary research goals contributing to the knowledge base, professional transformation, and personal growth. This position fits in a tradition of practitioner research, autobiography, narrative research, and self-study. At the other end of the continuum we find outsiders studying insiders. This version can hardly be called action research anymore: it would be a traditional academic research project studying the transformation efforts that the insiders conduct through action research methods. The goal of the researcher in such a scenario would be to contribute to the knowledge base, not to practice as such (Herr and Anderson 2005). More conventional criteria for validity may apply, for example those of the case study method (Yin 2003; George and Bennet 2005) or the grounded theory of Strauss and Corbin (1998).

The action research I present in chapters 5 and 6 can best be characterized as involving "outsiders in collaboration with insiders." The research team, called the Kafka Brigade, has worked with fifteen different groups of insiders on the diagnosis of particular instances of bureaucratic dysfunction. The researchers played an important role: they initiated and structured the research process, conducted the interviews, and moderated the collaborative inquiry meetings (which we called collective performance reviews). However, insiders too had an important role to play. Without their participation, initiative, diagnostic qualities, leadership skills, sensitivity to group dynamics, problem-solving capacity, commitment to following up, and willingness to reflect and evaluate, the researchers would not have been able to do their work. The goal of the research was to contribute to organizational transformation (by engaging the insider groups in a diagnosis of bureaucratic dysfunction) and empowering those inside organizations to effect change (by increasing their awareness and problem-solving capacity). In doing so, the research team also captured lessons that transcended the particular situation and the specific group of insiders.

Methodologically, the question of validity is very much related to the research goals of action research, which in turn are related to the

Table 4-2. **Goals and Relevant Quality/Validity Criteria of Action Research**

| Goals of action research | Quality/validity criteria |
| --- | --- |
| Generation of new knowledge | Dialogic and process validity |
| Achievement of action-oriented outcomes | Outcome validity |
| Education of the researcher and participants | Catalytic validity |
| Results relevant to local setting | Democratic validity |
| Sound and appropriate research methodology | Process validity |

*Source:* Adapted from Herr and Anderson (2005).

positionality of the researcher. The goals and quality/validity criteria, as noted by Herr and Anderson, are shown in table 4-2.

As the emphasis in the research project was on generating new knowledge, the achievement of action-oriented outcomes, and the execution of sound and appropriate research methodology, considerable attention was paid to dialogic and process validity. Dialogic validity, understood as "peer review in action," was institutionalized in the research project from the beginning. Frequent reflection meetings were held with fellow researchers and expert practitioners in a variety of formats. To promote both democratic validity and dialogic validity, some have insisted that action research should be conducted only as a collaborative inquiry (Herr and Anderson 2005). This was the case throughout the entire project, from initial conception to final reflections, as I wrote this book. Process validity, according to Herr and Anderson (2005, p. 55), "asks to what extent problems are framed and solved in a manner that permits ongoing learning. Are the findings a result of a series of reflective cycles that include the ongoing problematization of the practices under study? . . . Such a process of reflection should include looping back to reexamine underlying assumptions behind problem definition."

This is where our overall research design was particularly helpful: every step of the research process was extensively documented over time. The materials produced through standardized methods within each episode (such as narratives, case studies, action plans, and results) were reviewed and discussed by the research team at every point of reflection. The team's understanding of how bureaucratic dysfunction manifests and how it could best be dealt with accumulated over time, not only because more research was done but also because there was continuous reflection on previous research in the light of newly gained insights. The concurrent theoretical exploration (literature study) helped make the reflection sessions a richer and more productive element of the research project.

One objection to research that combines understanding and fixing is that, yes, fixing is clearly important, but when you include solutions in your methodology, it will be at the expense of objectivity. This is true. By employing these methods, the team sacrificed objectivity to get a more qualitative and in-depth understanding. To minimize the loss of objectivity, the research team and I took measures. We sought to make our biases explicit, actively looking for disconfirming evidence and soliciting dissenting perspectives by means of structured reflection and deliberation with insiders and outsiders, as well as in the academic arena. I have found that the advantages of doing action research on this topic outweigh the disadvantages of not being able to produce the most objective and generalizable research outcomes. Any other method would have sacrificed the rigor of an in-depth, clinical diagnostic approach for (the illusion of) more generalizable scientific knowledge. At this stage of knowledge creation and theory development, action research seemed both the most appropriate method and the most helpful step toward the larger goal of finding a better way to identify, define, diagnose, and remedy bureaucratic dysfunction.

## Design and Management of the Action Research Effort: The Kafka Brigade's Projects and Method

The Kafka Brigade is an independent, nonprofit action research team comprising a network of action researchers from Amsterdam, The

Hague, Boston, Northern Ireland, and Wales. Its mission is to tackle bureaucratic dysfunction that prevents people from accessing the public services they need or fulfilling the obligations they are required to fulfill. The Kafka Brigade's projects often focus on the groups in society who depend on the government for services or information but who get lost in a maze of rules and regulations created by a multiplicity of agencies. The Kafka Brigade method was developed in the Netherlands by a small group of academics, innovators, and activists, myself included, as a practical approach to promoting improvement in public service delivery. Its name is an homage to Franz Kafka (1883–1924), who brilliantly described the problems of modern bureaucracies, with their lack of transparency to outsiders and bureaucratic behaviors that isolate people both outside and inside the system.[4] At the time of the research reported here, the team varied in size between five and fifteen researchers. It was funded primarily by grants from the Dutch national government.

While the initial conception of the Kafka Brigade as an action research team predated its official launch, we started piloting the action research approach to dealing with bureaucratic dysfunction in October 2005. Dissatisfied with the state of affairs—much was being written about the inability of government to improve itself, and very little was being done to put ideas into practice—we established a visible, recognizable action research team with a distinct methodology (Docters van Leeuwen and others 2003; de Jong and others 2004). In a way, the launch of a team named the Kafka Brigade was an intervention in itself: it challenged the perceived complacency of the academic and administrative establishment and deliberately reached out to practitioners with potential and ambition to become change agents. The Kafka Brigade was positioned as an independent actor focused on catalyzing processes of organizational learning in Kafkaesque situations: situations in which private and public value was

---

4. A lesser-known fact about Kafka is that his daytime job was as a clerk in an insurance company. In that capacity he was known to be an intraorganizational activist who was concerned about problems that clients encountered as a result of organizational errors (Wagenbach 2003). In that spirit, the Kafka Brigade not only investigates the problems of citizens but aims to help solve them structurally in close collaboration with (potential) agents of change within organizations.

being lost but it was unclear to clients, professionals, managers and policymakers what mechanisms were causing this phenomenon.

The Kafka Brigade method consisted of a six-step research process that combined stakeholder interviews, documentation analysis, business process analysis, and collaborative inquiry. The method drew from a number of different disciplines and techniques, including change management, operations analysis, leadership theory, and public narrative, as well as democratic theory, public policy, public administration, and public management.

The centerpiece of the approach was the collective performance review, a moderated session during which representatives from all involved agencies (frontline workers, managers, and top administrators) convened around a case emblematic of the larger issue. Informed by the case study of a "victim" of bureaucratic dysfunction, a thorough analysis of the de jure and de facto business processes, and an in-depth analysis of policy documents, the participants in a collective performance review would engage in a collective diagnosis of what had happened and why, before identifying what might be done to remedy the problem. As fragmentation of service delivery and law enforcement was the major common denominator in all cases of bureaucratic dysfunction, the very fact that all involved agencies actually got together in one room resulted in a lot of new, previously unshared information. The collective reviews also created tension, which sometimes transformed into constructive relationship building and productive energy and sometimes precipitated anxiety, friction, and reticence to engage. By evaluating and reengineering our action research approach permanently, we eventually arrived at a model that worked reasonably well in terms of our ability to facilitate a process of collective diagnosis of a case of bureaucratic dysfunction. Tapping into a wide variety of data sources as well as into the (tacit) knowledge of a wide variety of stakeholders from different agencies and different levels within each agency gave us an unprecedented opportunity to undertake a deep analysis of complex cases of bureaucratic dysfunction. The next section describes in more detail what we learned and how we learned when we were prototyping the Kafka Brigade approach (Huijboom and de Jong 2005).

## Refining and Defining the Method

We began by looking for problems that would fit the requirements discussed in chapter 2: technically and politically complex and with a high likelihood of value loss, not just to the individual but to the community at large. We sought the help of senior administrators and politicians to "sponsor" the research project. We found four sponsors who were willing to give us the opportunity to work on a case we had selected independently within a broad problem area we had agreed on with them. The sponsor's commitment meant first, that the sponsor funded the research; second, that it agreed not to interfere with either our methods or our conclusions; and third, that it would be present at a collective performance review and at a follow-up session to discuss outcomes and the implementation of any future action. Our part of the agreement was, first, to act responsibly; second, to maintain confidentiality with the media before and during the research; and third, to commit to delivering an action plan that would be less abstract than conventional research and consultant reports. We phrased our own part of the process as an effort to solve both the case in question and the whole category of cases to which it belonged.

To prepare for these four initial cases, we officially named ourselves Kafka Brigade, we wrote a mission statement, and we wrote up our methodology, in which we laid out both the principles that guided our research and the steps we would take with the sponsor, starting with exploration and ending with follow-up:[5]

- *Case selection* The Kafka Brigade investigates only cases that are typical of a larger problem at hand. The case research is never just about an individual problem or the problem of an individual; it is about drawing lessons from concrete, real-life situations that may be applied to a broader group of clients.
- *Putting the problem of the client front and center while involving all stakeholders* To fully understand the roots of excessive bureaucracy, all stakeholders are invited to contribute to the analysis: clients, civil servants, public managers, policymakers, and government officials. The Kafka Brigade involves them in the problem

5. Adapted from the Kafka Brigade Website: www.kafkabrigade.co.uk.

definition as well as in the discussion of solutions. Invitations may be sent out on the sponsor's authority, and the sponsor attends the collective performance review in person.

- *Open attitude toward rules* Laws, rules and procedures: they are necessary for a well-functioning government. But sometimes rules and procedures are not the most effective or efficient way to achieve public purposes. They may—over time—have ceased to produce the intended value, or have unintentionally given rise to altogether new problems. The Kafka Brigade does not fight bureaucratic administration per se but rather aims to detect and understand unnecessary, problematic, or outdated red tape.
- *Under the radar* The Kafka Brigade flies under the radar of the media. The Kafka Brigade tries to avoid media exposure for the project during the research. This discreet approach provides the participants in a Kafka Brigade project with space to reflect on their practices honestly and develop solutions without being subjected to distorting media pressure, messages, or timelines.
- *Creating a safe environment—public servants at all levels are part of the solution* Critical reflection and creative problem solving flourish in an environment where individuals are commended for their honesty and supported for their willingness to rethink their collective and individual capacity to create public value. This often requires challenging assumptions and current practices. With this in mind, the Kafka Brigade strives to provide a safe yet stimulating environment for all involved participants.

By communicating and abiding by these principles, the Kafka Brigade was able to convince most invited participants to attend, most of the time. After a critical mass of participants had accepted the invitation, a five-step process would ensue over a period of approximately three months. At the end of the pilot phase, we came to the conclusion that an additional step was needed. This step is discussed in more detail at the end of this chapter. The five-step process follows:

- *Step 1—Explorative research and case selection* The Kafka Brigade begins by conducting an initial appraisal of the problematic situation. How frequently does the problem occur? Who experiences the problem? Is anyone already working to address the situation? If so, what resources do they have at their disposal? Which parties are responsible for the issue, directly or indirectly? These and many other exploratory questions are examined in order to define with greater precision the causes, characteristics, and gravity of the problem.

- *Step 2—Case research and preliminary reports* A second, more detailed investigation is then performed focusing on one or more specific cases that are representative of the broader problem. This stage of research involves interviews with clients and dossier analysis. Drawing on the insights of the exploratory and case analyses, two preliminary reports are prepared. The first report is a narrative description of the client, the entrepreneur's or client's (subjective) experience, sometimes accompanied by a short videotaped interview. The second is a factual, step-by-step description of the process or procedure under scrutiny.

- *Step 3—Expert critique of the preliminary analysis* During the expert critique, the narrative and the step-by-step descriptions are carefully reviewed with frontline staff, managers, policymakers, and expert practitioners and academics. By subjecting these descriptions to critical scrutiny, the Kafka Brigade gains additional insight into the problem and corroborates its initial analysis.

- *Step 4—Collective performance review* Now it is time to bring everyone with a stake in solving the problem together. A round table meeting is held with members of the public, frontline staff, managers, policy professionals, and other concerned parties. The meeting is carefully moderated to ensure that all participants remain engaged, focused, and committed to dealing with the problem. The challenge here is to avoid talking about grand redesigns or simply pointing fingers or blaming the system. The three desired outcomes of this meeting are, respectively, to (1) arrive at a shared definition of the problem, (2) identify and explore possible solutions, and (3) agree on an initial set of corrective actions that will lay the foundation for a broader, more systemic remedy. Commitment from all parties to carry out the first set of corrective measures is necessary to move the process forward and build support and momentum for subsequent reforms.

- *Step 5—Final recommendations and action plan* The Kafka Brigade presents its final recommendations in the form of a concise, high-impact action plan. The plan includes a practical list of actions for all participants in the project. The recommended actions are designed to address structural weaknesses in the organization, not just remedy the original problem (or specific dysfunction) that sparked the investigation.

The Kafka Brigade method was developed through trial and error and much iteration. The methodology of action research teaches us that whatever your initial idea may be, once you engage in actual practice, you may find that your method does not match the nature of your case and must be changed. The subjects with whom action researchers work are also responsive (Herr and Anderson 2005; Reason and Bradbury 2008). We found it nearly impossible to approach the topic of bureaucratic dysfunction without getting close to those involved, and we could not get close to those involved without interfering with their work (whether we wanted to or not). In some cases, our very presence as researchers provoked the Hawthorne effect (the subjects of study thrived on the sudden attention devoted to their work). At other times it triggered the opposite effect: the fact that we were studying bureaucratic dysfunction led to counterproductive defensive routines and elusive behavior. In both kinds of instances, it is not possible to simply record the situation "as it is." Action research therefore presents its own methodological challenge in that, in conducting research, researchers are also changing the initial situation they set out to study (Stringer 2007). The best an action researcher can do is to explain as clearly as possible what, how, and why something was done, and what the results are in terms of contributions to knowledge and practice.

## Reflective Spirals, Wide and Narrow

Our primary method of ensuring rigor throughout our six years of research practice was that we always lived up to the instruction of "no action without reflection and no reflection without action." "Reflection" here means the critical examination of empirical observations, as well as the critical assessment of the interpretations of these observations. This has been the guiding principle and driving force

Figure 4-1. **Episodes of Action Research: Narrow Spiral**

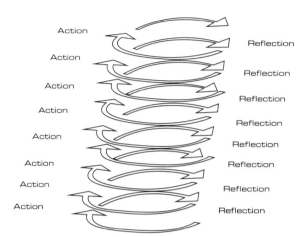

behind everything we have done. We have planned every activity and evaluated carefully what each project meant to bureaucratic dysfunction and to our method of study.

However, we did not anticipate all the events we eventually became participants in. Some episodes emerged because an opportunity occurred, but even if we did not plan a particular activity or event, we would still subject it to our process of action and reflection. We did so by establishing an alternating process called, in the literature of action research, a "reflective spiral" (Dick 1999). At every turn of the spiral, each project is subjected to a process of critical reflection on both substance matter and research method. The adjusted method is then applied to new research and the project is reevaluated accordingly at a new turn of the spiral, thereby bringing the knowledge about subject matter and research matter to a still higher level. In looking back at how we organized our reflective process, it would be most accurate to distinguish two spirals, a wide spiral and narrow spiral.

The narrow spiral (see figure 4-1) refers to our progress from one *episode* to another: at the beginning and end of every episode (in other words, every case study and publication), we took the time to reflect.

The reflection on particular episodes was not equally thorough in each phase, but we always asked how an episode contributed to our overall goal of developing a method to understand and solve bureaucratic dysfunction.

Figure 4-2. **Phases of Action Research: Wide Spiral**

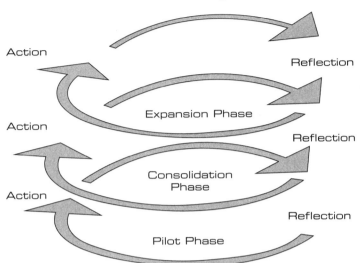

The wide spiral (see figure 4-2) refers to the progress we made from one *phase* to another: at the beginning and end of each of the three phases (pilot phase, consolidation phase, expansion phase), we reflected on what we had done and evaluated the method.

In the pilot phase (see table 4-3), informal Kafka dinners were convened approximately every three months, as were structured evaluation and design meetings. In the consolidation phase, we intensified the reflection process. Each project team evaluated how the case study project it had just finished contributed to the larger project of researching government dysfunction. In this phase, we also had regular meetings every two to three months so that project teams could share findings with one another: the Kafka breakfast sessions, which were three-hour meetings from nine to twelve o'clock at which the whole Kafka Brigade gathered to share lessons from each project.

The wider spiral of our evaluative process (see figure 4-3) turned at the beginning and end of each project phase. For example, at the end of the pilot and consolidation phases, we undertook a comprehensive evaluation of what we had done to produce lessons for the succeeding phases and adjustment of design. Most of these evaluations

Table 4-3. Reflection Narrows the Reflection Spiral

| Phase | Reflection per phase | | | |
| | Type | Frequency | Content | Participants |
| --- | --- | --- | --- | --- |
| Pilot phase | Kafka dinners (4-hour meetings) | Every 3 months | Project and research design | Core Team Kafka—*Avant la lettre* (4–6 researchers) |
| | Mentoring sessions (1-hour meetings) | Twice per mentor, once as a group | Goals and strategy for research and action | President, Court of Audit; President, State Council; and President, Advisory Committee on Institutional Transformation; plus core Team Kafka |
| Consolidation phase | Kafka breakfasts (3-hour meetings) | Every 2 months | Sharing experiences, evaluating methods | Entire Team Kafka Brigade (10–15 people) |
| | Case project meetings (2-hour meetings) | Before, during, and after case study | Research strategy, dilemmas, interpretation of results | Kafka case study team (2–4 people) |

Figure 4-3. **The Reflective Spiral in Episodes (Narrow Spirals) and Phases (Wide Spirals)**

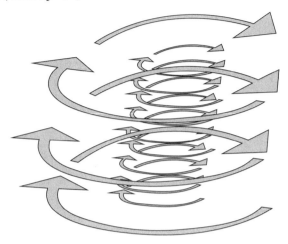

have been documented and discussed by people both within and outside the project, and details of our methods have been made available on the Kafka Brigade website and in articles and booklets. We have been active in the world of public forum discussions, in which we have engaged with both academic and public sector representatives to discuss the merits and the limits of our method.

## An "Intersubjective" Chronological Account

Each phase of the Kafka Brigade's development was roughly two years long. However, we did not plan the whole course of the work in terms of yearlong increments. What we did was trial and error, and we never thought ahead more than one or two episodes at a time. What we did was continuously to look back critically and formulate next steps. We then tried to create new research opportunities and seize them as they emerged. The most honest way to describe this progress is through a chronological account, without any pretense that this was a carefully planned-out research project. It is important to note that a chronology often looks like a plan, and individual episodes in a history can appear to be the causes or effects of other episodes. Without denying that some episodes directly emanated from earlier episodes, we suggest the reader take this narrative history as a chronological account of what happened, colored by our process of critical reflection and interaction with outsiders. The evidence in support of this narrative account includes the publications we put out along the way, the evaluation reports we made, and the transcripts of evaluation and reflection meetings held over the years. Of course, we cannot escape the fact that the following sequence is shaped by our own perceptions and documentation: this is a particular narrative of the Kafka Brigade's evolution. What we did do to be as objective as possible with respect to our own thoughts was create a more intersubjective account by sharing this material with colleagues, both inside and outside the project, and solicit critical feedback. This effort resulted in a more intersubjective and externally validated account of the course of events.

## Conclusion

The Kafka Brigade pertinent to this study consisted of an action research team of between five and fifteen researchers that conducted the fourteen projects this account draws on. The research community was broader than the core researchers of the Kafka Brigade, for it included the clients, frontline professionals, managers, policymakers, and sponsors who took part in collaborative inquiry, interviews, and case studies in the individual cases. The research community also included the expert practitioners and fellow academics who engaged in critical feedback during our institutionalized reflection process. To clarify the position of the researcher, it is important to emphasize that when I use the word "we" in chapters 5 and 6, I refer to the Kafka Brigade as a team of outsiders working with insiders on individual case projects. This grammatical inflection reflects the fact that action research is necessarily a collaborative learning effort. In subsequent chapters I describe each phase and episode of the action research project by focusing on how the spiral turned from action to reflection and from reflection back to action. The episodes are loosely described in terms of the goals and results of the work the research community did in that episode. The subsections of the discussion are organized around important topics, dilemmas, or insights that emerged. I refer to all the relevant sources when discussing phases and episodes. Each description concludes with the lessons learned from that episode with respect to the central elements of our research problem: the identification, definition, diagnosis, and remedy of bureaucratic dysfunction.

# 5

# Kafka Cases I: The Pilot Phase

*The government . . . covers the surface of society with
a network of small, complicated rules, minute and
uniform, through which the most original minds and
the most energetic characters cannot penetrate, to rise
above the crowd. The will of man is not shattered, but
softened, bent, and guided; men are seldom forced by it
to act, but they are constantly restrained from acting.
Such a power does not destroy, but it prevents
existence: it does not tyrannize, but it compresses,
enervates, extinguishes, and stupefies a people.*

ALEXIS DE TOCQUEVILLE, *Democracy in America*,
vol. 2, book 4, 2000 (1835)

In this chapter and the next, I present fourteen cases of bureaucratic
dysfunction as experienced by public sector clients. The cases are presented clinically, as if they were medical cases. I first describe the
"pathology," the combination of symptoms, and then the process of
identifying, defining, diagnosing, and remedying the problem (sometimes referred to as IDDR). In this chapter the first four cases taken
on by the Kafka Brigade are detailed. Two cases concerned entrepreneurs in the food sector, one was about school dropouts, and one had
to do with licensing a communal-garden barn. These first four cases
constituted the pilot phase, during which the Kafka Brigade was figuring out how to properly research a case and facilitate the process of
finding a solution. The lessons learned in this phase informed the

design of the systematic approach to case research that is presented in chapter 6. I use thick description to present the first four cases in order to convey the multifaceted character of the situation, the intricacies of engaging with the situation, and the difficulties of making sense of the issues and implementing changes in this initial phase. The chapter concludes with the lessons that informed the consolidated, systematic approach to case research described in chapter 6.

## CASE 1: A Sandwich Shop in Amsterdam

The first case, briefly foreshadowed in chapter 3, was that of Tamer Akgün, a twenty-nine-year-old Dutch entrepreneur of Turkish descent who attempted to open a sandwich shop in western Amsterdam. Although he managed to obtain all of the required permits and licenses from the city's authorities, punctiliously visiting the dozens of relevant agencies that monitor commercial restaurant activity in the city, the long bureaucratic delays in approving his paperwork left Akgün without the necessary funds to actually open the doors of his beautifully furnished, well-equipped shop. Many entrepreneurs in Akgün's neighborhood, particularly nascent immigrant entrepreneurs, felt too daunted or frustrated by the prospect of applying for the many required licenses and permits to bother opening their businesses through Amsterdam's formal economy. They set up shop hoping that law enforcement officials would not come calling. However, Akgün's family had had an unfortunate encounter with the Dutch tax office as a result of lacking familiarity with business regulations. Learning from this experience, Akgün wanted to abide by the law. Yet Akgün's efforts to navigate Amsterdam's licensing regulations cost him a great deal more time, effort, and money than simply opening a shop and paying fines after the fact would have.

One example of the many catch-22 situations in which Akgün found himself as a result of his conscientiousness began with the requirement that Akgün had to lease the real estate for his sandwich shop in order to apply for permits. However, to lease the real estate in his business name, he had to demonstrate to his landlord that he would have enough money to pay the rent. To collect the capital he needed, he would have had to borrow from the bank, but the bank would not lend him money until he had rid himself of debt. A debt clearance program would take over his past debts, but he would then be placed on a stringent repayment program that would not allow him to possess any property, let alone a sandwich shop. So, in order to start his sandwich shop, Akgün would have to show a debt clearance company that he would not start a sandwich shop.

Enter Amsterdam city manager Erik Gerritsen. Gerritsen was an energetic civil servant with an ambitious agenda to make city administration leaner, more flexible, and more responsive to the needs of its clients. Though he had already implemented many initiatives to increase the performance of the municipal government, he wanted to test these solutions on a problem that showcased the many inconveniences and challenges that red tape presented to the ordinary client. As a concrete example of what Gerritsen wished to see changed in Amsterdam's administrative culture, Akgün's sandwich shop seemed like a superb test case.

Gerritsen arranged a meeting between fifteen civil servants and Akgün himself, which was held in Akgün's empty sandwich shop. Akgün laid out the story of his good-faith effort disappointed by bureaucratic inefficiency. A lively discussion followed in which each of the civil servants attempted to defend his or her own agency's procedures and interactions with the public. When the discussion began to bog down because of individual civil servants' defensiveness and refusal to take responsibility for the challenges Akgün faced, Gerritsen did not accept the deadlock.

Gerritsen pressured the agencies involved to issue Akgün the paperwork he required. Akgün was able, with Gerritsen's patronage, finally to open the doors of his sandwich shop. However, while Gerritsen was relieved that he had been able to help, and that "his" government was not the only party to blame for the excessive bureaucracy that had almost ruined Akgün, he now faced a new problem. To what extent could the city improve its business climate if bureaucratic problems extended beyond the jurisdiction of any one civil servant? He was able personally to grease the wheels in one case, but what of the thousands of hotels, bars, and restaurants operating in Amsterdam, possibly under conditions similar to Akgün's sandwich shop?

Gerritsen worked to bypass this question of jurisdiction with the HoReCa1 project (HoReCa is the Dutch acronym for the hotel, restaurant, and café industry). While Amsterdam had already established several one-stop-shop application sites for entrepreneurs, their services were disconnected from each other and inefficient. The great innovation of the HoReCa1 project was that it combined the digitization of application procedures (which increased ease of access to these materials) with a comprehensive administrative overview of civil servant knowledge. As officials worked to place business processes online, they were also able to identify disparities between regulations and the actual service provisions offered at city offices. Thus, officials could find inconsistencies and overlaps in bureaucratic legislation that had gone unnoticed within individual agencies (while making the lives of entrepreneurs more difficult). The process of formalizing e-government became an excellent opportunity for municipal practitioners to rationalize their processes and to make application criteria transparent not only to applicants but also to the civil servants themselves.

The results of this project have been wide-ranging. Not only has the HoReCa1 project reduced both the administrative burden and costs to the city and to entrepreneurs, it has also become part of a citywide program to improve access to all city services. The scope of this initiative has encouraged general acceptance and participation on the part of the city's civil servants.

However, some of the problems in Akgün's case were not addressed by this initiative: the catch-22 situation involved private sector organizations (the bank) and semipublic organizations (the Housing Authority, Chamber of Commerce) that did not participate in the joined-up government effort of HoReCa1. The sandwich shop opened its doors for a while, as a result of the efforts of Gerritsen and others to intervene in the case, but eventually the doors closed again because too much money and energy had been lost to make it work after all. The lessons learned did inform the creation of a system that benefited many other businesses a couple of years later. At the same time, complete streamlining of information flows, services, and compliance assistance was still out of reach simply because some important agencies were not part of the city government and could not be incorporated in the HoReCa1 system.

This case was the very first case studied by the Kafka Brigade. It wasn't a success, and it wasn't a failure either. It did prompt the Kafka Brigade to think carefully about how to take on a case, whom to involve, and what to expect. These lessons were applied in the very next case, about entrepreneurs in The Hague.

## CASE 2: Entrepreneurs in The Hague

In The Hague, the Kafka Brigade had the opportunity to research two cases with similar problems to the one in Amsterdam: two nascent immigrant entrepreneurs struggling with the city bureaucracy.

### *Delays, Confusion, and Frustration*

Entrepreneur Jansen's saga with the local government in The Hague started when his application for a license for reconstruction was turned down because it contravened an environmental bylaw. The municipality granted him an exemption from the bylaw, but only after ten months of processing delays, because Jansen initially had applied for the wrong category of business permit and then had to supply additional information three times. Although the process is burdensome to entrepreneurs, civil servants at his local municipal office made it clear that they felt that in requiring entrepreneur Jansen to supply additional information they were doing him a favor, and that they could simply reject his request out of hand. Entrepreneur Jansen expressed frustration that he could not understand why all of the additional information was needed. The application process for the exemption Jansen received is highly opaque and also largely unknown to entrepreneurs.

Obtaining the building license took an additional four months, and was by no means the end of entrepreneur Jansen's administrative troubles. He was under the misapprehension that the exemption he received also covered an additional "exploitation" license (a license to run a particular kind of business in a particular building), but an inspection soon after the opening of his lunchroom revealed that he had misunderstood the application form, and he had to apply separately for the license. Although the licensing itself went smoothly, Jansen had to wait an additional six weeks to clear the "BIBOB procedure" (BIBOB refers to the Public Administration Act, or Probity in Decisionmaking Act), a process meant to prevent individuals with criminal records from starting a business. Further complicating these applications was a lack of operational transparency: interviews with municipal agencies involved with entrepreneur Jansen's case showed that some civil servants had no knowledge of the existence of other relevant agencies, let alone their requirements or procedures.

Entrepreneur Petersen's experiences both overlapped with and differed from entrepreneur Jansen's. The zoning plans Petersen consulted were out of date and nearly incomprehensible. After laboriously choosing a site, entrepreneur Petersen applied for a building license, which, unusually, was granted without a definitive exemption from environmental bylaws. The local municipal office also took the maximum application time of four and a half months to review his application, without a definitive cause for the lengthy review time (when asked later, the local agency cited lack of capacity). Like entrepreneur Jansen, he had to send in additional information twice. The real stumbling block came when entrepreneur Petersen applied for a permanent exemption to local environmental ordinances. His initial application was granted, again, after the maximum allowed time of twelve weeks had elapsed. The official application was approved after an additional eight weeks. However, over the course of this five-month wait, the local residents' and entrepreneurs' associations had raised objections to the opening of a takeout restaurant, and Petersen's exemption ended in a lawsuit.

Petersen faced delays piled on delays. Like Jansen, he thought that he was applying for his exploitation license at the same time as he was applying for his exemption, whereas in reality each item required its own application. Although he discovered his mistake in time, the BIBOB procedure slowed his applications further. Moreover, he had not yet established business partnerships for his enterprise in The Hague, leaving him without the necessary affidavits of his character. Instead, he was forced to call on one of his partners from another business to issue a certificate of moral conduct. Finally, he applied for a certificate of fire safety, but the fire department never processed it. While explaining these many obstacles, entrepreneur Petersen expressed distress that his local municipal agencies thought he was "bothering" them with his applications, even though their demands and procedures remained unclear. Yet the civil servants involved in the case commented that if an entrepreneur fails, it is his fault, and he probably caused the trouble himself.

Local policy in The Hague aims to direct entrepreneurs first to the local business desk, a government information desk maintained by the central city government, but in these two cases the entrepreneurs were unaware of this procedure and first went to the district office, a government service and an information center at the lower district level. Even though the district offices could not help these beginning entrepreneurs to the full extent necessary, the would-be entrepreneurs were never directly referred to the appropriate office. These breakdowns in communication extended to the agencies' websites, which, both entrepreneurs commented, had information that was often incorrect and out of date.

### Reflection on the Cases

In both of these cases, it became clear that longer application processes result in higher cost to applicants. Entrepreneurs have to pay rent on empty storefronts while awaiting official approval of their startups. As they continue to rack up costs during the application process, the entrepreneurs often delay their own applications through their poor understanding of bureaucratic procedure. Unused to the system, they quickly become frustrated with numerous license applications and repeated demands for the same information. During the collective performance reviews we held with civil servants in the presence of both the entrepreneurs and the responsible alderman, we distilled a number of mechanisms that impeded these immigrant entrepreneurs.

First, applying for licenses requires a high level of skill from entrepreneurs. Forms and procedures are often written in official jargon and are difficult to follow, for both applicants and administrators. In our case studies we found that few civil servants are able to understand all of the materials produced by their fellow public officers. The licensing process demands a wide range of additional documentation and information, materials for which the need is often not made clear to the entrepreneurs themselves.

This exacting application process stands in sharp contrast to the laxness with which regulatory laws are enforced. Entrepreneurs who choose to start their businesses informally can easily get away with not filing for legal documentation. This was fully acknowledged by the enforcement officials, who said they did not have enough capacity to enforce the regulations. Naturally, entrepreneurs run the risk of being fined, but the advantage of a quick start to their business often outweighs that risk. According to our respondents, this poor law enforcement makes a level playing field impossible.

Second, registering with the Chamber of Commerce is only the first order of business in starting an enterprise; an entrepreneur cannot open a business formally without holding all relevant licenses. There is a cumulative order to the application process whereby several permits will only be granted once an entrepreneur has received approval of initial documentation. By making license applications dependent on one another, government regulation has made the process of starting a business unnecessarily long and costly. The high costs to the entrepreneur in terms of both time and money make opening a business without some or all required permits seem the only profitable option. To a large extent this is the result of a lack of cooperation, both among government agencies and between agencies and their clients. Many civil servants openly acknowledge the poor functionality of the current system, yet they are resigned, feeling there is no alternative to the endless red tape. The result of this apathy is a lack of genuine one-stop shops for access to government agencies and a critical absence of appropriate guidance for entrepreneurs regarding regulatory procedures.

One thing that became clear from the case studies is that entrepreneurs and government agencies have completely opposing perspectives on the same application procedures. Government agencies struggle with a lack of capacity, generally taking the maximum time allowable for any given procedure. Entrepreneurs, by contrast, want to start their businesses as soon as possible, and they have no understanding of or patience for bureaucrats and their processes.

Civil servants implicitly understand their role to be that of guarantors of the public interest, and they often regard markets and businesses as private interests that are not to be trusted. Such bureaucrats generally do not recognize that the workings of government can actually damage public interest by impeding opportunities for clients and residents. At the lower or street levels of bureaucracy, by contrast, we find civil servants who are as frustrated with regulatory bureaucracy as the entrepreneurs they serve, going so far as to recommend not bothering with the licensing process when starting a new enterprise.

The cases in Amsterdam and The Hague were rich and provided the Kafka Brigade with many insights into how bureaucratic dysfunction manifested and why it was difficult to simply "cut" red tape. However, we lacked a structured approach to triage the situation and diagnose the problem. Therefore, we developed a simple four-step process based on our initial experiences that we set out to use in the next case. This process involved (1) exploratory research, (2) the case description, (3) a stakeholder meeting to discuss collective performance, and (4) a report to the sponsor.

## CASE 3: Dropouts in Amsterdam

The third case we investigated was sponsored by the Ministry of Education: dropouts in Amsterdam. After approximately a decade of research and initial policy efforts to remedy rising dropout rates, the Ministry of Education determined that it had not come close to addressing this problem adequately. From the ministry's perspective, part of the difficulty in lowering dropout rates was that it did not have accurate information about who was dropping out of school, when, and why. In 2000, one of the first efforts that the ministry undertook to counter these rising trends, the establishment of regional centers for the registration of dropouts, was supposed to answer precisely these questions. Yet these centers relied on information shared from schools about dropout rates, and there was general suspicion that these figures were inaccurate because neither the schools nor the regional centers were able to collect, clean, and process the data in a timely manner.

In 2005 the Ministry of Education came under increasing political pressure to provide a more accurate estimate of the size and nature of the school dropout problem, as well as effective remedies. However, the ministry did not feel comfortable with this assigned responsibility: after all, once a student drops out of school, he or she is no longer directly under the jurisdiction of the ministry. In fact, because they have dropped out, the one place these youths *cannot* be found is in the schools. The agencies that potentially interact with these youths include those in social services, health care, law enforcement, social benefits, and welfare-to-work training. What is more, it is not at all clear that people who drop out of school are experiencing problems: at least some may have found employment that they prefer to school.

These jurisdictional issues led to a prevailing sense among politicians and administrators that the school dropout problem might be bigger and more serious than they knew; at the same time, it remained undefined and thus difficult to address with policy. There were suspicions among politicians and civil servants alike that the system in place to fight truancy and dropping out was dysfunctional itself. The permanent secretary of the Ministry of Education commissioned the Kafka Brigade to find out what dropping out of school looked like from the dropout's perspective, with the intention of getting at this problem from a new direction. Instead of looking at dropouts from the perspectives of the respective agencies, he wanted to look at the whole delivery system from the perspective of a dropout.

## Step 1: Exploratory Research

First, we conducted a review of existing legislative policies, especially those governing the network of organizations involved in addressing this problem. We found that existing policy had—at least in theory—three priorities:

- Preventing dropping out in the first place, through strict enforcement of truancy laws;
- Investment in the registration of dropouts; and
- Providing services to at-risk youth in the Netherlands' urban areas.

The city governments in the Netherlands were responsible for coordinating these policy priorities. We interviewed professionals and managers working at this level to find out how the policy priorities were actually executed. The execution of dropout-related policy was characterized (by most of them) primarily in terms of *problems* in implementation:

- Many small, local initiatives were funded by the national government, with no coordinated efforts and no structural improvements.

- A high level of fragmentation existed between social services, education, mental health care, and welfare-to-work organizations. Each policy silo's own priorities prevailed over the crosscutting dropout policy.
- Many social workers seemed to be resigned to a situation in which a huge number of young people could not be helped, not because this would be inherently impossible but rather because supply would never meet demand. Given institutional constraints on supplies, these practitioners were unable to create tailor-made solutions to help their clients; furthermore, few had the time to engage completely with any one case.

We resolved that, if dropout numbers could not be assessed by any one government agency, and if dropouts' problems were considered too diverse for individual organizations to manage, then selecting cases from the rosters of these organizations was probably not going to be helpful. Instead, we found three cases through other channels. We connected with three adolescent dropouts who were then between the ages of twenty and twenty-two and enrolled in a nonprofit initiative not directly under the aegis of the Ministry of Education. These individuals were old enough to reflect on the upheavals of their teenage years and could tell us what had led them to leave school. What is more, as all were currently enrolled in the same skill-building workshop, they had already found a safe environment in which they could share their stories with us.

*Step 2: Case Descriptions*

The three young men in our cases came from completely different backgrounds. One had experienced problems at home after the divorce of his parents: his father fell ill, and he felt that he had to drop out of school to make money to support his family. However, because he was below the legal age for employment, he went from job to job in the black market. At one point, this young man had also experienced mental health problems. When he visited social services to seek financial and health assistance, he was given two options: go back to school or go abroad, to a summer school in a juvenile training and detention facility. He decided that school was no longer an option, and soon found out that his time abroad only drew him further away from his life goals in the Netherlands: finding regular employment and leading a normal life.

The second case was that of a young man who had experienced problems in the transition between primary and secondary education. Both socially and academically he was an outsider, so he began looking for friends out of school. He fell among the proverbial bad crowd, began using drugs, and started committing crimes. After several encounters with the police, this youth was placed in a juvenile detention and education facility. Attempts to return him to school failed, and his social workers finally decided to approve his eligibility for adult social benefits. After spending about four and a half years sunk in a deep depression, lying on his couch, he heard about the workshop in Amsterdam through a friend. He was also accepted on the sole condition that he would behave and work hard. At the time, for him this seemed the only viable way out of his predicament.

Our third case was a different story yet again. The young man had enjoyed a wonderful childhood and was a talented soccer player. At one point he had hoped for a career as a professional soccer player, and had practiced more and more to that end while neglecting his schoolwork. However, he sustained an injury that ruined his eligibility for that career. Only then did he realize that he had not received his high school diploma and was too old for school. He took many jobs but found them all pointless; he also felt that the service organizations with which he interacted were neither useful nor trustworthy. No one showed real dedication to helping him get back on track. He began to live on social benefits as soon as he was eligible but found that to be profoundly unsatisfying as a livelihood. As in the first and second cases, he heard of the Amsterdam workshop informally through a friend; there he discovered an environment in which practitioners took both his interests and his hopes seriously. It wasn't exactly a soccer career, but at least he felt as if he mattered to the people with whom he worked.

We wrote up narrative accounts of these three young men and their cases alongside all of their contacts with public institutions. In all three cases, the young men in question had had contact with at least ten different organizations, sometimes repeatedly. It seemed that all of these encounters had done nothing more than generate increasing disappointment among their supposed beneficiaries with what both society at large and the government in particular had to offer. This disenfranchisement itself became an obstacle to their finding gainful employment until they met a person whom they could trust, the manager of the workshop. The irony was that this manager was one of the few points of contact that were *not* part of the set of organizations responsible for antidropout policy.

### Step 3: Collective Performance Review

We organized a meeting with all stakeholders that had been involved, *should* have been involved, or *could* have been involved. The idea was to discuss, without any finger pointing, what had happened to the young men and how it was possible that none of them had been taken care of by the formal system of social and educational services. We invited policymakers from the Ministry of Education, including the director of school dropout policy, who was a true sponsor of the process, along with teachers and managers working in primary and secondary education, social workers, policemen, local government officials—everyone who was in some way involved with the problem of rising school dropout rates. We hosted this meeting in the Amsterdam workshop space where our three young men were working and where they felt comfortable. Interestingly, the policymakers we had invited did not feel particularly comfortable outside their usual working environment, which proved to be a lesson for us: the location and nature of the venue matter.

Although we had provided all of the participants with the young men's narratives, we interviewed them in front of our assembled practitioners to give them an opportunity to speak for themselves. Most in the audience were surprised by the insights the young men expressed, not only about their own situations but also about the support systems with which they had interacted. After their introductions, we asked the assembled group, "Could anyone have done anything to change the course of events in these three cases?" The second question was, if so, who should have taken the responsibility to do so? Most of the participants responded that they were each doing as much as they could to intervene in cases like these. However, the complexity of these particular life stories is something that no single civil servant can either fully anticipate or manage. Many professionals resolve to do what they can, but often that is not nearly enough.

From this overarching first conclusion, we began to speculate about what the causes of this institutional mismatch with real complexity might be. First, the policy definition of "school dropouts" in no way resembled the way that dropouts view their own problems. In fact, in all three cases, the real issues facing these youths included family dysfunction, lack of work, drug abuse, and other psychological, social, and economic difficulties. Dropping out of school was the least of their worries.

Second, without exception, the service professionals noted that there was a great deal of pressure on them to meet their service targets within a narrowly defined job description. These two things together, institutional pressure and limits on their tasks, made it impossible to deal with cases that did not fit a given profile. Given the extreme mismatch between the needs of young people with multiple problems and the policy definitions that structure a civil servant's work, practitioners were being actively discouraged from even contacting potentially difficult beneficiaries.

The third conclusion we reached was that the fragmentation in service delivery arose, at least in part, from the disjunction in governance of the various policy areas involved (for example, employment, education, social services, and law enforcement). Sometimes the national government, the regional government, or the city government might take responsibility for a given policy; otherwise, implementation may be subcontracted to private agencies. Even though school dropout policy is funded by the national government and implemented by the city government, all other policy areas have their own methods of administration, making it extremely difficult to coordinate across policy areas.

Fourth, the participants concluded that, in all three of these cases, there *should* have been someone who worked beyond the immediate call of duty to help these youths. The unanimous opinion of the group was that this person could have been anyone: a teacher, neighbor, employer, or social worker. When a student in trouble has been dissuaded from dropping out, there is usually an individual who has cared personally for the youth and helped him or her through. However, the problem with this solution is that, if any one person can mean the difference between staying in school and dropping out, it becomes very hard for national policymakers to direct resources. To whom do you give the authority to act if anyone can come to the rescue?

### Step 4: Report

In our report to the Ministry of Education, we summarized the conclusions drawn from our collective performance review, to which we added our own analysis. The recommendations for which the client had asked were directed particularly at their new policy agenda. The ministry wondered, in effect: We have a new budget for dropout policy; on whom and how should we spend it? We answered that the ministry should not limit eligibility for these funds to any particular organization. This was a radical idea for the ministry, since it had always had specific institutions such as schools or training programs in mind when writing bills. However, based on our research, the ministry officials decided eventually that the new funds would be submitted to any organization with a convincing approach based on the needs of young people. In other words, their goals had to be demand-driven rather than supply-driven.

### Step 5: Follow-up

After we completed this project, a proposal guided by some of our recommendations (restructuring the funding) was passed into law. The national policy to reduce early school leaving changed, and the director of the initiative credited the Kafka Brigade as one of the initiators of that policy. Eight years later, the number of early school leavers had plummeted dramatically—a 40 percent decrease. At the time, however, although the sponsor was satisfied, we were not. The Kafka Brigade had been able to influence policy, but we were not at all convinced that we had been able to motivate anyone to execute these policies. We also felt that we had failed to encourage local reform. In some of our earlier episodes, we had been able to drive local change, but we had been unable to scale up. In this case, it was the reverse: we were able to make large-scale changes, but we had lost touch with execution on the ground. We felt strongly that we could only really be impactful if we worked toward case-level solutions and category-level solutions at the same time.

---

## CASE 4: Small-Structure Permits in Leiden

Our fourth case involved the needs of people who are part of communal gardening associations, in which a group of people owns several acres of land in common on the outskirts of a city, each tending a small plot of his or her own. The Ministry of the Interior, which had received complaints from communal gardeners in the city of Leiden, sponsored this case because it wanted to learn whether the local situation was a result of national regulation (as Leiden claimed) or local interpretation (as the Ministry of the Environment claimed).

### Step 1: Exploratory Research

Communal gardening is a relatively common practice in the Netherlands: the community's members may cultivate all of their land, they may build a small barn or structure for relaxation or for storing tools, or they may use their plot for recreation. This is an excellent alternative for city dwellers who cannot afford a real vacation home or who enjoy gardening for its own sake but lack the space in their own homes to pursue it. Our particular case involved an association administering a communal garden in the city of Leiden, which consisted of a cooperative of about 100 people. To build a structure on any individual plot, whether for storing tools or for recreation, association members had to apply to the city government for a building permit. The city government managed this licensing process, but the general guidelines for building approval were laid out at the national level. Because the national government's prescriptions were fairly general and meant to be interpreted by each municipality, many cities had wildly different application procedures, requirements, and turnaround times. Because the national government had begun receiving complaints about these between-city differences, in 2004 it chose to put out a directive concerning application procedures to each city in the Netherlands, without actually changing any rules or regulations.

The 2004 directive established a broad framework for cities to apply in their permit approval process. It included stipulations regarding, for example, the maximum amount of paperwork the city could demand from individual applicants, or the minimum necessary quality of floor plans accompanying the application. The result of this unifying approach was that, essentially, the application procedures for building a cathedral became the same as those for building a barn. There was literally no difference between the two in the national government's guidelines. The responsibility for interpreting these directives sensibly fell to individual city governments. The manner in which the city government of Leiden approached this new framework confused communal-garden owners, who found that almost none of their applications for building permits were being approved after the national measures were implemented in the city. One example of this kind of bureaucratic dysfunction was that of an applicant who had done everything in his power to apply correctly for his permit to build a barn on his plot. His application was still turned down. He brought his case to the attention of the Ministry of the Interior as an extreme example of a typical case of the impossible building situation in Leiden. The Ministry of the Interior is the national government agency responsible for local government; a second ministry that became involved in the case was the Ministry of the Environment, which had initiated the 2004 framework.

The Kafka Brigade examined the individual case, the city government's procedures, and the communal-garden association to determine what the problem was and how it could be remedied. We followed our five-step process (exploratory research, case research, collective performance review, report, and follow-up) developed in the previous case, but we also inserted a step in between the case studies and the collective performance review that we called the "expert critique," to contrast both the factual and narrative accounts of the client with the way other organizations perceived both this individual case and the larger problem.

## Step 2: Case Research

To return to our particular case, our applicant had filled out pages and pages of answers to all the city government's questions. Some of these questions were truly difficult to answer because they did not apply to his project, including queries about the nature of the soil, the division of units within the proposed structure (a barn, in most cases, has only one room), and numerous other questions irrelevant to his project. He also went through the time-consuming, costly process of commissioning official architectural drawings from a professional firm and taking photographs of adjacent structures to support his application. Because the local government's workers would only answer his questions after he had submitted his formal application, he received no advance guidance in how to prepare his paperwork.

After the applicant's conscientious efforts to dot all the i's and cross the t's, his application for a recreational barn structure, where he could rest after cultivating his plot of land, was rejected. He contacted a city civil servant after this rejection to ask whether his application was rejected simply because he used the term "recreational barn"; in other words, would his application have been approved if he had used the appropriate terminology of the "communal-garden home"? The practitioner answered that, yes, if he had called his structure a communal-garden home, his application would have been approved. Hearing this, the applicant said, well, why not simply take my application, reopen my file, and replace the word "barn" with "communal-garden home"? The practitioner answered that once an application had been rejected, it could not be reopened; in fact, the city of Leiden had already destroyed the applicant's expensive plans and documentations!

Undeterred, our applicant went through the whole process again, only to have his paperwork rejected again. This time the reason was that the legal period for resubmitting the application had just expired (by one day). Now he would have to start all over again. Finally he gave up, going so far as to buy the property next to his own, which was for sale and already had a barn, and selling off his own barnless plot. In other words, this individual gave up his previous piece of land and purchased a new one simply out of frustration with the Leiden city government's building permit procedures. It seemed to us that what this person wanted was completely within the letter of the law and in compliance with all regulations; the bureaucratic process according to which he was rejected was incomprehensible.

### Step 3: Expert Critique

We went to all of the relevant civil servants at the Ministry of the Environment, who said that their original idea was to provide a broad framework to help unify basic elements of the business permit application process across Dutch cities. However, city governments must apply this information in a rational manner. It is not at all mandatory for the city government to ask for *all* of the information in the broader framework in all cases. The problem, these practitioners argued, was not with the legislation but with Leiden's interpretation of the national framework. Officials in the Leiden city government replied that this was not true. They argued that they did not have the freedom to handpick what information they would collect in every building permit application. Despite the national government's claims, its framework was inflexible. In effect, this particular case study became an example of Leiden's word against the central government's.

### Step 4: Collective Performance Review

We wanted, first, to invite a person with authority in the Leiden city government, the alderman for public works and land issues. Although we wrote a carefully phrased invitation, the whole involvement of the Kafka Brigade was not very much appreciated; it was seen as unnecessary interference from outsiders. Relatively upset, the alderman called our organization. The first person with whom he spoke was an intern who was researching the case for us. The alderman gave him a stern lecture about the role of city government in obstructing building and said that the interference of the Ministry of the Interior was unwarranted. The Kafka Brigade should stay out of local business, the alderman argued: there was no problem with their building permit application process in the first place, and if there were, the communal gardeners should come to him directly with their complaints. We were taken aback by the vehemence of his response and told the communal gardeners that they had permission to visit the alderman directly.

The communal gardeners, for their part, were disappointed. They had gone through so many appeals processes as individuals that they were now interested primarily in discussing structural problems in Leiden's procedures. The case's complainants did accept the alderman's invitation to go to his office, but when they arrived at Leiden's City Hall, they received another lecture on procedure. The city government essentially told them again that the problems they were experiencing were not the fault of Leiden's application processes and that nothing could be done to remedy cases that had already been rejected.

We reported back to the Ministries of the Interior and the Environment. We could not organize a collective performance review because the situation had escalated to such a fever pitch that all parties appeared firmly entrenched against one another. We had also managed to offend the potential participants, making the creation of a productive, safe environment next to impossible. We decided that it would be best to split up the collective performance review into a series of bilateral meetings with one stakeholder at a time. We asked a mediator from the Ministry of the Interior to assist us in gaining the cooperation of Leiden's local government. At first it appeared that this effort had failed to work, and that the alderman was refusing to concede anything to anyone. However, after a couple of months the alderman did set in motion a process to address some of the construction issues in communal gardens. It remains unclear to us if and how our intervention may have contributed to this outcome, but it appears that the alderman felt much more comfortable in the role of the man solving problems in his jurisdiction.

The meeting immediately after that was with the Ministry of the Environment. We told the officials that this problem in Leiden was the result at least in part of their unifying efforts at the national level, and that they should at the very least check in periodically with city governments after the institution of such directives to be certain the directives were being implemented productively. The ministry's representatives agreed, but they also said that they were working on an e-government process for permit application that would render all of these discrepancies and challenges obsolete. We were skeptical about this claim because, even if all application forms were to become available online, the form itself remains lengthy, and the amount of supporting information required is substantial. Many of the questions may also remain irrelevant. It remains to be seen whether this e-government application will be effective in remedying Leiden's problems.

Our third meeting was with the Ministry of the Interior. We reflected on the way that the ministry is seen by local governments and raised questions about what roles the Ministry of the Interior might play in remedying bureaucratic dysfunction at the municipal level. The ministry does have jurisdiction over the system of lower-level government, but it does not actually have the authority to intervene in particular municipalities. If city governments do not function well, people may complain to the ministry, as the communal gardeners did, but other than "soft powers" the ministry does not have any tools to act.

### Step 5: Action Plan

These three meetings with the alderman, the Ministry of the Environment, and the Ministry of the Interior replaced the collective performance reviews. Given the fragmentation of the Kafka Brigade's interactions with this case, we did not produce a single action plan or report. Instead, a series of agreements emerged, which have led to some results. Procedures at the Leiden municipal level for building permits have become simpler. The Ministry of the Environment claimed that it would take into account this issue of narrow interpretations of its broad framework when planning future directives (although as yet, we have seen no results from this resolution).

## Lessons

Our own difficulties led us to the realization that we needed to refine how the Kafka Brigade worked between tiers of government. This resulted in our final adjustments to the Kafka Brigade method in this initial phase, a more consolidated action research design that structured our next phase of work. Our research design now consisted of five steps, all focused on understanding what the problem is and mobilizing the potential to come up with remedies:

1. Exploratory research into broader contextual issues;
2. Case research that would address structural problems through a focus on a specific situation;
3. Expert critique, in which we conduct in-depth interviews with the stakeholders involved in a case;
4. Collective performance reviews (that is, a moderated discussion to define problems and explore solutions);
5. Action plans summing up all of the actions to which participants in the collective performance review have committed themselves.

These action plan commitments work on three levels: (1) the case level, addressing bureaucratic dysfunction identified in a particular instance; (2) policy-level solutions that will potentially affect all similar cases at the level of legislation; and (3) capacity-level solutions, which refer to the ability of an organization or network of organizations to identify and remedy problems of bureaucratic dysfunction. This last type of solution would ensure that future problems could be detected and dealt with more effectively; it is this type of solution that would make initiatives like the Kafka Brigade redundant in a perfect future.

To conclude, this project design was the cumulative result of what we learned from our first Kafka Brigade projects. With this design in hand, we began the second phase of our project, which is described in the next chapter.

---

## Lessons Learned from the Pilot Study

Through trial and error in the pilot phase we learned a great deal with regard to the process of dealing with bureaucratic dysfunction. In what follows we summarize the lessons in the chronological order of the episodes (case projects) we conducted. Most lessons took the form of questions. We answered these questions by adjusting our approach, fine-tuning our methods and techniques, and reframing and rephrasing the way we wrote and spoke about the work. The result was the improved research design that we started with in the consolidation phase, discussed in the next chapter.

## Identifying Bureaucratic Dysfunction

Bureaucratic dysfunction is hard to identify. How do you prove that government performance is dysfunctional and that indications of dysfunction are more than just exceptions? How can you support plausible intuitions with data rather than anecdotes?

It is tempting to look for general solutions, but finding solutions that make sense to practitioners requires remaining focused on particular problems that they can relate to and work on. Mechanisms to identify structural bureaucratic dysfunction are virtually absent in or around the responsible organizations. Only extreme incidents and general performance statistics get attention (there is no mechanism in most organizations that spots the trouble in between). In particular, those working at the policy level and those working on the front lines have stunningly different mind-sets, which are expressed in different language and different attitudes.

In developing or nominating specific cases as emblematic of bureaucratic dysfunction, the following should be considered:

- Under what conditions does the use of well-selected cases, written up as structured narratives, provide a clear point of entry to the identification of bureaucratic dysfunction?
- Under what conditions will involving the client (the "victim" of bureaucratic dysfunction) as a source of information be helpful in identifying problems?

Even with hard proof of bureaucratic dysfunction, the issue can be denied and ignored. Ultimately, the question is how stakeholders can be convinced to accept that there is a problem, and then be persuaded to work on it.

## Defining Bureaucratic Dysfunction

Bureaucratic dysfunction can be (and has been) defined from many different disciplinary and practical angles. People within bureaucracies tend to define the nature and relevance of bureaucratic dysfunction in terms of their own organizational task and to the extent that they are responsible for that task. Clients have their own experience and definition of bureaucratic dysfunction.

Defining bureaucratic dysfunction in terms of suboptimal social outcomes (public value perspective) is a political choice rather than a scientific one. To keep deliberation open, it is necessary to avoid fixed definitions of what problems and solutions look like. The public value perspective helps define bureaucratic dysfunction because it focuses on "what could be" or "what could have been" instead of "what is" or "what has to be." Encouraging this perspective can help those involved define the problem in terms that everyone can understand.

In defining bureaucratic dysfunction, the following should be kept in mind:

- The combination of factual accounts (process maps) and narrative accounts (perceptions) helps describe the experience of alienation of clients and bureaucrats.
- Without the willingness, ability, or opportunity to define the actual problem, a collective performance review does not have much value. We have to invest in a productive working environment and open-minded attendants.
- If a case is not defined through deliberation and interaction with relevant stakeholders, it may end up being defined in terms of the interests of the dominant player, such as the most vocal advocate or the highest-ranking entity or official.
- The initial problem definition (case description) is more likely to be accepted as a valid starting point if it is contrasted with an expert review that includes the perceptions of the involved stakeholders as well.
- In the case of opposing and contradictory problem statements, it is important to leave the issue undefined or half defined. The initial question for the collective performance review then becomes, is there a problem?

## Diagnosing Bureaucratic Dysfunction

Without robust evidence, any analysis is vulnerable. The challenge is to use the limited resources for research wisely and strategically, which means selecting cases carefully. To make adequate and relevant diagnoses of bureaucratic dysfunction, we must get closer to the problem and closer to the people involved. It is important to keep in mind that diagnosing a case is already part of a change process that has political implications. It may provoke anxiety, undermining behavior, and resistance.

Because the process of diagnosing bureaucratic dysfunction is conducted in a forum with many stakeholders, all holding different views and perspectives, the facilitator may find the following points useful in working toward a consensus:

- Facilitating a diagnostic process requires moderating skills, as well as a blend of knowledge of the case at hand and general knowledge about change management.
- Tone of voice matters a great deal. A diagnosis can easily be perceived as an attack or an accusation. Communication and facilitation skills are extremely important.
- If a diagnosis is focused only on one dimension, such as organizational culture, business processes, or legislation, it is not likely to yield much insight into bureaucratic dysfunction.
- Even though the collective performance review is case-based, diagnosis takes place on many different levels of abstraction.
- It is important not to let the diagnosis be monopolized by one stakeholder's perspective. A policy-focused diagnosis, for example, may not bring out issues on the delivery side (and vice versa).

### Remedying Bureaucratic Dysfunction

There is not necessarily a direct or logical relationship between a diagnosis and a remedy, if it is left up to others' interpretation or willingness to act. And if there is no full agreement on the problem definition, it is hard to achieve consensus on a solution.

The following points summarize the insights gained by the Kafka Brigade during the initial phase with respect to remedying bureaucratic dysfunction:

- Solutions originating in an external context can be dismissed as not fitting the current or local need.
- To contribute to the solution, one must strike a balance between becoming a darling and becoming an enemy.

- The authority of policymakers can be used strategically to focus attention and to sustain momentum in change processes.
- Focusing on small steps that the individual manager or professional can take may have a larger overall effect than trying to force a consensus on larger changes.
- Empowering the individual manager or professional to successfully maneuver in his or her environment may be key to unleashing change.
- Remedies may be defined and implemented at three different levels: the case level, the category (policy) level, and the capacity level.

The research design and method may not enjoy the support or approval of some stakeholders. In those cases, applying them too rigidly will not produce a better analysis or result. The more exposed or challenged people feel by the Kafka Brigade's approach, the more important it is to make them feel they are part of the solution and can take credit for it. The reactions that an unconventional case-based approach provokes are part of the process and should be carefully managed and analyzed.

# 6

# Kafka Cases II: The Consolidation Phase

*Someone must have slandered Josef K., for
one morning, without having done
anything wrong, he was arrested.*

FRANZ KAFKA, *The Trial*, 1998 (1925)

This chapter presents the results of the second phase of action research on bureaucratic dysfunction by the Kafka Brigade. The research method was much more structured, systematic, and consistent in its design and application in this phase than in the pilot
phase. Whereas the pilot phase encompassed a variety of heterogeneous episodes in which each episode built on and improved on
the previous episode, the consolidation phase consisted of ten case
studies (numbers 5 to 14) that were conducted in an almost identical
manner.

The chapter begins with an outline of the research design, the case
selection process, and the basic analytical distinctions we used to organize the material. Summaries of the ten cases are then presented,
including a compact overview of the people affected, their major complaints, and the agencies involved. Each case description includes the
results of our attempt to identify, define, diagnose, and remedy bureaucratic dysfunction at a particular place, at a particular time, with a
particular group of people. The chapter concludes with some general
lessons about effectively identifying, defining, diagnosing, and remedying bureaucratic dysfunction.

## A Breakthrough Opportunity

After the first four cases, we reflected on the lessons learned and were looking for an opportunity to apply the emerging method of research and intervention to a larger set of cases of bureaucratic dysfunction. We had learned from previous projects that high-level sponsorship was necessary for convening people and creating urgency around a problem, and for ensuring that the ensuing plans would be acted on. An opportunity to obtain such a sponsor presented itself when the Dutch Minister of Public Sector Reform resigned and a new minister came into office to finish the last three months of the four-year government term. Because he would have only three months in office, had little to lose, and saw an opportunity to launch an interesting experiment, he was willing to fund a large-scale project (ten cases), along with a comprehensive evaluation of the methodology, and was also willing to become personally involved, if needed. It was a perfect window of opportunity for the Kafka Brigade.

### *Consolidating the Research and Intervention Design*

First, we ensured that the Kafka Brigade would operate as it had all along, continuously alternating action and reflection. A considerable part of our budget was allocated for reflection; not only on each particular case but also on the project as a whole. The Ministry for Public Sector Reform gave us a formal research assignment to draw lessons about bureaucratic dysfunction and our methods. Another condition that we agreed on from the beginning was the personal involvement of the minister, which would be instrumental in convening the relevant parties and generating a sense of urgency around both the problems and solutions they identified. If, for some reason, the participants in the collective performance review could not address action points, then the minister would commit to taking the problem to a higher level. We decided to start every collective performance review with a statement about this commitment pledge. The minister, who would be present on at least a few occasions, or a civil servant speaking on his behalf would announce that he invited everybody, first, to contribute to the problem definition; second, to nominate a step or an action that he or she could take to remedy the problem; and third, to mention whatever was needed from others—or from him, for that matter—to make that happen. This was our plan to build a degree of commitment that would empower participants and mobilize the resources of those involved. These conditions consolidated the research and intervention design that we had been developing and became the starting point for the next ten cases.

## Case Selection

After we had agreed on the project conditions and fine-tuned the research and intervention design, we had to select the cases. We immediately agreed that we should include a variety of policy areas because we had learned that bureaucratic dysfunction was not limited to one or even a few policy areas but was ubiquitous. We also chose to take on only cases involving more than one government agency. These cases would also have to concern more than just a particular incident; they had to have relevance for a larger category of cases. We also made feasibility a criterion: we wanted to be sure that something could actually be done about the problems the cases presented within a relatively short time frame (three months to a year). The question then became, where would we find these cases?

Another project of the Ministry of the Interior came in handy. In 2005 the ministry had launched a new website, Lastvandeoverheid.nl (BotheredBytheGovernment.com). This website allowed citizens to file complaints about the government in general, but also about particular cases. Civil servants had used this information to notify other agencies about the complaints, but they were often stuck with cases that were too complex to be directed to a particular agency. We began working closely with the civil servants to read, interpret, discuss, and act on the written complaints. Because many complaints were hard to understand without more information, the civil servants started calling the complainants in order to better assist them. Together we gradually developed a working method that enabled the civil service workers to sort the submissions to the website into various categories. One of the categories was labeled "complex." This meant that even after the civil servants had gathered more information from the complainants and other agencies, they still could not figure out what the problem really was, let alone what a solution might look like. This category of complaints provided useful material for the Kafka Brigade. We started selecting cases from this category that satisfied the criteria we had developed.

## *Presenting the Cases*

The Kafka Brigade method involved exploratory research, case research, expert interviews, a collective performance review, an action plan, and a follow-up meeting. The written products of the first three steps were always a narrative account of the situation of a client and a factual account of his or her encounters with agencies. These documents, supported by desk research and nuanced or contrasted by the expert interviews, formed the written input for the collective performance reviews. In a way, this input was the result of the problem identification and initial problem definition of our method. The collective performance reviews would produce the expanded or corroborated problem definition and diagnosis of the problem, as well as a list of corrective actions or remedies. The written result of the collective performance review was an action plan, with a summary of the collectively conducted diagnosis and individually nominated actions for improvement.

## Ten Cases of Bureaucratic Dysfunction

The cases (numbers 5 through 14) presented in this chapter follow the first four cases that made up the pilot phase of the study and were presented in the previous chapter. Below, the issues of each case are distilled and presented both in an "At a Glance" box and as a discursive narrative featuring the client who experienced the problems. (All client names have been changed for anonymity.) After that the theoretical perspectives described in chapter 3 are used to organize the findings from the collaborative performance review: "Red Tape" (the perspective of the public sector client), "Structure" (the perspective of the public manager), "Culture" (the perspective of the public sector professional), and "Statecraft" (the perspective of policymakers).

## **CASE 5**: Medical Assessment Certificates

**Service Providers Require Helena to Have Her
Chronically Ill Daughters Tested Repeatedly**

*At a Glance*

| | |
|---|---|
| Those affected | Disabled and chronically ill people who depend on public services for assistance |
| Major complaints | Unclear application procedures, lack of information |
| | Repeated demands for similar or identical information |
| | Cost of compliance (time and effort) |
| Agencies involved | City government (multiple divisions) |
| | Insurance company |
| | Tax authority |
| | Hospital |
| | Ministry of Health |

Helena was the mother of two daughters with disabilities. Her elder daughter suffered from multiple sclerosis, and her younger daughter, Gwen (not her real name), had a rare and incurable disease called TNF-receptor-associated periodic syndrome (TRAPS), which had left her confined to a wheelchair. There were fluctuations in her condition, but overall, her situation was deteriorating rather than improving.

Because Helena's husband worked full time, much of the care for Gwen and her sister fell to their mother. It was highly physical work. Helena had to lift Gwen frequently, and traveling in conventional cars required her to dismantle and reassemble Gwen's wheelchair, causing serious back pain. To make Helena's life easier, the family decided to buy a wheelchair-friendly van so that Gwen could travel without dismantling the wheelchair. This van had a gray license plate, indicating that tax deductions applied on the vehicle taxes. In 2004 Helena discovered that new restrictions on tax deductions would soon make "gray driving" more expensive. She wrote a letter requesting more information and was told that the current vehicle tax relief her family received would be continued because of Gwen's medical condition. However, the family would need to reapply annually to continue the exemption.

The first year Helena reapplied for her vehicle tax refund after the new pricing went into effect everything went well; she filled out the stack of forms and submitted the necessary paperwork to prove Gwen's illness. The second year she submitted her tax application early, in the hope of receiving her refund sooner. Five months after filing, she received a notice from the tax collection office that it had not received an application with a medical assessment certificate for extension of the exempt status. Helena did not understand this. The same tax authority had provided a tax refund because of her daughters' medical conditions every year without annual certification by a doctor. It seemed a complete waste of both her family's and her doctor's time to have to file and refile a new medical assessment certificate every year; after all, TRAPS is an incurable disease.

Helena's troubles with certification requirements continued as she dealt with other agencies and organizations. Each time her daughters required a new service or undertook a new activity, Helena needed to apply with a new medical assessment certificate: for a government contribution to a new van that could accommodate Gwen's wheelchair for trips to and from school, for a designated parking spot near their house (stating *how far* the children were was able to walk), for specific medical aid reimbursement (the insurance company required additional certificates, including an indication of *how long* the children were able to walk). A government inspector came by to check whether Gwen's condition justified the received support from the government. He caught her on a good day and judged negatively. The inspector did acknowledge he had never heard of TRAPS and was not aware of fluctuations in the patient's condition. He said he just needed to base his decision on what he observed that day. It was not clear if this was a rule or just his interpretation of the rules.

As her daughter's condition worsened, Helena found herself spending more and more time on the paperwork and legwork associated with the assistance she received, taking her daughter to the doctor five times a year just to obtain assessment certificates—wasting the doctor's time and causing undue pain and distress to Helena and her daughter. Helena could not understand why one universal medical assessment certificate for all purposes once and forever could not be issued.

## *Diagnosis*

The collective performance review for this case was held at a family restaurant in the village where Helena lived. The minister for public service reform and representatives of all of the agencies involved, both at the frontline and at the management level, attended, along with Helena and Gwen. All participants acknowledged the problems facing Helena and her daughters and confirmed that her complaints were legitimate.

### Red Tape: The Perspective of the Public Sector Client

- The red tape facing Helena arose not only from the government but also from private sector agencies such as the insurance company. Only Helena had a complete overview of who was involved.
- In the case of the automatic extension of a vehicle tax exemption, Helena's own assumptions were wrong.
- The tax authority's website was unclear, and the representative of the tax authority confirmed that this may have contributed to Helena's incorrect assumptions.

### Culture: The Perspective of the Public Sector Professional

- The frontline officials dealing with Helena's case had known about her difficulties but were unable or unwilling to resolve them. According to these officials, they did not have enough discretionary authority to design new solutions for her case; if they did have such authority, they were unaware of it, and were certainly not encouraged to use their own discretion.
- The agencies involved seemed to be speaking different languages, down to the basic definition of what it meant to be "chronically ill." There were frequent misunderstandings about other agencies' certificates, which led to demands for more information from the client rather than from the agencies in question.
- Because there are legal constraints on the exchange of information between government agencies, and especially between public and pri-

vate organizations, these agencies preferred to ask the client for more information directly rather than getting in touch with one another.

■ The doctors in particular felt that they could alleviate the administrative burden for their patients if they could communicate their assessments directly to the relevant agencies, but they have a confidentiality clause in their professional ethics oath and law that prevents them from doing so.

### Structure: The Perspective of the Public Manager

■ All the involved agencies lacked a feedback loop with frontline workers. They affirmed that this was the primary reason why Helena's problems were not brought to the attention of the responsible managers.

■ Even within small organizations, but especially in larger ones, divisions operated relatively disconnectedly. For example, within the tax authority, different offices had different guidelines and editing rights when it came to handling personal information.

■ When the attention of a local politician was drawn to this case, improved responses to Helena's demands seemed possible after all. The participants confirmed that the way their work was structured and evaluated generally did not include an incentive or an organizational principle for treating clients decently. Both managers and frontline workers acknowledged this situation.

### Statecraft: The Perspective of Policymakers

■ The legal term "renewal of certification" had caused untold problems as a result of its range of interpretation among officials. Those who took the term literally demanded that clients provide new certification with every application. Those who applied the term more loosely simply asked whether any information had changed or been added since the patient's last certification.

■ The civil servants at the municipal level acknowledged that they often had trouble translating generic policy language into procedures and forms understandable to themselves, their colleagues, and their clients.

■ All participants admitted a complete lack of feedback from the front line, all the way up to the policymakers, when it came to Helena's problem.

- The minister of public affairs confirmed that neither Helena's problem nor problems like hers had ever been discussed at the political level or raised by pressure groups or professional associations.
- Health care policy in the Netherlands is generally not focused on proactive service delivery. It is reactive in nature; it always requires action from the client to begin its processes.

## Remedies

The collective performance review revealed that the challenge of burdensome medical assessments for the purposes of certification of eligibility for benefits was bigger, more serious, and affected more people than anyone had imagined. Because most of the participants agreed on both the problem definition and diagnosis, there was considerable willingness to do whatever was necessary and within their power to rectify it, which led to a list of remedies to which the participants committed themselves.

### Case-Level Remedies

- The city government decided that all decisions regarding the continuation of Helena's daughter's benefits and licenses would be based on the existing case file, and no new assessments or certificates would be needed in the future.
- The insurance company decided that Helena would not need to get approval for reimbursement of every trip to the hospital. This would significantly reduce paperwork for Helena.

### Category-Level Remedies

- The municipal government immediately reversed its business processes with regard to service delivery to disabled and chronically ill people. The civil servants resolved to deliver services first and then to conduct randomized checks for verification of claims afterward. They also abolished the rule that patients had to reapply annually for handicapped parking permits in cases of incurable disease. They concluded by drafting a letter, which was sent to all the city governments in the Netherlands, explaining what they had learned and encouraging managers in other cities to follow suit.
- The health insurance company also changed its business processes to ensure that certain services would be delivered immediately, with

checks afterward to verify patients' conditions. The insurance company also agreed to share its learning with other companies in the sector.

■ The tax authority immediately changed its website to provide greater clarity about its rules.

### Capacity-Level Remedies

■ The Ministry of Health agreed to communicate with the Ministry of the Interior and municipal governments to assure frontline workers that they did indeed have the discretion to organize proactive service delivery.

■ The Ministry of Health also created a website that municipal governments could use to allow clients to apply for multiple services at once.

---

## CASE 6: Conflicting Benefits

**Partially Disabled Johan Did Not "Benefit" from His Social Security Benefits**

*At a Glance*

| | |
|---|---|
| Those affected | Disabled and chronically ill people who depend on public services for assistance |
| | Small entrepreneurs who also receive some form of benefits |
| | People who receive benefits from more than one agency |
| Major complaints | Unclear application procedures, lack of information |
| | Lack or responsiveness to the problem by officials |
| | Fiscal and income uncertainty |
| Agencies involved | Council for Pensions and Benefits (PUR) |
| | Institute for Employee Benefit Schemes (UWV) |
| | Tax authority |

Johan was a child of a couple who were deeply affected by World War II and was considered a second-generation sufferer from the aftereffects of that war. He had an assortment of psychological and physical problems. In the Netherlands, one agency is responsible for managing any benefits to which such individuals are entitled by law, the Council for Pensions and Benefits (PUR). Benefits for second-generation war victims guarantee a fixed basic income, from which PUR deducts any other supplemental income that its beneficiaries receive. In other words, if the total fixed income for beneficiaries is $50,000 per year and a given individual makes $30,000 per year, PUR will pay that person $20,000 a year. Johan did not make much money, and his income varied widely from year to year as a result of his physical and mental fitness. Thus, PUR had to recalculate his income annually to determine how much should be deducted from his war-sufferer benefits.

Johan's physical ailments had become acute enough to prevent him from working his regular job; a doctor declared him unfit to work. As a result, Johan became entitled to disability payments from the Institute for Employee Benefit Schemes (Uitvoeringsinstituut Werknemersverzekeringen, UWV) in addition to his preexisting war-victim benefits. His physical constraints kept Johan largely confined to his home, but he also wanted to do something to keep busy and to contribute to society. He began to volunteer two or three hours a week at a rehabilitation center for blind people. Johan enjoyed this work. Eventually the rehabilitation center decided it wanted to pay Johan for his help. The center requested that Johan submit an invoice for his hours. To do this, Johan had to register as a business with the tax authority—and here is where he began to encounter serious problems.

With the addition of this tiny business venture, Johan discovered that the two government agencies from which he was receiving benefits, PUR and the UWV, had very different rules for income calculation. Combined with the beneficiary's small business on the side, these rules created a highly variable yearly income for Johan. The fluctuations led the tax authority to flag Johan's case as a result of suspicion over the variable calculations of his income. Once the tax authority audited his records, it discovered that he had made $150 more than was allowed by the terms of his disability benefit, which moved him into a higher tax bracket. As a result, Johan was fined $15,000.

Johan's problem was not only the fact of this colossal fine but, more important, that he was completely unaware of the consequences of registering as a business for his two hours of work per week. Because of the lack of clarity surrounding the rules of his pension disbursement, he was unable to calculate for himself the maximum amount of money he was allowed to make on the side. Furthermore, now that he was officially running a business, he found that for every two to three hours of work, he had to spend a full day working through all of the corresponding bureaucratic paperwork. The third challenge was that, while he had documented his case very carefully, neither the disability agency nor the tax authority nor PUR understood the rules of his case well enough to take responsibility for resolving conflicts between jurisdictions or regimes. Johan did not know what to do or where to go for assistance, which led him to report his problem to the government website.

## Diagnosis

The collective performance review took place in a village restaurant close to Johan's residence. The minister for public service reform, senior management from the involved agencies, and frontline officers from UWV and PUR, but not from the tax authority, all attended the review. In their opening remarks, all of the participants acknowledged their embarrassment at the responsibility they bore for causing Johan's difficulties, but also their happiness that the case was brought to their attention.

### Red Tape: The Perspective of the Public Sector Client

- Johan's problems were revealed to be quite exceptional. There are only a few dozen individuals like Johan who are simultaneously entitled to two different government benefits and are running a small business on the side. Because his case was so unusual, many agencies were unable to manage it.
- The agencies' failures to respond to Johan's inquiries and to share information about their decisions regarding his case caused Johan to feel excessive anxiety. This was of material importance because Johan was already mentally ill.
- All of the frontline officials with whom Johan dealt lacked sufficient knowledge or skills to manage his situation. The information

they needed to deal with Johan's needs was not available, either to them or to Johan.

- Frontline responses to Johan's problems were generally one of the following three: first, giving no response at all; second, providing him with standard brochures; and third, claiming to consider requests and leaving Johan waiting indefinitely. The participants recognized that these were all defensive routines on the part of the frontline people.

### Culture: The Perspective of the Public Sector Professional

- All of the organizations involved repeatedly directed Johan to one of the other agencies. They were aware of the existence and importance of other organizations but not of the particular work those organizations did or the rules they had to follow.
- The organizations never contacted each other. Johan was used as a mailman between agencies.
- All three organizations acknowledged that it was not customary to bring complex cases to the attention of higher management so that they could take action to prevent similar cases from occurring.
- No single organization considered the possibility of using its own discretion to solve Johan's troubles.

### Structure: The Perspective of the Public Manager

- While there was some doubt as to whether the origin of Johan's problems was Johan himself or the performance of the organizations with which he interacted, it was clear that streamlining the business processes of these organizations was not a feasible solution. Because Johan was subject to multiple laws under the auspices of several agencies, it was legally impossible to improve the business processes that were keeping Johan in limbo.
- All three agencies were managed with the aim of meeting production targets. Because employees were not rewarded for solving problems, the usual practice was to procrastinate on any complex cases that arose.

### Statecraft: The Perspective of Policymakers

- All the participants agreed that the major cause of Johan's problems was that different programs had been initiated at the national level without anyone anticipating the possible effects of contradictory policies in particular cases.

- Both benefit programs used their own measures for income, which caused problems for the tax authority.
- The tax authority failed to distinguish between small and large enterprises; all individuals had to comply with the same administrative regulations. This policy put a disproportionate burden on Johan, who worked only a couple of hours a week.
- Participants agreed that there was no possibility for any employee of any of the agencies to report problems of this kind. In other words, this was an issue where no single person or organization was at fault but in which a particular case revealed a design flaw.

## Remedies

### Case-Level Remedies

- Johan got clarity about his situation and learned how the system works and where it went wrong in his case.
- The PUR agreed to take responsibility for coordinating Johan's benefits and to be Johan's sole point of contact with the government in the future. The agency also assigned Johan a personal case manager.

### Category-Level Remedies

- The PUR actively identified similar cases and notified these individuals that it would be coordinating their benefits from now on.

### Capacity-Level Remedies

- Management of the PUR and UWV, with help from officials at the Ministry of the Interior representing the minister for public sector reform, the sponsor, resolved to work together to develop a means that would enable employees of any organization to identify and act on problems caused by the problematic convergence of government programs or regulations in individual cases. This resolution resulted in a device called the Kafka Button, which is an internal alarm procedure signaling to senior management that a given case requires interagency communication at a higher level.

## CASE 7: Appeal and Redress in Health Care

**Rheumatic Niek Seeks Redress Concerning Health Care Payment Decision**

*At a Glance*

| | |
|---|---|
| Those affected | Those appealing a decision regarding direct payments in health care<br>Those filing a complaint without knowing what the problem is and what agency is responsible |
| Major complaints | Inability of client to fully understand and deal with application and appeal procedures<br>No "address" to file a complaint |
| Agencies involved | Care Assessment Agency (CIZ)<br>Care administration office<br>Home care provider<br>Social Insurance Bank (SVB)<br>National Ombudsman |

Fifty-five-year-old Niek suffered from chronic rheumatism, which left him unable to live on his own. He had been staying in an assisted living facility with minimal services, surrounded by people who were, on average, eighty years old. Niek's best friend had been looking after him, but Niek's physical needs had grown more serious than his friend could manage. He wanted to be elevated to a higher service level. As a result, Niek approached a government health care organization to request more household assistance.

This agency conducted an assessment of Niek's condition and determined that Niek was entitled to professional care in his home for one and a half hours per week. After a month of this care, Niek received another letter raising his entitlement to three hours per week. This notice also informed him that there was a new system in place, called Direct Payments, in which the government, instead of assigning the client a particular care provider, would pay its benefits directly to the care provider of the client's choice. This system was intended to observe the principle of customer choice, and Niek opted in. He chose a care provider, and the SVB (Sociale Verzekeringsbank, the Dutch Social Insurance Bank) began to remit money on his behalf to his chosen organization.

At some point, however, Niek realized that the SVB had been paying the care provider less than what the provider charged for his services. Niek had been completely unaware of this discrepancy since he saw neither the money nor the bills. Yet the government held him accountable for the difference, and Niek received a bill for approximately $1,500. He approached the Dutch Care Assessment Agency (CIZ), the care provider, and the SVB in an effort to appeal the bill. All of these agencies identified Niek as the one responsible for the situation, and none of them accepted his appeal. It did not help matters that Niek, assuming everything was taken care of, had lost track of the documentation needed to prove his case.

Niek turned to the National Ombudsman, but the ombudsman also could not resolve the case, citing, first, a lack of hard evidence that promises were made to Niek, and second, the fact that some of the agencies in Niek's case, such as the care provider and other semipublic or nonprofit agencies, were not government organizations; the ombudsman can only take action in the case of a complaint about a particular government agency. After reaching this impasse, Niek submitted his complaints to the government website.

### Diagnosis

The collective performance review in this case was difficult to organize because the agencies involved were reluctant to participate: they believed there was no problem. Since Niek's problems had arisen, the Direct Payments structure had been changed. In Niek's case, the Ministry of Health had sent money to the SVB, which in turn was to pay the provider of the client's choice. The policy had since been changed to allow money to be sent directly the client, who would either pay his care provider directly or approve an automatic transfer from his bank account to the SVB, which then would pay his provider. The ministry claimed that with this change of policy, clients were more responsible for their own money and could see for themselves how much they had and how much they had to pay.

While this system may have prevented Niek from becoming confused about his responsibility for payments, the problem remained that other clients, like Niek, would not know where to seek recourse if they encountered problems. Thus, we were able to convince the agencies involved that it would still be useful to diagnose this case and see if additional remedies were needed.

*Red Tape: The Perspective of the Public Sector Client*

- Niek was not able, either physically or mentally, to administer his own direct payments. This is a problem that occurs in many cases in which individual clients are expected to take responsibility for a new program. This issue was confirmed by the participants, who agreed that it was difficult for them to decide whether Niek was suitable for the Direct Payments program.
- Niek and his caregiver did not know where to file their complaint and could not understand the whole system and how it worked. The participants in the collective performance review shared his confusion: no one could figure out where the complaint should have been filed.
- Because Niek was physically and mentally unable to take full responsibility for the direct payments, he lost paperwork and documentation, which caused further difficulties in his case, particularly when he wanted to appeal decisions.
- It became clear that the responsibility for information and advice on the Direct Payments program did not belong to a single agency. This caused fragmentation, lack of clarity, and inadequately informed clients.
- Only after choosing the Direct Payments program did clients receive full details of what their choice entailed.
- Most officials' performances were not measured by the number of solutions they achieved or satisfied clients they served but by the number of cases they could file per day, which made them reluctant to deal with exceptional cases.

*Culture: The Perspective of the Public Sector Professional*

- Participants acknowledged a complete lack of cooperation between agencies when problems arose. All of the processes were automated, and there was no direct contact between employees of any of the agencies.

- The design of the Direct Payments policy meant that the burden of the integrative work rested with the client. Thus, the lack of inter-agency communication was a matter of the policy itself, and not an incidental problem of implementation.
- A significant lack of flexibility was found in all of the participants when tackling this case. No one seemed able to take the discretionary authority to make exceptions.

### Structure: The Perspective of the Public Manager

- There was no particular problem with the internal business processes in this case. However, if problems arose, there was no one in a position to manage them.
- Because the Direct Payments program reduced operational costs for both health care providers and administrative agencies, the dominant performance metric was to produce, in the most efficient way, incentives for clients to choose Direct Payments.
- When individuals chose Direct Payments program over care in kind, this was taken as a signal that the individual was willing and able to take responsibility for the management of direct payments. Managers did not create any incentives for frontline people to be concerned about the capacity of clients who chose the direct payment option even when they needed it.

### Statecraft: The Perspective of Policymakers

- There was virtually no feedback from the implementation to the policy level, although the Ministry of Health had a systemic responsibility for the Direct Payments program in particular and for health care delivery in general.
- There were no mechanisms in place to bring problems in execution to the attention of the ministry.
- The Ministry of Health also did not feel it bore responsibility for correcting these issues, which it labeled implementation problems. The other agencies involved claimed that Niek's difficulties were either the client's or another agency's problem.
- The political decision to introduce Direct Payments into health care was informed by the belief that clients should have choice in their providers; it was assumed that clients would be able to decide for themselves whether they were fit enough to take on the responsibility.

- The Direct Payments system was generally understood to be a way of saving implementation costs, because the clients themselves would undertake much of the administrative work.
- The challenges faced by individuals who took on responsibility they could not handle were not brought to the attention of either higher officials or politicians.
- The way the Direct Payments system was supposed to work had been poorly communicated to frontline professionals and clients. If everything worked well, there was no issue, but as soon as things did not work well, it was hard for people to find out where they could go to solve their problems.

### Remedies

When responsibility for a particular problem is divided among multiple agencies, a client has nowhere to turn to appeal or seek redress for decisions. Even the National Ombudsman had difficulties, because that office could step in to deal with a problem only when there was documentation and a complaint about a particular agency. When no one agency seemed to be at fault, there was no way to address the dysfunction or to learn how to prevent these cases from happening in the future.

#### Case-Level Remedies

- Niek basically had one request: he wanted his money returned. No single agency was willing or able to grant that request because each felt it could not justify such a decision without proper documentation or proof that it had made a mistake.

#### Category-Level Remedies

- No significant remedies were nominated at the category level. None of the participants committed to taking action to improve general policy regarding the administration of the Direct Payments program.
- Most participants agreed that the Ministry of Health should improve the provision of information to clients. Some participants also pointed out that the ministry should not allow people who were not capable of dealing with the responsibility for direct payments to apply for one.

*Capacity-Level Remedies*

■ The CIZ, the SVB, the Care Administration Office, and the care provider agreed to have case meetings whenever a case like this arose in the future.

■ The National Ombudsman office agreed to further explore ways to better address these types of cases in which both the problem or complaint is unclear and multiple agencies are involved. The agency also committed itself to training its employees to better recognize and deal with "Kafka cases."

## CASE 8: Licensing a Restaurant

**Building a Pancake Restaurant, Maaike Gets Lost in Licensing Procedures**

*At a Glance*

| | |
|---|---|
| Those affected | Clients, especially entrepreneurs, who apply for a building permit |
| Major complaints | Lack of information and certainty about regulation and procedures<br>General attitude of government officials<br>Duration of the entire procedure |
| Agencies involved | Municipal government: Division of Building and Construction<br>Municipal government: Parking Division<br>Municipal government: Fire Department<br>Ministry of the Environment |

Sixty-seven-year-old Maaike lived in a small, rural town in north Netherlands, in a farmhouse she shared with her son. Because of her age, Maaike and her son began to consider giving up farming in favor of starting a pancake restaurant in their home. The two of them knew nothing about the rules governing how to start a restaurant, so they wrote a letter to the town hall asking what guidelines they should follow.

They learned that the first set of rules addressed concerns about potential traffic disruptions in Maaike's neighborhood. They would also be required to change their zoning designation from agricultural to commercial space. The aesthetics of the building would have to be approved, and Maaike's neighbors would have to be consulted to determine whether the restaurant would generate problems or disadvantages for them. Maaike wanted to put up an extra barn on the property for storage, which would require an additional permit. Their property would have to conform to fire safety guidelines. And finally, the building licensing procedure of Maaike's town required two application stages: "initial" and "additional." Although Maaike and her son had been in touch with the government, they still did not understand the exact difference between these two layers of procedures.

Maaike's challenges began with the immense amount of time and energy it took just to discover and comprehend the rules. But her real problems arose when she and her son began to prepare their applications: they were asked repeatedly for additional information and expert assessments, including a business plan and a chamber of commerce registration number. Maaike was reluctant to write a business plan or register at the chamber of commerce *before* knowing whether she and her son would be permitted to open a restaurant in their farmhouse. In addition, the terms of each procedure were often incompatible with the time it took to collect the additional requested information. For example, there was a six-week time limit for submitting completed building license applications but the documentation required took longer than six weeks to prepare, so it was virtually impossible to comply within the time frame.

Maaike also struggled with the general attitude of the city government. She thought she was doing something positive for her community, her town, and the local economy, but in all of her encounters with government, she felt that the civil servants were neither supportive nor encouraging. Maaike's and her son's negative experiences of both the procedures and the attitudes accompanying their licensing applications led them to register their complaints on the government website.

## *Diagnosis*

The collective performance review took place in the village where Maaike lived. All of the involved agencies were represented at the review except the architect whom Maaike had engaged to help with procedure. It became clear over the course of the review that this architect could have been a more competent intermediary, but all of the participants agreed to focus on the general lessons that could still be derived from the case.

### *Red Tape: The Perspective of the Public Sector Client*

- Everybody agreed that the problem arose as a result of the complexity of procedures and regulations, which was a problem for both the civil servants and Maaike's family. Everybody agreed that Maaike's complaint about the length and variety of procedures was legitimate.
- Maaike had created some problems for herself by making repeated changes to her own plans and by hiring an architect who was unfamiliar with city government procedures to act as an intermediary between Maaike and municipal agencies.
- The lack of clarity Maaike experienced when asking for more information was the result of a lack of understanding among the civil servants themselves regarding national regulations. They were not sure what was and was not allowed, and so relied on formal rules and language that were often opaque to Maaike. This led to a great deal of uncertainty and to mistakes further along in the process.

### *Culture: The Perspective of the Public Sector Professional*

- There was no contact between the various city government departments. Maaike had become the main nexus of communication between agencies, and so it fell to Maaike to inform one agency of another's stand on a given issue.
- The civil servants involved had all the knowledge that they needed to pursue their own procedures and apply regulations; what they did not have was the capacity to look beyond the letter of the law to apply these rules in a manner sensitive to Maaike's particular situation. For example, there are ways for a civil servant to prevent an application from expiring, but no one used these methods because the civil servants involved were not willing to think outside the box.

*Structure: The Perspective of the Public Manager*

- Even though all of the divisions were part of the same city government, including the fire department, they could only work sequentially. Thus, an individual could start an application procedure with one division only after completing the procedure of another division. This was not a legal requirement; it was simply the way things were organized.
- The participants agreed that, within city government, there was no mechanism to bring problems from frontline offices to a higher level. Thus, complex and problematic cases were generally delayed, and senior management was asked neither to intervene nor to make structural changes to prevent these cases from recurring.
- For most civil servants, their performance metric was based on the number of applications processed and not on the duration of a single application procedure (or on client satisfaction, for that matter). According to participants, this fact explains why no one intervened when Maaike's case was left pending too long and became too complicated.

*Statecraft: The Perspective of Policymakers*

- The perceived complexity of regulations for construction licenses led to rigid behavior on the part of city government officials, according to participants.
- Most participants agreed that the city government had not been invested in learning from implementation problems, nor had they communicated with the Ministry of the Environment to determine how to improve service delivery to clients.
- Regulations were biased toward risk management to protect customers of the business rather than toward enabling people to start businesses within the limits of the law. The general attitude toward entrepreneurs was skeptical, with no distinction between really dangerous enterprises, such as places working with biohazard materials, and relatively harmless family restaurants in rural areas.

## Remedies

It took a long time before all the participants showed a genuine willingness to contribute to the diagnosis of the problems that had been identified. A number of additional meetings took place, but in the end, no positive results were accomplished at the case level and only very marginally at category and capacity levels.

### Case-Level Remedies

- It was inevitable that Maaike would have to go through another application procedure and basically start all over again. However, she continued with her construction plans while waiting for formal approval. The city government ordered her to stop building, and Maaike fought that order in court. The court ruled against her, as building without a license is illegal. Maaike was forced to stop, and was left disillusioned.

### Category-Level Remedies

- The Ministry of the Environment has begun experimenting with a licensing process that would automatically issue a construction license if a client develops a construction plan in cooperation with a certified architect or construction company. If the government later discovers that the plan fails to comply with official regulations, the contractor or architect in question would lose certification. This experiment was not prompted by this particular research, but the Kafka Brigade's case led to insights that were later also incorporated in this initiative.
- While participants did resolve to simplify the construction licensing procedure, the Ministry for the Environment was reluctant to do so because it was investing its energies in a new, updated electronic form.

### Capacity-Level Remedies

- The Ministry of the Environment made no suggestions other than to say it was working on digitizing the whole licensing system, which would eventually increase the capacity of city governments to deal with such applications.
- Though city government officials represented themselves as willing to improve capacity, no concrete solutions were offered.

## CASE 9: Benefits for Ex-Convicts

**From Jail, Martin Applies for Social Benefits**

*At a Glance*

| | |
|---|---|
| Those affected | Ex-convicts depending on public services or social benefits<br><br>Communities, taxpayers at large |
| Major complaints | Flawed process design<br><br>Lack of information and certainty about regulations and procedures<br><br>General attitude of government officials |
| Agencies involved | City government: Division of Building and Construction<br><br>Municipal government: Parking Division<br><br>Ministry of the Environment |

Martin, an ex-convict living in Amsterdam, had a fifty-year-old wife who was ill and could not take care of herself. They had been married for a long time, but when Martin committed a crime and was sentenced to spend time in jail, he could no longer take care of his wife.

Martin's wife received some help from the city government, and an exception was made that entitled her to receive additional benefits. But the problem was not solved, for on Martin's his release from his six-month jail sentence, he would not have a job and would have to apply for social benefits. The problem that Martin and his wife ran into is that to apply for welfare, you need a postal address where you actually live. You cannot apply for welfare from prison. Once you have applied, the waiting time for the application to be processed is about thirteen weeks. This meant that Martin and his wife would have to wait an additional thirteen weeks on top of the six months of hardship they would have endured while Martin was in prison.

Two social workers working on Martin's rehabilitation became concerned about his situation and that of other ex-convicts. People like Martin come out of jail but do not have a place to go or money with which to buy food and clothes. In many such cases (according to the social workers, about 90 percent), ex-convicts quickly start committing crimes to get by. The social workers thought that society would benefit if convicts were able to apply for social benefits from prison.

The law requires welfare applicants to have a home address, which entails having a lease on a property. However, many ex-convicts have high debt loads, which make them unable to obtain a lease. Thus, to start receiving money, you need an address, and to have an address, you need to have money. This catch-22 situation was not being addressed by the Institute for Employee Benefit Schemes (UWV), social workers, prisons, or relevant agencies of city government.

The city government does make an exception to these rules for homeless people, who, if they prove they are homeless, receive a postal address that can be used for all official purposes. However, this policy does not apply to ex-convicts, and nobody really knew why that was, or if the policy *could* apply to the former prisoners.

In this case, we started out with the story of Martin and his wife, but during our research we were less and less able to get access to Martin until even the social workers no longer had contact with him. In a way, this was a case in point: the rehabilitation failed, perhaps because of the difficulties in transitioning from incarceration to regular life. We were able to continue work on the case with the social workers, who could speak on behalf of their clients and the communities in which former prisoners are supposed to reintegrate and were willing to make a change.

## Diagnosis

The collective performance review took place in the office of one of the social workers, and all of the agencies involved sent representatives from frontline and middle management levels. Martin was not present, but his social worker spoke on his behalf.

### Red Tape: The Perspective of the Public Sector Client

■ Martin's problem was a hidden one because many of those formerly incarcerated prefer not to deal with government at all. If something goes wrong, they would rather leave the situation entirely than deal with the government directly.

- Social workers are aware of the difficulties facing former prisoners, but find it challenging to act on behalf of clients who will not help themselves. In attempting to assist former prisoners, social workers are working on behalf of the general public; they are trying to prevent their clients from winding up on the street, either becoming homeless, going back to crime, or both.
- Many ex-convicts have trouble keeping appointments and are hostile to the government. This is, of course, counterproductive.
- Ex-convicts can be difficult for frontline officers to reach because they may not have a permanent place to live.

### Culture: The Perspective of the Public Sector Professional

- Agencies redirect clients to each other but acknowledge they do not do anything more than that. Either the ex-convicts themselves or their social workers are left to sort out the problems that emerge from conflicting legislation and lack of interagency cooperation.
- Most frontline officers have far more discretionary authority than they realize. Even when upward of 50 percent of their clients are in exceptional situations that require flexibility, workers may be either unaware or unwilling to use their own discretion to solve problems.
- Although senior management pays lip service to the idea of improving agencies' collective performance, they are not willing to hold their employees accountable for contributing to solutions for cases.

### Structure: The Perspective of the Public Manager

- Conflicting legislation has led to business processes that reveal a problematic convergence of programs between the UWV-administered disability administration and the city government's welfare system.
- Most participants agreed that the individual agencies implicitly expect other agencies to do the integrative work for their clients.

### Statecraft: The Perspective of Policymakers

- The policymakers consulted before and after our collective performance review were aware of the complexity of the problem but did not know how to prevent it or what their role should be in solving it.

- The issue of former prisoners and entitlements provokes ideological and political responses. Many citizens feel that ex-cons have only themselves to blame for their situations and should not be receiving excessive assistance in the first place. This reduces the willingness of politicians to invest in improving the situation.
- Social workers responsible for the successful reintegration of former prisoners into society see an increasing danger of recidivism but have problems bringing that danger to the attention of politicians.

## *Remedies*

### Case-Level Remedies

- Because Martin had vanished, no action could be taken to benefit him directly.

### Category-Level Remedies

- The UWV has appointed contact persons for prison and city government employees to improve communication between agencies.
- The city government of Amsterdam has agreed to improve service delivery to ex-convicts across the board, but it remains unclear what that might involve and what results would emerge from such an initiative.

### Capacity-Level Remedies

- Remedies at this level have not been identified. It appeared that there was no willingness to address the most pressing issues that were identified during the collective performance review, either because of political sensitivities or because of personal preferences. It also became clear that most practitioners wished only to support the expansion of already existing programs that had been politically mandated.

## CASE 10: Immigration, Marriage, and Employment

**Engaged to a Dutchman, Maria Applies for
Permanent Resident Status**

*At a Glance*

| | |
|---|---|
| Those affected | Immigrants who fit more than one of the following profiles: immigrate to marry, immigrate to study, immigrate to work |
| Major complaints | Lack of information and assistance regarding eligibility criteria and application procedures<br><br>Apparent incompatibility of policies and regulations<br><br>Lack of coordination between agencies<br><br>General attitude of officials and agencies |
| Agencies involved | Immigration and Naturalization Department (IND)<br><br>Center for Work and Income (CWI)<br><br>Information Administration Agency (Informatie Beheer Groep)<br><br>Universities<br><br>City government (multiple divisions) |

Maria was a twenty-two-year-old Polish woman engaged to a Dutch IT professional. Two years into their relationship they decided to move in together, and chose the Netherlands as their place of residence. Because Maria was a Polish citizen, she qualified for an extended stay in the Netherlands, since both countries are part of the European Union and have an immigration treaty (which did not necessarily mean that she would be eligible for all benefits and would enjoy all the rights a Dutch citizen would). There are many different rules that govern foreigners' eligibility to seek employment, study, and qualify for public services. Maria did not know how to go about obtaining the right permits but decided to figure that out while staying with her fiancé in tourist status, for which no permit is required.

The first thing Maria wanted to do was learn to speak Dutch, not least because all government forms are in Dutch. To be admitted to a course in Dutch for foreign residents of the city, she had to register with the city government. In order to register, however, Maria needed already to have applied for permanent resident status. The problem was that Maria still did not know what kind of permit she needed. She was allowed to stay in the Netherlands as a citizen of a country in the European Union, and she was allowed to study in the Netherlands as an exchange student. In both capacities, there would be limitations on the right to employment. Maria also needed to work a part-time job while she studied but did not know whether she qualified for employment.

First Maria tried to get information about employment eligibility from the Immigration and Naturalization Department (IND). The IND, instead of listening to her specific questions, provided her with a lot of brochures and forms for different situations and intended for different target groups. There were separate procedures for obtaining permits to marry a Dutch citizen, get a job, become a permanent resident, and pursue education, but Maria wanted all of the above. She wanted to marry her Dutch fiancé, work a part-time job to make ends meet while she was studying, and live in the Netherlands permanently with her fiancé. Because all of the forms were for different procedures, choosing one procedure would practically exclude the others.

Maria and her fiancé had a lot of questions, and nobody could answer them. They were sent from one agency to the next and given all kinds of information that raised more questions than it answered. After two years of inquiries, Maria found out that in a neighboring city it was possible to register with the city government without also registering for permanent resident status. Maria still didn't know which visa she needed, but she was happy that she could at least register with the city government so that she could begin to learn to speak Dutch.

Still, she needed an answer to the question of whether she was allowed to work on top of her studies. The city government sent her to the Center for Work and Income (Centrum voor Werk & Inkomen, CWI), where she was told that because the department deals with people who come to the Netherlands for employment, not to study, they did not know the answer. Apparently most of the foreign students who also work do not officially register with the authorities. The official that they dealt with advised her quasi-seriously to find a job on the black market. For more information, they sent her to the "Information Administration Agency" (Informatie Beheer Groep), the Dutch national bureau for student affairs, a part of the Ministry of Education. This bureau did not have an answer to the question either; they said it was a case for the IND.

Finally, an administrator at the university where she was studying told her that the best option was to apply for a student visa. Even though she wanted to get married and live in the Netherlands permanently, Maria would be better off pretending that she just wanted to study, and apply for another visa later. The student visa would allow her to work at a job, but had a clause that she had to work a minimum of eight hours and a maximum of ten hours per week. She did not understand the specificity of the rule but was happy to find out, after two years, that she was able to get a job. When she applied and was accepted for a job at the university, the university required her to get a work permit from the CWI. Maria applied for and received the permit, but it did not mention the fact that she was a student. When she asked the CWI to correct the mistake, the officials there did not respond to her request. She did not get the job.

Not only was it difficult to obtain the right information or find any official willing to listen to Maria's story and help her troubleshoot the problem, it also took a long time to obtain any one permit, often only to discover later that another permit or additional documentation was required. In the end, it took more than two years for Maria and her fiancé to sort out the issues. Adding insult to injury, the treatment she received from the government made Maria feel very unwelcome. Maria and her fiancé found this strange, because what Maria wanted was not a favor from the government. Legally, she was allowed and even encouraged to study and seek employment in the Netherlands. Maria and her fiancé were left with a lot of questions, a lot of frustration, and no understanding of why Maria had had to go through this ordeal or how she could have handled it better.

### Diagnosis

Immigration is always a controversial issue in the Netherlands, and debate on the subject is both highly polarized and highly politicized. The execution of immigration policy has come under sharp criticism from both the left and right, which led to increased tension and anxiety in this particular case. The fact that the case was a closed one, meaning the situation had resolved itself and there were no further claims or appeals by the client, was a prerequisite for most of the participants to agree to join the collective performance review in the first place. The minister of public service reform, representatives of frontline and midlevel management from all involved agencies, and Maria and her fiancé attended the review (senior management declined to attend, for unknown reasons).

*Red Tape: The Perspective of the Public Sector Client*

- The long duration of the process was not entirely the result of governmental procedures but was reflected the additional time Maria and her fiancé took to think over their situation before applying for another work permit.
- Everybody also acknowledged that the case was resolved not *because of* government agencies but *in spite of* them, since Maria had learned from a colleague rather than from an official what course she should follow to resolve her situation.
- Maria filled out her forms in English but always received responses in Dutch. Fortunately, she had friends who could translate for her, but since the language of the letters was highly specialized and legalistic, much depended on how it was translated. This problem particularly disadvantages immigrants as a group.
- The officials Maria contacted were unable to provide clarity and, in most cases, their advice was contradictory.
- The encounters Maria had were extremely short; she was almost never able to explain her situation and sort out the case completely with any one official.
- Any advice Maria received concerned only the particular jurisdiction of the agency with which she was dealing. She could never get answers regarding the consequences of particular decisions for contracts outside the government, such as a mortgage or a lease.

*Culture: The Perspective of the Public Sector Professional*

- A de facto lack of cooperation and coordination was evident between the agencies involved in this case. It became clear that the frontline people literally did not know what kinds of work their colleagues were doing.

- It also became evident that Maria herself was the only means of communication these agencies had with each other. Even when one agency made a mistake and another noticed the error, the second agency would not call the first; instead, it let Maria solve the problem.
- Both frontline officials and their managers acknowledged that the discretionary authority of frontline officials was extremely limited. Because of this, as well as issues raised in the previous points, the behavior of most frontline workers was generally inflexible and reactive, even in cases like Maria's, when it would have been relatively easy to help her.
- The frontline people also pointed out that the guiding values of their agencies did not include solving problems, satisfying clients, or looking beyond their own jurisdictions.

*Structure: The Perspective of the Public Manager*

- All the participants confirmed that the performance metric for their work had to do with the number of cases they could process in a day. They were rewarded neither for solving cases nor for satisfying clients, only for processing demands as quickly as possible.
- The competence and knowledge of most frontline employees were clearly insufficient to deal with the kinds of questions that people with complex problems have.
- Because of the political tension around this particular policy area, there was a lot of apprehension within organizations that manage immigration. Participants confirmed that, at all levels, people resorted to formal hierarchy and official job descriptions to protect themselves. There was a general fear of creating incidents that might come to media attention and further fuel political debate.
- All the participants noted that immigration services had been subject to numerous policy changes that their organizations were incapable of absorbing. There were many concerns about continuity in the organizations, particularly in light of the lack of funding. Given this turbulent environment, many employees felt they had to concentrate on production and keep their heads down, out of trouble.

*Statecraft: The Perspective of Policymakers*

- Frontline workers acknowledged that they found it hard to translate policy into understandable language for clients, and especially for the target group of immigrants.

- Owing the political tension surrounding issues of immigration, there was a lack of energy and willingness among administrators and policymakers to sort out the problems. They felt that unless the issue was dealt with at the political level, they would be unable to make progress.
- That immigration policy is permanently contested had made it problematic to fund immigration services in a sustainable manner.
- There was an incentive not to bring implementation problems to the attention of politicians because they would immediately be politicized.
- Some participants speculated that the whole system of procedures and services was organized as a de facto policy of bureaucratic disentitlement. Because it was not feasible to keep out immigrants, it became the practice to dissuade them by making immigration procedures more laborious and by underfunding agencies. A participant admitted that he had created the rule about the number of hours foreign students were allowed to work specifically to discourage foreign students from finding jobs.

### Remedies

After diagnoses had been made during the collective performance review, the minister of public service reform had to leave the meeting but encouraged everybody to suggest actions that they could undertake personally to alleviate the situation. She also committed herself to doing whatever was beyond the scope of their authority. After a break, we resumed our collective performance review by asking, "What can you or your organization do to make even a small difference for people in Maria's situation?" Nobody spoke. The moderator waited for a full two minutes, but the deafening silence persisted. Everyone felt increasingly embarrassed that they had contributed to the problem definition but were unable to think of remedies. Asked about their embarrassment, most participants replied that they felt so constrained by the overall authorizing environment, their specific management conditions, and the particular regulations with which they were dealing that they were unable to think of anything they could do personally, even though they wanted to.

We asked what could be done to create more room to address these issues. Most of the participants offered to talk to their management but could not think of remedies beyond that. Thus, our results from the second half of this collective performance review were disappointing. We decided to lower the bar even further, asking for the smallest steps that they could imagine, and these remedies are what resulted from this exercise.

*Case-Level Remedies*

■ Case-level remedies were not necessary because the case had already been closed and Maria had obtained all the licenses she needed. What is more, Poland was an EU member, so there were no restrictions on her work, and there should be no difficulties in future in terms of either her employment or her permanent resident status.

*Category-Level Remedies*

■ Romania and Bulgaria were at the time both countries in the same situation that Poland was in when Maria arrived in the Netherlands. Many students were expected to come from these nations to the Netherlands and to wind up in the same position as Maria. Thus, the first action at the category level suggested by the IND) and the Ministry of the Interior was that they would look into the website of the IND to clarify procedures and provide more information tailored to this particular group.

■ The IND, the CWI, and the University of Rotterdam all agreed to join forces to provide better information to Bulgarian and Romanian students. The IND agreed to take the initiative in this area.

■ Both the University of Rotterdam and the Ministry of the Interior agreed to try to identify more risk cases by identifying foreign students studying in Rotterdam. Thus, when problems arose, they would be able to do additional case research in tandem to accumulate more evidence needed to change the situations.

*Capacity-Level Remedies*

■ Only one remedy emerged at the capacity level, relating to the use of discretion among city governments, especially at the Department of Civil Affairs. The Kafka Brigade had encountered the challenge of lack of use of discretion by this agency before (in our cases dealing with certification). We decided that this case would serve as another example of what could go wrong if the turf war between the Ministry of Justice and the Ministry of the Interior was not ended. The Ministry of the Interior resolved to take up this issue at a higher level to force progress in this unproductive situation.

---

### CASE 11: Legal Documents

**Ilse Tries to Report a Death, Sven Tries to Acknowledge an Unborn Child**

*At a Glance*

| | |
|---|---|
| Those affected | Dutch nationals who have lived abroad |
| | Dutch citizens who were born or have died abroad and their relatives |
| | Foreign nationals who live in the Netherlands |
| Major complaints | Cost of compliance with procedures |
| | Arbitrariness of procedure application |
| | Lack of options for appeal |
| | General attitude of officials |
| Agencies involved | Municipal government: Department of Civil Affairs (Burgerzaken) |
| | Municipal government: General Municipal Database (Gemeentelijke Basisadministratie, GBA) |
| | Ministry of the Interior |
| | Ministry of Justice |
| | Ministry of Foreign Affairs/Dutch embassies abroad |

This case concerned two different individuals with similar problems, Sven and Ilse, who experienced problems with the official certification system in the Netherlands.

Sven worked for a Dutch bank, in which capacity he was stationed for three years in Brazil with his girlfriend, with whom he lived in qualified domestic partner status (civil union). After his stint in Brazil, Sven returned to his hometown and had to reregister with its city government as a resident. The city government maintains two divisions for managing citizen information. The first is the Department of Civil Affairs (Burgerzaken), which documents major life events, including birth, marriage or civil union, and death. The second is the General Municipal Database (Gemeentelijke Basisadministratie, GBA), which holds personal records of numerous other kinds, such as home addresses, social security numbers, whom citizens live with and in what house, and so on. This second system is the root source of information for all public services. The Department of Civil Affairs is a much older organization and is staffed by civil servants with a separate judicial status rather than a managerial one. Because of the significance of the kinds of events the department documents, its practitioners have a special legal responsibility to ensure that its documents are entirely true. The GBA, on the other hand, is not as strict in its recording processes.

Sven, upon his return to the Netherlands, registered with the GBA using a lease on a property to prove his residency. He was unaware of the difference between the Department of Civil Affairs and the GBA and did not to visit the first in addition to the GBA because he was not aware he had any reason to do so. Three years later, Sven's partner became pregnant, and, because they remained unmarried, Sven wanted to legally acknowledge the child to resolve concerns about custody or inheritance before they could even appear. Sven visited the city government offices again and discovered that the civil servant he consulted could not continue the acknowledgment procedure without a certification that Sven was currently unmarried and had not been married in Brazil.

Sven contacted the Brazilian authorities and learned that the only way to get a document certifying that he was not married in Brazil was to ask two people who knew him to visit a notary and declare that Sven was not married. This procedure would have taken four to five months, would have cost a lot of money, and would have been too late in any case because the child would have been born before the procedure was completed. Sven consulted friends and colleagues and learned that civil servants in other municipalities had been known to accept claims without certificates, but because workers had broad discretion to demand certification or not, there was no way to know whether any given civil servant would do so. One civil servant whom Sven consulted replied, with some hesitation, that he would give Sven the opportunity to declare under oath that he and his partner were both unmarried. However, this statement would only concern this child, and Sven would still need to acquire a statement of his unmarried status for the future, if he decided to have another child or to marry his partner. As a result, Sven continued his procedure with the Brazilians. He also discovered that there was another way around the problem: if a civil servant refused a request to acknowledge a child without certification that the applicants are not married, the applicants could ask her to put this refusal in writing so that they could appeal. This appeal would immediately go to the Department of Justice, but it would also take a long time to process.

Ilse, the second person stymied by certificates, had traveled to the Dominican Republic with her husband on vacation. After three days her husband died suddenly of a heart attack, leaving Ilse in shock. She cannot remember what happened immediately after his death; she recalls that she flew home in one plane, her husband's coffin in another. The funeral home Ilse selected to handle the coffin and other arrangements required a death certificate from the Department of Civil Affairs before it could proceed with the interment of the body. Officials in the Dominican Republic faxed over their own official death certificate, autopsy report, and a statement from the Dominican mortuary all attesting to Ilse's husband's death.

Ilse's son-in-law submitted this documentation to the city government in an attempt to apply for a Dutch death certificate, but the city government refused to issue one until all of the documents could be translated into Dutch. Ilse and her family spent time and money getting these documents translated, but the Department of Civil Affairs still refused to register the death because the Dominican documents had not been certified by a third government agency.

Because the situation involved a corpse, and resolving the case was an urgent matter, a civil servant gave Ilse a temporary pass to cremate or bury her husband's body. Flabbergasted by this absurd decision—how can a license to cremate be temporary?—Ilse and her family invited the civil servant to come to the mortuary himself if he would like to see whether a cremation could be reversed. The official certificate was issued four months later.

Beyond the frustration of handling so much paperwork at a time of such emotional distress, a delay in obtaining a death certificate has a profound impact one's financial life: pensions, social benefits, mortgage contracts, and life insurance terms all change with the death of a spouse. Ilse found it hard to believe that the civil servants at the Department of Civil Affairs appeared to favor a piece of paper with the right stamp on it over the good word of a doctor or funeral director in the Netherlands. Why should a certified document be more valuable than eyewitness observation?

As the Kafka Brigade investigated the certification problems of these two Dutch citizens, we stumbled across a civil servant who had worked at both the Department of Civil Affairs and the GBA and who had experienced the differences and incompatibilities between the two organizations and the problems these created for clients firsthand. However, he had learned in attempting to streamline processes between the two that their issues could not be resolved within City Hall. The two organizations do not operate under the same jurisdictions: the Department of Civil Affairs operates under the Ministry of Justice, while the GBA works, first, under the city government, and second, under the Ministry of the Interior. What is more, he found that the civil servants working at the Department of Civil Affairs had virtually no room to be flexible in executing their procedures. Because of their special status as part of the judicial system, they had a legal liability that often made it impossible for them to craft tailor-made solutions to their clients' problems.

### Diagnosis

The collective performance review brought together representatives from all of the involved agencies, the minister of public service reform, and relatives of the two principals. First, Sven and Ilse told their stories, followed by comments from a civil servant with copious experience with these types of cases. This civil servant confirmed that these cases emerged from structural problems with the certification process.

#### Red Tape: The Perspective of the Public Sector Client

- In both cases, going abroad had caused problems that would not have occurred had the citizens stayed in the Netherlands. Proof or lack thereof from foreign governments was inadequate in the eyes of the civil servants at the Department of Civil Affairs and had resulted in Sven and Ilse being denied government-issued documents they needed urgently.

- The real complaints of each client emerged because they felt were not being treated decently. This was especially so in the case of the Department of Civil Affairs, which a citizen visits only in moments of major life change, such as a birth or death in the family. Given the importance of these events, the clients were particularly furious that they were not treated humanely or with respect.
- The lack of a straightforward appeals process made the clients feel even more disenfranchised and disrespected.
- The lack of awareness on the part of the clients was caused by a lack of accurate information and knowledge on the side of the government. Of course, it is impossible for frontline officials at the Department of Civil Affairs or the GBA to know everything about all possible circumstances, so they resort strictly to procedure and legislation and do not provide contextual information or assistance.
- In both cases, the clients needed to return several times to the Department of Civil Affairs desk with additional documentation, and each time they were sent back with new homework. This was a waste of time and energy and increased each client's anxiety level.

### Culture: The Perspective of the Public Sector Professional

- Even though both divisions are usually located close to one another, sometimes even in the same office building, they have no contact with each other; all communication is through the client. The burden of integrative work once again belonged to the clients.
- Representatives of both divisions acknowledged that they do not trust each other's data, nor do they understand one another's business processes. They do not see why they should cooperate on a regular basis. The participants attributed this mind-set to each office's organizational history and culture: the Department of Civil Affairs belongs to the realm of the judiciary and vital statistics, while the GBA has emerged in the realm of government operations and information management.
- Because these two divisions are not very familiar with one another's business processes, they do not know the consequences for clients if they must apply for documents from other agencies.

- The lack of flexibility perceived by both complainants was explained by the participants as a result of three reasons: first, although they do have discretionary authority, they have enormous difficulties translating that into daily practice. Second, they are extremely cautious about fraud or forgery because it has serious ramifications for benefits claims and other matters. Third, the back-office structure of the Department of Civil Affairs consists of lawyers looking over employees' shoulders. The participants reported being afraid of reprimands from this back-office organization, which made them more inflexible.

- At the same time, there were wide variations in how office employees dealt with these kinds of situations. The participants acknowledged that they were aware of such variety but that it was not conditioned by the needs of the case so much as by individual perceptions of how flexible they were allowed to be.

*Structure: The Perspective of the Public Manager*

- The two main divisions of the municipal government that played a role here did not feel responsible for solving these certification issues. They were both very much focused on their own business processes and remained disconnected from legislation at the national level.

- The problems with the certification system have been known for decades at the senior management and higher levels. Failure to resolve these issues was blamed on political turf wars between the Ministries of the Interior and Justice.

- The organization of services seemed to be directed at issuing documents to people who fit an average profile and denying them to those who do not. There seemed to be no emphasis on solving problems that arose from special circumstances or from flaws in regulation or procedures. Frontline employees were not rewarded in any way for solving problems for clients.

*Statecraft: The Perspective of Policymakers*

- Participants acknowledged that there was not a sufficient sense of urgency to make certification problems a priority at higher levels of government or operating agencies. The lack of urgency has resulted in procrastination on this problem.

- No one felt responsible for this issue. High-level officials claimed that frontline people did not adequately use their discretion, while frontline workers argued that the legislation was unclear, inadequate, and left insufficient room for discretion.
- Because the involved actors at both the agency level and at higher levels of government had not collectively worked on the problem, they also did not see the size of the problem.
- When civil servants from the GBA make mistakes, they fall under administrative law, and workers cannot be personally prosecuted. When employees of the Ministry of Justice working in the Department of Civil Affairs make mistakes, however, they can be prosecuted under criminal law. This explains the lack of flexibility at the department.
- Most of the participants felt that legislation was skewed toward preventing identity fraud and abuse of services and was in no way designed to serve the great majority of people who were there for genuine reasons.
- Some participants also explained that the process for generating legal documents provides one political means to discourage foreigners from coming to the Netherlands; there is no incentive in the process to facilitate the acknowledgment of foreign documentation. That Dutch citizens experience problems as a result of living abroad or going on vacation internationally seemed not to matter.
- An additional issue was that neither the Ministry of Justice nor of the Ministry of the Interior wanted to acknowledge its errors because to do so would have meant ceding ground to the other. This could potentially lead to a lower ministerial budget and layoffs in their field. The two divisions remained at a stalemate.

## Remedies

The collective performance review was very well received by all participants and caught the attention of many people at both ministries. It became the starting point of a productive process of consensus building, which led to the following remedies.

### Case-Level Remedies

- There were none, as both cases had already been resolved and closed.

*Category-Level Remedies*

- The Department of Civil Affairs began to institute more training for frontline people, especially in the use of discretion. They worked to make their front-office employees more aware of their options within the limits of the law.
- The Department of Civil Affairs abolished the requirement that those attempting to acknowledge a child born out of wedlock produce a certificate proving they were unmarried.
- The National Association for Civil Registry has suggested the creation of an information package for people who temporarily leave the Netherlands to inform them of what they need to do to return, and what the consequences might be of leaving.

*Capacity-Level Remedies*

- The Ministries of Justice and Interior have created a ministerial task force to see if the Department of Civil Affairs and the GBA could be merged. The latter would lead the new system. The minister of justice has agreed to this arrangement and broken the stalemate between the two ministries. As of early 2009, it had been officially announced that this merger would take place, which would force communication between the two divisions, prevent discrepancies between their records, and minimize potential conflicts.

---

## CASE 12: Licensing a Supermarket

Derek had owned a local supermarket franchise in a medium-sized Dutch city for about fifteen years. Business was going well, and he wished to expand into the house next to his store. To find out how to get approval for this plan, he went to the municipal government's Service Desk for Entrepreneurs, which was supposed to be a one-stop shop for information. He got information about the various departments that might have to be involved in the project. The first order of business was to have an architect draw up a design and construction plan in order to apply for a building license. In the summer of 2006, Derek submitted an application for a construction license. The license is issued fourteen months later.

**Derek Wants to Expand His Supermarket**

*At a Glance*

| | |
|---|---|
| Those affected | Clients, particularly entrepreneurs, applying for a building permit |
| | Entrepreneurs inquiring about government licenses in general |
| Major complaints | Lack of information and certainty about regulation and procedures |
| | Cost of compliance with procedures |
| | General attitude of officials |
| Agencies involved | Municipal government: Division of Building and Construction |
| | Municipal government: Service Desk for Entrepreneurs |
| | Municipal government: Fire Department |
| | Ministry of the Environment |

Like Tamer Akgün in the case of the sandwich shop, Derek had to pay rent on the house for the entire fourteen months it took to obtain his construction license. Every time Derek submitted an application, after a waiting period he would receive a request for additional information or instructions to apply for additional licenses with other departments. For example, the proposed expansion meant that he also needed to provide more parking space for customers. This rule applied even though his business plan stated that 85 percent of his customers were pedestrians. Derek was unable to discuss this with the relevant civil servants. He had to apply first and then appeal.

The government also required Derek to have archeological research done on the property. He learned about this requirement only after his first application was rejected. Regulations also seemed to require an assessment by acoustic experts to determine whether the noise level would becceptable for the neighborhood. Only after the assessment had begun did he find out that this was not necessary in his case—the rules had not been clear about that. Finally, Derek learned that after all the research, he had to sign an agreement that would render him liable for any claims from people in the neighborhood whose property value might decrease because of his construction plan. Because Derek had no way of knowing whether losses in his neighbors' property value would occur or whether his planned extension would cause such losses, this liability made Derek very anxious.

Throughout the process, the two major problems confronting Derek were the costs associated with the long wait time to get his applications approved and the general uncertainty about what he needed to do, when, and why. The so-called one-stop shop could direct him to different places but could not give him more insight into the correct sequence and interrelations of procedures.

In addition, Derek felt that nobody was willing to help him or encourage his business enterprise. He felt that officials hid behind rules and procedures, leaving the burden of discovering regulations and figuring out how to comply to him. The general attitude of the city surprised and annoyed him.

## Diagnosis

The collective performance review brought together representatives of the city government, as well as the business association and the Service Desk for Entrepreneurs, both of which are nongovernmental organizations. The city manager of Derek's city was also present. The participants agreed quickly that the primary goal for the session was to find out what had gone wrong in general, and to determine how encounters at the Division of Building and Construction's service desk could be improved. The problem definition was not particularly controversial. Most participants agreed on the problem and its causes; what did cause disagreement was what should be done to change it.

### Red Tape: The Perspective of the Public Sector Client

- Derek did not report his problem with any official authority, but the business association of which he is a member was aware of his difficulties, and it was his business association that nominated his case for scrutiny.

- Derek did not see the government as monolithic and was aware of the various organizations responsible for the parts of his case. The only thing he did not understand was why there was nowhere to go with questions.
- It was not only the government but also private sector parties, such as the landlord and the supermarket franchise chain, that needed to supply information for Derek. The waiting time for all of these parties to come together contributed to the problem.
- There were many unproductive encounters between Derek and the municipal divisions that manage building and construction, parking permits, and entrepreneurial services.
- There is a checklist of requirements for entrepreneurs starting new businesses, but this checklist applies only to standard permit applications and not to cases where zoning plans must be changed, as they did in Derek's case.

### Culture: The Perspective of the Public Sector Professional

- The Division of Building and Construction was dependent on the advice of other agencies (environmental, fire, and so forth), which contributed to waiting time. There was no streamlined process: every time the Division of Building and Construction asked for advice, its request wound up on top of a pile of similar paperwork other divisions had on their desks.
- Each division had its own operational and legal issues. Participants did not necessarily agree that it was problematic that the applicant was the main means of communication between divisions.
- Participants did not feel that employee management contributed to a lack of problem-solving capacity. They felt there was sufficient capacity to manage complex cases. In Derek's case, the problem was that no single employee was able to provide all the answers on a particular point.
- The manner in which priorities were set for the involved divisions of the municipal government was influenced by some incidents the city had had with poor-quality construction in the past. The city's focus was therefore very much on preventing new construction defects. Thus, frontline workers wanted to be sure that every license issued met legal criteria completely and that official procedures were followed to the letter.

- Derek's problem with the general attitude of the city government was a direct effect of this role interpretation—making sure nothing bad would ever happen, and that the city government would always be covered by strict enforcement of the rules—on the part of its civil servants.

*Structure: The Perspective of the Public Manager*

- Participants agreed that the business processes of the Division of Building and Construction and the Division of Parking Permits were relatively disconnected but saw this as inevitable because the legislation governing the two was very complex and also disconnected at a higher level. They did agree that service delivery could be improved by finding ways to work around this split.
- Frontline employees downplayed the role of top management in the city government. They believed that they were executing legislation enacted at a higher level of government. Frontline employees also thought that their main task was to apply official procedures and enforce the law, and much less to facilitate the applications of their clients.

*Statecraft: The Perspective of Policymakers*

- Much of the regulation governing Derek's case is phrased in technical, juridical language, and because the frontline employees involved were particularly cautious, they adhered to this language and did not translate it into more colloquial terms for their applicants, which created confusion and misinformation among their applicants. Some of the participants frankly acknowledged that the average entrepreneur does not understand what the law says.
- The participants agreed that the Service Desk for Entrepreneurs was equipped with neither the authority nor the capacity to be meaningful for entrepreneurs, despite the good intentions with which it had been created. Instead of providing case managers or answers to specific questions (which applicants tend to have), the service desk had become a place to obtain general information or to be directed to other agencies.
- The focus on preventing accidents by rigidly applying the law has emerged as a policy priority, but there has never been a political debate that formally established this as a focus over client assistance and service delivery. The review revealed a tension between

these priorities, and because politicians have not made an explicit choice, the bureaucrats have, choosing to favor rule adherence over proactive client assistance.

## Remedies

### Case-Level Remedies

- No actions could be determined because the case had already been closed.

### Category-Level Remedies

- There were no remedies suggested here either: all the participants felt there was nothing wrong with the rules.

### Capacity-Level Remedies

- The Division of Building and Construction and the Service Desk for Entrepreneurs resolved to meet to look into applicant scenarios and to redesign client services.
- The Division of Economic Affairs is exploring an opportunity to train frontline employees to serve applicants more proactively, especially entrepreneurs.
- The Division of Building and Construction agreed to grant access to the Service Desk for Entrepreneurs so frontline workers would have the information necessary to answer entrepreneurs' questions. This would also relieve some of the administrative burden on the Division of Building and Construction.

## **CASE 13**: Youth Care

Kirsten and her husband had a fifteen-year-old adopted daughter. Kirsten and her husband noticed that something was wrong with their daughter early on in her social and mental development. When she was ten years old, a psychologist had diagnosed a learning disability in mathematics and behavioral problems stemming from an attachment disorder.

Kirsten's daughter did not feel at home at her regular elementary and secondary school, and the school decided that she would be more

**Adequate Mental Care Is Hard to Find for Kirsten's
Adopted Daughter**

*At a Glance*

| | |
|---|---|
| Those affected | People in urgent need of mental care and their relatives |
| Major complaints | Lack of information and certainty about application procedures |
| | Mismatch between supply and demand in mental health care |
| | Frontline workers' lack of flexibility and lack of focus on solving problems |
| Agencies involved | Youth Care Agency (Bureau Jeugdzorg) |
| | Ministry of Health |
| | Schools |
| | Youth treatment or detention facilities |

comfortable if she could transition to a special high school early. Unfortunately, this particular school had a waiting list. In the meantime, she was placed in another school with people who had autism spectrum disorders. This turned out to be a worse fit than her original school because her autistic classmates made it more difficult for her to strengthen her social skills. She felt very alone and eventually stopped going to school. The truancy officers from the city government would not intervene to help Kirsten because *she* was willing to send her daughter to school but couldn't get her to attend in a meaningful way. Truancy officers can act only if the parents are not willing to enforce truancy laws, not if they are simply unable to. They did not feel responsible for helping Kirsten find another school where her daughter might be more inclined to attend. Over time, Kirsten's daughter's problems became so serious that when space became available at the high school she was going to attend in the first place, her problems had become too complex for the teachers in that school to manage, and Kirsten and her daughter had to look for yet another place to go.

Kirsten decided to contact the Youth Care Agency (Bureau Jeugdzorg) for professional social services. The Youth Care Agency conducted an assessment but, owing to capacity problems, could not provide appropriate treatment. Kirsten's daughter was placed in the crisis shelter of a facility in another part of the country, which provided only noneducational activities. Her problems worsened, and she became involved with some dangerous men. Her parents were unable to prevent her from seeing these men because the crisis shelter was not a detention facility, and their daughter could walk out whenever she liked. She was out of reach of her parents, who felt powerless.

When their daughter's behavior hit rock bottom, a court ruled that she had crossed the line and could be detained and admitted to a youth detention center with a treatment facility. Legally, after the court decision, she had the right to be admitted within twenty-four hours. However there was another capacity problem: no detention center was available. When she was finally admitted to a facility, because the group she was supposed to be in was full, she was placed with a group of girls with drug problems. This again had a bad influence on Kirsten's daughter. When her behavior deteriorated even further, the facility intervened, moving two other girls out of the group she was meant to be in so she could be placed into that group.

On top of this ordeal, Kirsten had to contend with all the usual red tape associated with all the different schools and facilities. With every application to a new (temporary) facility, her daughter had to submit to another assessment, which always reached the same conclusion.

At the time of our research, Kirsten's daughter was doing well and improving slowly. However, she still was not in school getting an education, which is what she and her parents were looking for in the first place. Overall, Kirsten found the youth care in the Netherlands extremely disorganized, fragmented, inefficient, and ineffective.

## Diagnosis

The collective performance review brought together a wide range of representatives from organizations concerned with youth care and other policy areas, including health care, juvenile justice, and education. The main question we posed from the beginning was, what are the root causes of the problems that Kirsten experienced in this case?

The participants all agreed that Kirsten's difficulties were widespread problems and not exceptions. There is a continuous mismatch between what young people need and what organizations can provide. The participants were noticeably anxious, and their frustration was evident in the way they defined the problem and the powerlessness they displayed when making resolutions to remedy the problem.

### Red Tape: The Perspective of the Public Sector Client

- Kirsten and her husband were perfectly capable of articulating the help they needed and were well aware of which organizations they should apply to for that help. The challenge was that the officials they encountered were unable to assist them.
- In part because the appropriate placement was never available, Kirsten's daughter's situation worsened over time. Her mental health deteriorated more quickly than the system could respond.
- The professionals working with Kirsten's case were almost never able to provide adequate information. It was unclear whether this was caused by a lack of expertise among frontline people or whether they simply did not understand the client's particular situation.
- It was, however, clear that encounters were highly formalized to deal with cases as efficiently as possible. Performance metrics valued the number of encounters managed per day over the effectiveness of the encounter.

### Culture: The Perspective of the Public Sector Professional

- Participants recognized a common problem within youth care, which is that many divisions and agencies engage in mutual referrals that leave the client lost between organizations. Thus, in many cases, particularly complex ones, the client was the only one with an overview of all of the agencies involved. Divisions rarely communicated with one another, and if they did, it was as a last resort, through central government youth care organizations.
- Even though many professionals wished to do more personally, they felt constrained by their circumstances and unable to lead their clients by the hand to ensure that their problems were solved. They remained largely unaware that they could take a flexible approach to complex cases. Flexibility was not emphasized or encouraged in standard business processes.

*Structure: The Perspective of the Public Manager*

- Although special cases and exceptions were business as usual, business process design in the various agencies involved here did not anticipate demand from cases that did not match supply. This paradox became clear during the collective performance review.
- All participants agreed that the way the agencies were funded was a major impediment to proactive work. Most participants felt that their organizations were underfunded. They had to serve as many clients as possible with limited resources, which resulted in rigid ways of working.

*Statecraft: The Perspective of Policymakers*

- There was a high level of discontent among both professionals and managers in youth care about the legislative framework and governance structures. This discontent is neither translated into constructive criticism nor channeled through feedback mechanisms that policymakers can actually use. Practitioners feel stuck, but do not know how to move beyond their counterproductive relationships with higher levels of government.
- It became clear that the public has high expectations of the government in regard to youth care. Citizens expect the state to prevent tragic incidents from happening; they also react strongly to accidents and problems reported in the popular media. The efforts of politicians, on the one hand, and practitioners on the other have not led to more effective or efficient youth care. This predicament puts stress on all relevant actors but particularly on frontline workers.

## Remedies

The remedies in this case were noteworthy in that none of the suggested actions could be directly linked to anyone present in the room. The only solutions they could develop were ideas for others to accomplish, such as changing rules for medical and mental assessments of young people; starting a rule-free experimental zone in youth care in a particular province in the Netherlands; improving policy regarding designated places for treatment and detention to ensure space for urgent cases; and altering the way the Ministry of Health (not present at the meeting) holds its agencies responsible. All of these actions and interventions might very well be beneficial to youth care, but they were all defined abstractly. The fact that the participants could not suggest anything they could achieve themselves reflected their helplessness in the face of the daunting challenges presented by youth care in the Netherlands. No actions were volunteered at any of the remedy levels—case, category, or capacity.

## CASE 14: Direct Payments

**Direct Payments Don't Pay Off for Lisa's Caregiver**

*At a Glance*

| | |
|---|---|
| Those affected | People eligible for the Direct Payments program in health care and their relatives |
| Major complaints | Lack of:<br>—information and certainty about the requirements and responsibilities that come with direct payments<br>—responsiveness of government officials and agencies<br>—problem-solving infrastructure |
| Agencies involved | Ministry of Health<br>Care administration office (Zorgkantoor)<br>Ministry of Social Affairs and Labor<br>Social Insurance Bank (SVB), or Social Security Administration<br>Ministry of Finance/Tax authority |

Lisa was a ninety-one-year-old woman who had been experiencing medical problems not serious enough to warrant going to an elder care facility or hospital. Her sixty-year-old daughter had left her job to look after her mother on a daily basis. She could afford to do so because the government's Direct Payments system paid her as it would any other caregiver.

This program was designed to ensure customer choice (including the choice to designate a family member) and, as described in case 7, was revised in 2003 to involve the client in the payment process. The client would receive direct payments from the government, which the client would then return to the social insurance bank (Sociale Verzekeringsbank, SVB), which in turn would pay for the care provision. This extra step in the process gave patients some autonomy in managing their own bank accounts and care budgets. The SVB then gave patients the option of setting up automatic monthly payments from the patient's bank account to the SVB. Obviously, though, if there is no money in the patient's bank account, this debit cannot take place. If a patient defaults on her automatic payments, the SVB not only will stop paying the care provider, it will also cease all administrative work on behalf of the patient.

For Lisa, problems arose when, at some point, either the SVB or the government agency that disbursed these benefits made a mistake, and Lisa's daughter stopped receiving payments. When Lisa and her daughter began trying to trace the mistake, they found that the SVB had been unable to make its arranged debits from Lisa's bank account, so it had discontinued both administrative service and payments to Lisa's daughter. The problem was, who was at fault?

Neither Lisa nor her daughter was able to figure out which organization had made the initial mistake, but one consequence of the error was the involvement of the tax authority. Because the social insurance company had stopped providing administrative service, Lisa now qualified as an employer and was legally obligated to keep the books of her new business. The tax authority now regarded Lisa as her daughter's employer and therefore subject to regulations guiding not only taxes but also occupational health and safety and social security. The paperwork accompanying these regulations proved a huge administrative burden to this ninety-one-year-old patient.

Of course, neither Lisa nor her daughter was aware of their changed business status initially, and it took some time to sort out what they were being held responsible for. They had no idea where to go for help: to the government agency that paid their direct payments? To the social insurance company that administered their wire transfers?

To the tax authority? To the Ministry of Health, responsible for this whole system of care? Or to the Ministry of Social Affairs and Labor, now that Lisa was an employer? Because they were at a loss, they hired a lawyer to make a case on their behalf, but he did not know where to go either. In the meantime, the tax authority had frozen Lisa's bank accounts and put a lien on her property for nonpayment of taxes.

It was at this stage that one of the employees at the lower echelons of the tax authority became involved in the case. She had seen many other examples of cases in which individuals who were ill or very elderly and not capable of taking on such responsibility had mistakenly been labeled employers anyway. She brought the case to the attention of her employers at the tax authority but soon discovered that the matter was too complex for her organization to manage. Because those within the institution seemed unwilling or unable to do anything, she started looking for outside help. Ultimately the Kafka Brigade was asked to intervene by the Ministry of the Interior. We began to research the case and, though Lisa had unfortunately passed away by that time, we were able to talk to her daughter, the lawyer they engaged, the tax authority employee who responded to Lisa's complaint, and her employers.

*Diagnosis*

The collective performance review for this case united representatives of the tax authority, the SVB, and the Ministries of Finance, Social Affairs and Employment, the Interior, and Health. Three directors general of the four ministries attended, as did lower-level employees, including frontline officers at the tax authority. This case was without doubt one of the most complex the Kafka Brigade tackled. It took a great deal of effort to research the many facets of the issue, and it became clear, during the collective performance review, that few of the participants were aware of the breadth of the problem. Participants also acknowledged that their reluctance to take on the case arose, first, from its technical difficulty, and second, from a lack of political will to resolve the challenges besieging the new Direct Payments system. Criticizing the feasibility of the implementation of the Direct Payments program is not a very popular thing to do.

*Red Tape: The Perspective of the Public Sector Client*

- It was very clear from the beginning that Lisa and her daughter were not capable of taking on the responsibility of administering their own care payments. They were inattentive to the regulations with which they had to comply. Had they realized that the system would involve such a substantial administrative burden, they would probably not have chosen direct payments over care in kind.
- Lisa and her daughter were also unaware of the changes in policy enacted in 2003, with broad consequences for the Direct Payments system. Lisa was unaware that she would legally be labeled an employer, with all the responsibilities that accompany that position, resulting in the problems that emerged in her case over time.
- A third problem that did not affect Lisa but was a concern for anyone who qualified for direct payments was that while the caregiver was usually the one applying on the client's behalf for direct payments, the client bore all of the legal responsibility for this system and the caregiver none at all. This was allowing unscrupulous third parties to apply for direct payments and channel the money into their own bank accounts without providing enough care, or any care at all. There were no mechanisms in place to identify such fraud.
- No single agency ever contacted Lisa or her daughter to find out why payments had ceased. The SVB simply discontinued Lisa's service, and the tax authority claimed its money and put a lien on her property. This situation could have been avoided and corrective action could have been taken at an early stage if anyone had bothered to follow up with the clients about the interruption in payments.

*Culture: The Perspective of the Public Sector Professional*

- The frontline employee from the tax authority mentioned in the review session that she and many of her colleagues met clients at their desks who felt very lost and emotional. These clients often came to her office because the tax authority was the only agency that actually had a front office. It was difficult to dismiss people who were weeping at her counter, even though responding to their problems was outside both her job description and the jurisdiction of her agency.

- The Ministry of Finance is responsible for the tax authority, the Ministry of Health for health care and care payments, and Social Affairs and Employment for employer-employee relationships. All had a different stake in particular Direct Payment clients, and all functioned on a highly abstract and theoretical level. In practice, numerous problems occurred, perhaps more than were noted because agencies did not share information or communicate with each other about problems. The challenges of the Direct Payments system could be much larger than anyone knows.
- Most of the participants in the session concluded that their agencies were structured to perform efficiently only within their own jurisdictions: the tax authority demands that its employees collect taxes efficiently; the SVB instructs its employees to process payments and take care of client administration; and the health care agency focuses on distributing payments on time. None of these three organizations trained its officers to solve the problems that occurred as a result of lack of coordination between agencies.

*Structure: The Perspective of the Public Manager*

- Only after individuals have chosen direct payments do they receive all of the relevant information about the consequences of this choice. There is a flaw in the business processes governing the provision of information to clients.
- The business processes of payment, flagging accounts, and terminating funds are all automated. There is scarcely any human intervention. As a result, if something goes wrong, it triggers an automatic response without demanding any proactive problem-solving responses at any of the agencies involved.
- Agencies are also not incentivized to deal with anything more than their particular business with actual clients. They have no mechanisms in place to detect eligible nonrecipients of benefits, or people who have somehow managed to slip through the cracks. This type of proactive service delivery would be possible only if agencies compared databases, but because since no single group has the final responsibility for the Direct Payments system, no one has encouraged employees to take note of such problems.

- At the category level, the Ministry of Health designed the Direct Payments system to allow disabled people who in all other respects have complete control over their lives to administer their own care arrangements. The ministry intended to treat such people not as patients or as dependents but as clients in their own right. However, it quickly became difficult to draw the line between those who were eligible for direct payments and those who were not; as a result, the ministry decided to automatically qualify every patient for direct payments, including those who were neither mentally nor physically capable of executing the responsibility.
- Though policymakers assumed those who were not capable of taking on the extra work involved in direct payments would choose payment in kind, in practice, because of lack of information or abuse by third parties, many people entered the system without being equipped to manage it. These clients' problems rarely were conveyed from the frontline officials to management, and had not been brought to the attention of policymakers.
- Participants all agreed that the dominant philosophy of customer choice in the political arena on both the left and right of the political spectrum tended to preclude criticism on the implementation side. Participants did not feel that it would be desirable or feasible to suggest protecting people from accessing the Direct Payments system.
- Officials in politics are very much aware that the costs of health care are increasing with an aging society. The costs of direct payments are much less (sometimes as much as 20 percent to30 percent less) than care in kind, in part because the integrative and administrative work is done by the client. Although very few politicians would acknowledge it openly, the cost incentive to encourage people to use direct payments over care in kind has driven political will to make it work and to give people the right to Direct Payments, whether they are capable of taking advantage of that right or not.

## Remedies

The fact that politicians have been so forceful in their endorsement of the Direct Payments system has made participants feel powerless in terms of developing structural solutions. The one idea they did suggest in that regard, to make an official determination about which clients would be able and therefore eligible to use Direct Payments, was politically not feasible. We asked participants to develop a string of secondary solutions.

### Case-Level Remedies

- Lisa had already passed away by the time of our collective performance review, and the problems with her daughter and caregiver had already been solved.

### Category-Level Remedies

- In case of a client's obvious incapability, the tax authority would have the responsibility to separate out a bank account specifically for the purpose of budgeting for direct payments. This would mean that, when tax and compliance problems arose, instead of letting the problem go, the tax authority could channel money for the caregiver from the Ministry of Health to a separate account. While this remedy did not achieve universal agreement, it represented one possibility.
- The participants agreed to revisit the policy regarding the obligations for patients receiving direct payments who have become labeled as employers; the social insurance withholdings for their caregivers can still be administered through the SVB, but if for some reason something goes wrong, the responsibility for fixing it would not immediately fall to the client. At the same time, participants were keenly aware that this lesser responsibility for clients might actually make the system more vulnerable to abuse and fraud. Changing the practice would require deep rethinking and redesign, and probably a change in legislation.

### Capacity-Level Remedies

- The participants resolved to conduct a quantitative analysis of the number of Direct Payment clients who risk of getting into trouble with the agencies who administer their payments. They understood the risk profile is for this kind of client but did not know how many there were because the agency databases had not been combined. This action would increase capacity to prevent problems.

- The participants committed to change the business processes at the SVB so that when problems occur with deposits, officials would contact clients in person to identify what might be causing difficulties and what could be done about it.
- The SVB also offered to give those eligible for direct payments and labeled as employers the opportunity to let the SVB take over their administrative duties completely, not only with regard to payments to the caregiver but also in managing their bank accounts. Indeed, in problem cases, this administration could become a forced decision, in which the SVB would have complete control over a client's money, administration, unpaid taxes, and so on. This remedy is one that the SVB would have to discuss with the relevant ministries.
- Another suggestion was for the Ministry of Health to use the tax forms that clients must fill out anyway for accountability purposes, leaving clients with one less burden. They would have to account for their spending of their care budget on only one form, submitted to the tax authority, which would then share this information with other agencies. This idea would have to be discussed and implemented at the category level.
- More generally, participants suggested improving city government and health care employee training and information dissemination to clients so that clients could make more informed choices and frontline employees would be better able to assist them in doing so.
- A final remedy was to work with those city governments that did not do business with the SVB (about 59 of the 442 municipalities in the Netherlands) to make sure that potential beneficiaries were not falling through the cracks.

## Conclusion

As we were conducting our research, at times we thought our results were disappointing in terms of producing tangible actions that would improve the lives of clients the performance reviews generated. In part this owed to the inevitable time lag in introducing changes to large agencies: even though the participants in our collective performance reviews committed to remedies, they had to return to their organizations to begin the slow process of building consensus to implement their plans. However, over the course of 2008, as we worked on our report, we received more and more information on progress being made on many of the proposed remedies in almost all of the ten cases. By March 2008 sufficient progress had been made that the minister of public service reform sent a letter to Parliament announcing our results, which are briefly summarized below.

## Immediate Results

Not all cases yielded immediate results; here I discuss those that did.

### Case 5: Medical Assessment Certificates

- At the national level, the annual handicapped parking permit renewal requirement has been abolished. This means 120,000 fewer medical assessment certificates will be required per year by public service agencies.
- The health insurance company has also changed its method for checking eligibility for services. It now performs random checks after each application rather than universal evaluations before granting any assistance. This means an estimated 100,000 fewer medical assessment certificates will be issued per year in the Netherlands.

### Case 6: Conflicting Benefits

- The Council for Pensions and Social Benefits has improved the structure of its service to people receiving more than one social benefit so that they will no longer fall through the cracks.
- Both the Council for Pensions and Social Benefits and the UWV have established a "Kafka Button" for their officers. This represents an internal procedure that can be activated where there is a complex procedure that cannot be managed at a lower level of bureaucracy.

### Case 7: Appeal and Redress in Health Care

- The National Ombudsman has acknowledged that the Ombudsman's office has been ill-equipped to manage complaints in which no single agency is at fault. To remedy this problem, the office has changed its operating processes, and has committed to improving employee training to better apply this new way of working.

### Case 9: Benefits for Ex-Convicts

- The UWV has changed its procedures so that people serving prison terms may suspend their social benefits rather than terminating them entirely. This allows individuals released from prison to resume their social benefits rather than applying anew, from scratch.
- The city government in Amsterdam has also altered its system: while convicts do not have the option of pausing their benefits, they can begin the application process from jail rather than only on release. This prevents the problem of ex-convicts being released onto Dutch streets without money.

### Case 10: Immigration, Marriage, and Employment

- The Immigration and Naturalization Department (IND), the Center for Work and Income (CWI) , and the Information Administration Bureauc (IBG) have started building a joint portal website for immigrants in general and for foreign students in particular.

### Case 11: Legal Documents

- The minister of justice has resolved that the General Municipal Database and the Department of Civil Affairs will be merged; the GBA will be the leading source in the new system. This means an estimated 157,000 fewer certificates will be produced overall, because the new office will be able to draw on its own databases for information without requiring that clients produce new documents.

These were the immediate results to emerge after our 2007 collective performance reviews. Many of the other remedies proposed, and to which our participants committed, remain in the implementation or development stage. Through the sixth step of our method, the check-back meeting, we kept pressure on our groups. Nonetheless, in many cases, even in our check-back meetings, practitioners were still fine-tuning their remedies and could not guarantee that their plans would be realized. We were not sure that our action research had actually contributed to real solutions.

### Results after Three Years

In 2010 we conducted a follow-up study on the implementation of the action plans of our fourteen cases. We found that the actions

Table 6-1. **Results after Three Years: Implementation of Action Plans**

| | | Level of implementation | | |
|---|---|---|---|---|
| Case | Encounter | None | Part | Full |
| 1 | Licensing a sandwich shop | | | ✓ |
| 2 | Licensing a shop and a restaurant | ✓ | | |
| 3 | Access to services for school dropouts | | | ✓ |
| 4 | Licensing a community-garden barn | ✓ | | |
| 5 | Obtaining medical certificates | | ✓ | |
| 6 | Sorting out social benefits | | | ✓ |
| 7 | Appeal and redress in health care | | ✓ | |
| 8 | Licensing a restaurant | ✓ | | |
| 9 | Obtaining benefits as an ex-convict | | | ✓ |
| 10 | Sorting out immigrant rights | | ✓ | |
| 11 | Obtaining legal documents in case of birth or death abroad | | | ✓ |
| 12 | Licensing a supermarket | | ✓ | |
| 13 | Access to youth social services | | ✓ | |
| 14 | Sorting out problems with the Direct Payments system | | | ✓ |

formulated at the collective performance review session had been fully implemented in only six cases out of the fourteen. In three cases (the sandwich shop, medical certificates, and school dropouts), the process had continued after the session and created even more results. In five cases the work was still in progress after three years:

some actions had been implemented, some had not, and some had proven to be very time-consuming (such as changes in legislation). In three cases, nothing had happened at all, and our follow-up inquiry was sometimes met with defensive attitudes. Table 6-1 summarizes these three-year results by case.

### Evaluating the Kafka Brigade Approach

The report following this phase of the Kafka Brigade's development reflected on both the nature of bureaucratic dysfunction in the ten cases we encountered and on the effectiveness of our approach to the problems we had diagnosed. Most of the lessons we took away from this consolidation phase are discussed in the next chapter. It is sufficient to say here that we drafted an extensive report to disseminate our case study results and the current state of our method to a wider audience of academics and practitioners. We wanted to solicit constructive criticism, to generate discussion around what we had already accomplished, and to ask how (and if) we should move forward. To these ends, we wrote a 200-page report, including case materials, to document the development of our method to date. In addition to this report, we published articles on the Kafka Brigade method in practitioner and academic journals and in edited volumes.

The response of academia to our work was largely positive; many scholars were interested both in what we were doing and in how we were doing it. We were invited to write journal articles, present our methodology at a number of academic conferences, discuss our work with colleagues, and teach as guest lecturers. These experiences assisted us in better explaining our project and in thinking about what the essence of our method really was. There were no immediate reviews or critical discussions in response to our publications, in part because we had not yet drawn conclusions that could be generalized. We had published our raw material with minimal analysis of what bureaucratic dysfunction was and how it came about.

The response from practitioners was more straightforward: after the initial skepticism that we had encountered in previous stages, we noticed that our method and our project were enjoying more positive feedback. We had generated interest among public managers with these cases. As a result, we decided to organize reflection sessions to bring together those who had been involved in the project's consolidation phase and the mentors who had guided us in earlier phases with practitioners who were not directly involved in Kafka Brigade research but who had played a pivotal role in moving public service reform forward. From these reflection sessions, in which we explicitly asked participants to critique our method and to advise us on how to go forward, we derived a host of lessons, which we summarize below.

- *Look beyond red tape:* What the Kafka Brigade does is much broader than addressing red tape. By using cases of apparent bureaucratic malfunction, the Kafka Brigade can approach larger issues in public administration. Most notable among these problems are turf wars between domains, particularly policy or functional domains, as expressed through institutional forms such as agencies or networks of agencies. Our respondents advised us to look more deeply into these challenges because red tape is only a symptom of such underlying problems.
- *Challenge the status quo:* We were advised to acknowledge the fact that public administration represents the exercise and sometimes the abuse of power, which itself in numerous ways. By exposing dysfunction, the Kafka Brigade punctuated equilibriums; as a result, power can shift in unexpected ways. These challenges to existing status quos can be catalysts for rebalancing power dynamics, but they can also cause authorities to exercise more power.
- *Ensure follow-up*: The Kafka Brigade set in motion processes that entailed much more than remedying particular cases or categories of cases. According to some, these processes could, or even *should,* lead to organizational and institutional transformation. At its best, the Kafka Brigade would initiate such processes and then leave after its first intervention. However, we were advised to consider ways to think about the ownership and safeguarding of such processes. To ensure follow up, we needed to look at process and change management in general.
- *Remain skeptical:* With the Kafka Brigade becoming better known in the world of public administration in the Netherlands, we had to avoid becoming overly hyped. In new initiatives such as this, there is always the danger of being used by organizations as window dressing, to maintain the appearance of remedying problems in

their bureaucratic processes without substance. We were advised to remain highly critical of the organizations with which we worked and of our reasons for cooperating with them, and to avoid institutionalizing ourselves at all costs. At the same time, other practitioners told us that we should become an institution, that we should be feared but also respected by organizations in administration. These voices argued that becoming too elusive would also not serve our cause.

- *Embrace difficult cases:* Nearly all of the practitioners who gave us feedback appreciated that the Kafka Brigade's method focuses on the most complex 10 percent of clients by matching a face to a difficult case. This reminded practitioners that complexity itself should never be a reason to procrastinate or to neglect an issue because difficult cases still involve flesh-and-blood clients struggling with painful situations.

- *Recognize priorities*: The final piece of advice we received involved the nature of the work that we do. We were told that we would be mistaken if we limited our task to the remedy of organizational dysfunction in terms of improving business processes or making government interventions more effective. Commenters observed that, in part, the alienation felt by both professionals and clients toward public service systems arises from a new public management paradigm that dictates to government to deliver services in a businesslike manner. According to some, this approach to bureaucratic dysfunction is part of the problem, not part of the solution. In this model, what has been forgotten is that the work of government is also highly political, and there are priorities to rank and interests to balance. Our mentors appreciated that our method addresses problems in service delivery by creating a space for political deliberation, to rethink the values that should guide public organizations. In short, the Kafka Brigade method allows space to understand bureaucratic dysfunction not only in terms of delivery dysfunction but also as political dysfunction. The broader absence of politics from models of bureaucratic reform is something our method could address on a practical level.

Overall, we can conclude that the results of this consolidation phase in terms of lessons for our method include the following. First, elements of the identification and definition of government dysfunction have been consolidated and have proved efficacious. Second, we have been able to fine-tune our expertise and skill in accomplishing this first task, and we have further experimented with diagnosis and remedy. The most important challenge ahead is figuring out to what extent this method can be applied more universally: What do the lessons from our empirical exploration through action research mean for a more generalized understanding of the critical conditions under which one can effectively deal with bureaucratic dysfunction?

In other words, we have proved the efficacy of the approach that was developed in the pilot phase by applying it more or less successfully in ten different cases in the consolidation phase. We cannot infer universal effectiveness of the approach from these findings, however. Overall effectiveness and universal applicability can only be proved when we learn more about the main variables in real-life conditions. On the other hand, the action research has yielded a rich variety of lessons about dealing with dysfunction that will help inform more focused future action research projects, as well as more conventional social science research on the effectiveness of the interventions. The harvest from the research in the consolidation phase is therefore increased knowledge about and sensitivity to the most important characteristics of the independent variable (the approach to dealing with bureaucratic dysfunction) and the dependent variable (the outcomes of diagnosis and remedial action). In the next chapter I recap what we have learned from both our conceptual analysis and our operational inquiry in order to present the outline of what seems to the most effective way to deal with bureaucratic dysfunction, based on our research findings.

# 7

# Emerging Issues and Lessons

*Few problems, once solved, stay that way. Changing
conditions tend to "unsolve" problems that previously
have been solved.*

RUSSELL ACKOFF, *The Art of Problem Solving*, 1978

This chapter discusses the results of the Kafka Brigade's exploration
using the frameworks developed in the earlier chapters. It attempts to
capture the most salient lessons from the action research project and
illuminate them with insights from the conceptual and theoretical
work. In bringing together the lessons from these three kinds of research, we can begin to understand how we might deal effectively
with bureaucratic dysfunction. In chapter 2 I identified complex cases
of red tape as potential symptoms of underlying bureaucratic dysfunction. In chapter 3 I reviewed the literature to further explore the
meaning and root causes of bureaucratic dysfunction. To get a sense
of how bureaucratic dysfunction manifests in practice, I then examined fourteen different cases, organizing the lessons of each case
through the typologies and analytical frameworks that emerged from
our conceptual and theoretical explorations.

## The Nature of Bureaucratic Dysfunction

Bureaucratic dysfunction manifests in many different ways and in many
places, with many different causes and many different consequences

for stakeholders. It is a breach of both common sense and rational (or at least understandable) organizational behavior. It is an inherent characteristic of our culture and also a structural flaw in institutional design. The literature on the phenomenon offers a wide variety of perspectives, which table 3-4 shows organized into four broad categories emphasizing various dimensions of the problem.

As the case studies discussed in chapters 5 and 6 show, any or all of the mechanisms researchers and theorists have identified, from clumsiness in service design to misguided attempts to regulate society, from the risk-averse behavior of frontline bureaucrats to fragmented accountability mechanisms, can cause bureaucratic dysfunction. It is impossible to tell from the symptoms what the underlying cause of the problem is. Situations with the same symptoms may have different causes, while situations with similar underlying problems may display different symptoms. Therefore, the Kafka Brigade approached the problem in practice with a pragmatic but careful attitude, using a sophisticated diagnostic framework and a large number of working hypotheses. To keep an open mind with regard to possible causes, we needed a process that would bring a variety of perspectives to bear on the task of identifying, defining, and diagnosing the problem. It had to be broad enough to cover all levels of analysis represented in the framework yet focused enough to allow investigators to come up with specific remedies. The action research process of the Kafka Brigade revealed the underlying mechanisms causing the problems in fourteen different cases.

Because complex red tape was the main criterion for case selection, the Kafka Brigade knew these cases were both technically and politically complicated. What we did not know was what the underlying bureaucratic dysfunction looked like. Issues connected to "culture," "structure," and "statecraft" turned out to be relevant for diagnostic and remedial purposes in most of the cases, in the sense that we could see potential causes or remedies (or both) within these dimensions. The structural dimension was relevant in twelve of the fourteen cases, while the cultural dimension and the statecraft dimension were relevant in eight and nine cases respectively. In all of the cases, two or more dimensions other than red tape as such turned out to be relevant. In only one case, however, were all four dimensions of bureaucratic dysfunction pertinent (see table 7-1).

Table 7-1. Underlying Causes of Fourteen Cases,
Organized by Analysis Level

| Case | Encounter | Structure | Culture | Statecraft |
|------|-----------|-----------|---------|------------|
| 1 | Licensing a sandwich shop | ✓ | ✓ | |
| 2 | Licensing a shop and a restaurant | ✓ | ✓ | |
| 3 | Access to services for school dropouts | ✓ | | ✓ |
| 4 | Licensing a community-garden barn | | ✓ | ✓ |
| 5 | Obtaining medical certificates | ✓ | ✓ | |
| 6 | Sorting out social benefits | ✓ | | ✓ |
| 7 | Appeal and redress in health care | | ✓ | ✓ |
| 8 | Licensing a restaurant | ✓ | ✓ | |
| 9 | Obtaining benefits as an ex-convict | ✓ | | ✓ |
| 10 | Sorting out immigrant rights | ✓ | | ✓ |
| 11 | Obtaining legal documents in case of birth or death abroad | ✓ | | ✓ |
| 12 | Licensing a supermarket | ✓ | ✓ | |
| 13 | Access to youth social services | ✓ | ✓ | ✓ |
| 14 | Sorting out problems with the Direct Payments system | ✓ | | ✓ |

We concluded that while not all dimensions were relevant in all cases, bureaucratic dysfunction is a multidimensional problem. This confirmed our initial intuition that complex red tape is only a symptom of a *variety* of underlying problems. It is also a vindication of the decision to choose a heuristic approach to the operational part of the inquiry. At the same time, the categories are very broad, and further differentiation of the dimensions would probably result in more useful distinctions. As table 7-1 illustrates, dealing with bureaucratic dysfunction is likely to be more effective if the approach acknowledges multiple dimensions, both conceptually and operationally. This understanding has *implications for the diagnostic process* in terms of what data are important, what working hypotheses and questions are relevant, and who should be involved in the diagnostic and remedial process.

In customary practice, red tape is typically reduced to just one or two dimensions. Most efforts to reduce red tape focus on eliminating rules and redesigning work processes but fail to address misguided policies or counterproductive behaviors on the part of the people executing them. Other efforts focus on cultural change or capacity building but fail to look at what really happens in government encounters or how accountability systems (fail to) incentivize behavior. What the Kafka Brigade's action research has shown is that complex cases of red tape, which are characterized by a lack of consensus on problem definition and a lack of knowledge about the nature and size of the problem, provide a useful entry point for inquiring into bureaucratic dysfunction. But while these cases may be defined in terms of concrete criteria, their shapes, sizes, causes, and consequences are very different. This has important implications for approaches to dealing with the problem:

■ The symptoms do not tell you enough about the nature of the problem to know what the causes and consequences are, or what remedies are likely to be effective.
■ The problem is extremely varied and heterogeneous and requires a diagnostic process that helps unravel the structural and cultural aspects of the problem, as well as the elements of statecraft.

## The Process of Dealing with Bureaucratic Dysfunction

Earlier in this book I distinguished four important steps of the analytical approach to the operational inquiry into bureaucratic dysfunction: identification, definition, diagnosis, and remediation (sometimes referred to as IDDR).

### *Identifying Bureaucratic Dysfunction: Screening and Nominating Problems*

Identifying bureaucratic dysfunction means detecting problems and nominating them for discussion and action. Here it is important to pay attention to dysfunction that goes unnoticed because problems may not be reported by clients and professionals or may not be well articulated and handled by managers and policymakers. Complaint procedures and ombudsmen are useful mechanisms for addressing problems that clients and professionals identify (problems that may indicate structural bureaucratic dysfunction), but these institutions are less well positioned to deal with some of the inevitable blind spots. The analytics we developed to help identify some of the blind spots are phrased in terms of the capacities in which clients and government (fail to) encounter each other. We defined bureaucratic dysfunction as the mismatch between state capacity to deliver services and enforce regulation and client capacity to benefit from public services and comply with regulation, and we developed analytics aligned with the concepts of false positives and false negatives in service and obligation encounters.

Of course, once a problem is identified, one needs to be able to determine whether it is worth working on—and how deep one is willing to dig to understand it or spend time solving it. Since the existing mechanisms and institutions are well positioned to address less complicated forms of dysfunction, the potential to add the most value lies in those areas where it is more difficult to figure out what the problems are and what the solutions might be. Those are the cases that show signs of both technical and political complexity. When red tape is both technically and politically complicated, the chances are greater that the problem will go unnoticed or remain unsolved, or both. Therefore, complex cases of red tape can serve as warning signs of potential bureaucratic hazard. Bringing these analytical tools together, I presented a model of bureaucratic dysfunction in encounters between clients and the state (see figure 2-4). The results of the conceptual and theoretical exploration in turn influenced how we thought about the process of identifying bureaucratic dysfunction.

### Defining Bureaucratic Dysfunction: Assessing the Loss of Value

Defining bureaucratic dysfunction means determining what the problem is about, to what extent it is larger or more structural than meets the eye, whom it affects (directly or indirectly), and who needs to be involved in the diagnosis and remedy. The usual approaches to bureaucratic dysfunction rely on partial definitions of the problem concerning material or immaterial losses to the client or to the public at large. Ombudsmen typically focus on justice or welfare losses to individual clients; courts of audit scrutinize welfare losses caused by bureaucratic dysfunction from the perspective of the public at large; advocacy organizations focus on structural injustice to social groups caused by dysfunction, and so on.

While all these functions and institutions may or may not work very well, there is often a missed opportunity to see and understand the relationships between the loss of value to the individual and the loss of value to society. Especially in complex systems of public services, with many agencies involved, it is difficult to understand a problem and do something about it until the bigger picture is clear and the full array of values at stake can be assessed. To attain more comprehensive problem definitions, we have suggested using analytics rooted in public value theory, as shown in table 2-1.

Ombudsmen typically focus on welfare and justice losses from the private (client) perspective, but often make efforts to conduct their so-called own motion research research to better understand the root of problem and advise government organizations in efforts to improve overall performance in terms of both justice and welfare for the good of both clients and the public at large. Supreme audit institutions, such as courts of audit and audit commissions, typically define bureaucratic dysfunction in terms of welfare loss to the public. The most innovative among them, acknowledging that public policy achieves the desired social outcomes only if it is well executed, recognize productive encounters with clients as an important part of the puzzle. Reform agendas and initiatives in Western countries that have focused on reducing administrative burdens, extensively monitored and documented by the OECD and the World Bank, typically define the problem in terms of welfare loss to the client. However, behind these reform and red-tape-reduction agendas there is also a claim that reduced red tape for individual clients (especially businesses) will increase economic growth, which is a social outcome contributing to the welfare of the general public. Finally, many governmental and nongovernmental organizations define bureaucratic dysfunction in terms of losses in justice and fairness in the public realm. The United Nations Commission on Legal Empowerment of the Poor, for example, has connected dysfunctional justice systems to the structural exclusion of social groups. So there are many different actors working on solving bureaucratic dysfunction, but they typically define the problem in terms of just one or two of the quadrants in the matrix presented in table 2-1. The challenge is to orchestrate a process that affords a broader definition, both to facilitate a better understanding of the problem and to clear space for a better chance to deal with it effectively.

### *Diagnosing Bureaucratic Dysfunction: Engaging Clients*

Involving the people affected by bureaucratic dysfunction in the process of investigating and solving it increases the effectiveness of efforts to deal with the problem. Our research revealed two main ways in which clients add value: as a data point and as a proxy. The conditions under which the added value is most likely to occur depend on particular clients' representativeness, the various capacities in which they interact with agencies, and the political pressure their case is able to generate among the relevant parties. These considerations are explained below.

#### Data Point

As a data point, the added value of client engagement lies in the fact that clients (recipients of services as well as obligatees) do a lot of the *integrative work* created by fragmented systems of service delivery and rule enforcement. As such, they are an important part of the production function of the state. To understand what causes the mismatch between client and state, it is vital to learn what problems exist on the client side of the production function. Clients have always been important data points for improving government performance (especially when improving client satisfaction is an important goal), but typically as an indicator for outputs. Aggregate quantitative and qualitative data about client satisfaction are certainly helpful in improving the quality of public services. But the thick description of the experience of a person who encounters the state in many different capacities and through a variety of encounters provides a more helpful perspective for the purpose of dealing with bureaucratic dysfunction. It is interesting to know how people grade their experience with government encounters, but it is more important to know precisely what hurdles had to be gotten over and what other factors shaped the encounter, led it astray, or prevented it from occurring at all. Indeed, when looking at bureaucratic dysfunction, the point is often to focus on the eligible nonrecipients and noneligible recipients rather than on the clients who showed up and got what they came for. Similarly, focusing on the obligatee experience would not suffice, since bureaucratic dysfunction creates noncomplying obligatees and complying nonobligatees too. Understanding what exactly leads to these situations requires close investigation of encounters (and nonencounters) at the boundaries of bureaucratic agencies. In some cases, the affected individual helped the Kafka Brigade articulate the most relevant questions and nominated the most valuable ideas for improvement. In many cases the affected individual was the only one who had a full picture of the dysfunction, including all the various parties involved and each party's particular perspective. In other cases clients were simply lost in the woods, bewildered by the demands being made on them.

Because civil service professionals and managers of government agencies typically have a deeply held but necessarily partial perspective on the problem, client perspectives round out the view with crucial information that cannot be obtained elsewhere. Clients' overviews of the spectrum of agencies they encounter help lead to creative solutions across organizational boundaries. Combining factual accounts (process maps) and narrative accounts (perceptions) illuminates the experiences of both clients and bureaucrats. The narrative account helps express the dimensions of the problems that elude the institutional or legal perspective. But without a factual account to back the story up with objective data and information, government officials are less likely to acknowledge the more affective dimensions and the subjective experience of feeling powerless, frustrated, and bewildered as a result of bureaucratic dysfunction. It is the collision or collusion of rational and emotional elements, institutional and personal elements, system elements, and life elements that reveals the true nature of the problem.

### Proxy

As proxies, affected individuals represent a larger group of potentially or actually affected clients. If and when this function can be established through presentation of the data and persuasive logical reasoning, the individual may come to represent a wider group of people not just statistically but also politically. The affected client comes to symbolize a previously unknown or neglected constituency of the involved agencies. As such, he or she possesses public authority—the authority of a public that is called into existence through the process of inquiry. The affected individual comes to stand in for an anonymous group that the system has failed. The actual presence of a client in a forum where the problems are diagnosed and remedies are devised puts political pressure on the process. It establishes an urgency and immediateness that cannot be denied or downplayed. After all, there is immediate feedback from the client if the problem is misdiagnosed or if suggested remedies fail to constitute an adequate solution. If and when this pressure can be made productive, and if the client's situation is sufficiently representative of the larger problem, the outcome of the process is likely to be a more accurate diagnosis and a more specific and adequate set of remedial actions. We learned that to make the involvement of affected individuals effective and valuable, we had to consider and attend to three things: the relative representativeness of the individual's case, the multiplicity of capacities in which the individual was encountering the state, and the degree of anxiety the individual's presence caused in the discussion forum.

*Representativeness*

The more representative an individual's case is of a wider group of affected people, the more the role of the affected individual as a proxy can be emphasized and the more value his or her involvement has in terms of putting pressure on the process. Representativeness is not a given. Only after a comprehensive diagnosis can one define the most important characteristics of the group the individual may represent. If the argument for representativeness cannot be made because both the problem definition and the population data are inconclusive, however, an argument may still be made for the emblematic value of the case. In other words, it should be evident that the characteristics of a case of complex red tape should plausibly apply to a wider if still undefined category of cases. If that cannot be established, the involvement of affected individuals as data points and proxies is not likely to be effective.

In almost all fourteen cases, it was hard to establish conclusively that the case was representative. Because we were looking into complex problems with many variables, we refrained from using the term "representative" at all, preferring to look for cases that were "emblematic." We made this choice to indicate that while a case should bring out the most important factors of a problem, it need not necessarily present all dimensions found in all similar cases. There is a logical paradox here: the problem is that we do not know all of the relevant factors, dimensions, or data until we explore and discuss a case in a broader forum of interested and affected parties. At the same time, we want to have such a discussion based on concrete problems, exemplified by a real-life case. To resolve this issue at least to some degree, we learned that plausible intuitions are important. Throughout the exploratory case research, we developed our sense of what might be an emblematic case, but quickly grasped that such choices can never be fully justified. In light of the importance of establishing a case that will be accepted as an important and meaningful case to work on collectively, this is a weakness of the approach. Another weakness lies in the fact that those problems that go unnoticed by officials and practitioners often involve clients who are least able and least willing to complain or to articulate what they face. In such cases, it is crucial to do data analysis to establish where problems might occur, and to identify cases proactively. Simply relying on incoming formal complaints is insufficient to identify deep bureaucratic dysfunction. By using a variety of channels (such as letters, emails, ombudsman cases, accounts in the media, and cases brought to the attention of elected officials) and a proactive approach (actively reaching out to clients who may have experienced red tape but who are less likely to complain, for one reason or another), one is better able to identify particular instances of a suspected problem area.

### Multiplicity

The more a case emphasizes the multiplicity of capacities of an affected individual, the more diagnostic value his or her involvement has. If and when clients are involved, it is important to stress that they should be addressed in their multiple capacities, as service recipients and as obligatees complying with regulatory duties. Failing to acknowledge the multiplicity of capacities and the fact that these capacities may differ or change over time or as the situation changes will lead the discussion in a particular direction and may result in a missed opportunity to explore the whole problem and to consider all dimensions and affected interests. If affected individuals are difficult to find or to approach (such as ex-convicts, victims of child abuse and neglect or domestic violence, drug addicts, tax cheats), one can use the expertise and connections of frontline professionals to identify cases. If the problem concerns failure to obtain available services, eligible nonrecipients (such as school dropouts or nascent entrepreneurs) could be found through informal social or professional networks. And if proactive data analysis reveals problems that go unnoticed by practitioners because clients are unwilling or unable to complain, organizations may resist acknowledging a reality that makes their problems bigger.

An important point related to the issue of representativeness and multiplicity is that a case need not be "clean" in order to be useful for inquiry. Cases in which the client has done absolutely nothing wrong morally, technically, or legally are very rare. Nearly everyone makes mistakes, whether deliberately or not. Because of the complexity of their situations, clients sometimes act in ways that are detrimental to their cases. This aspect of human nature can be considered part of the problem.

*Case Anxiety*

Working with individuals affected by bureaucratic dysfunction, especially when they are present physically, is difficult because it creates anxiety among the civil service professionals involved. Typical responses include dismissal of the case ("issue not relevant," "case not representative"), refusal to engage ("involvement creates precedent," "creates false expectations for the client"), and general resistance ("too much confrontation," "no time," "no confidence in positive outcomes"). This is understandable because the diagnosis can easily be perceived as an attack or an accusation. A collective performance review aimed at diagnosing problems may provoke particularly high levels of anxiety since it may feel to some like an indictment of their role in the situation and an attack on their professional commitments and capacities. Facilitating a diagnostic process requires moderating skills, as well as a blend of case knowledge and general knowledge about change management.

One challenge we encountered in identifying cases was that an open case is sometimes preferable because it cannot be dismissed as easily as a closed case. On the other hand, a closed case may be preferable because it does not provoke the anxiety associated with an open case (such as potential legal ramifications or conflicts of interests). In the process of diagnosis, the anxiety level often rises because so much more misunderstanding and lack of collaboration between agencies and between implementation and policy levels becomes apparent than had initially been perceived. The process of diagnosis often alienates practitioners from one another in ways that can be unhelpful for the process, as happened in the immigration and pancake shop licensing cases. In both instances the diagnosis stage became painful and participants began holding back when the apparent lack of consensus became too much to bear. In selecting a case, it is important to assess what kind of case will be most helpful in getting to a productive level of anxiety, keeping in mind that too much anxiety may lead to explosion and shutdown, while too little anxiety may not produce the energy needed to galvanize change.

## Remedying Bureaucratic Dysfunction: Transforming Accountability

The remedial value of the approach we have developed and tested lies in its potential to transform the accountability system without the need to pass legislation or change institutional arrangements. Where the involvement and actual presence of affected individuals creates a close proximity to the task, the involvement and actual presence of senior administrators or politicians creates a close proximity to the authorizing environment. The client is a proxy for the negative consequences of bureaucratic dysfunction and the politician is a proxy for the accountability system. What happens in the process, and especially in the collective performance review, is that fragmented, task-oriented accountability systems are dissolved and restructured in better alignment with the desired outcomes. Involving senior administrators or politicians ("authorizers") in a process of collaborative inquiry has the potential to integrate fragmented client encounters and provide political cover for remedial action on the part of otherwise reluctant agency staff. Under the right conditions, this potential can work to galvanize and sustain meaningful change and revise the terms of accountability to improve performance.

### Fragmentation

The agencies that deliver public services and enforce laws specialize in creating specific types of encounters between the state and the client. From a client's perspective, there are many interdependencies between the encounters: to be eligible for service A, one needs to comply with rule B, which requires obtaining a document from agency C, and so on and so forth. The client does much of the integrative work. This is understandable and unavoidable to a certain extent. A government bureaucracy that accommodates all variation in society and serves clients in all their capacities simultaneously is neither conceivable nor desirable. The Weberian principles of bureaucratic organization, the more fundamental notions of separation of powers and checks and balances, and finally the need to divide labor in order to deal with large amounts of work imply and necessitate fragmentation. However, when things go wrong, fragmentation can become a serious problem. In the case of bureaucratic dysfunction, as defined in this study, it can become very difficult—even impossible—for clients to sort out their case. All agencies might be doing their jobs correctly but still collectively fail to deliver services or impose duties. An error on the part of agency A may cause agency B to deny a claim, causing the client to fail to comply with agency C's regulations in time. Even if the relevant organizations detect and acknowledge problems of this kind, officials may not be equipped to deal with the problem. The reason is that not only are the tasks of the state fragmented, the accountability structures among and within organizations are as well.

To break through the institutional version of the "bystander syndrome" and incentivize responsible action beyond an individual civil servant's mandate or jurisdiction, the existing accountability system needs to be dissolved. This means delegitimizing the way legitimate actions are currently organized or defined and legitimizing actions that would address the discovered dysfunction. Since no single agency can take legitimate action to resolve the problem under the current accountability system, some force is needed to legitimize transformation. We found that this does not have to be someone with absolute power over all involved parties (if such authority even exists). All it takes is someone at a senior level willing to take responsibility for managing the politics. It is not the actual formal position that somebody occupies in the authorizing environment but rather the official's experience and skillfulness in maneuvering in the political arena. Just as it is important to find a good emblematic case and a cooperative affected individual, it is important to identify an authorizer who is able and willing to take on this task.

### Politics

The process of inquiry is a political process. Diagnosing a case is already part of a change process that has political implications in two senses. First, it engages officials who operate at political levels that allow them to authorize lower-level officials to depart from what they have previously understood their duty to be. Second, it is political in the sense that it involves judgments about values to be protected, as well as about technical means to be invented. For this reason it is important to avoid fixed conceptions of what problems and solutions look like. In most cases no single organization or individual is able to fully define the problem to the satisfaction of others. People tend to define the nature and relevance of bureaucratic dysfunction in terms of their own organizational task and to the extent that they are responsible for that task. What is bureaucratic *dysfunction* to some are bureaucratic *responsibility* and virtue to others. If a case is not defined through deliberation and interaction among relevant stakeholders, it may end up being defined in terms of the interests of the dominant player. One person's view of bureaucratic virtue will triumph over others, and what may be useful and reasonable actions of others will be treated as dysfunctional.

When different actors or agencies have contradictory views of the problem, it is important to leave the issue undefined or half defined. The initial question for the collective performance review then becomes, is there a problem? This is where the role of the authorizer is of crucial importance: she can establish the urgency and importance of the problem as experienced by the affected individual. In doing so, she lends her authority to the community of inquiry to pursue the diagnostic and remedial process. We also found that it is not always necessary to establish a single definition of the problem. The act of defining can be as important as its result because it clarifies the variety of (perhaps contradictory) perspectives on the same issue. This is why, at the collective performance reviews, diagnoses often ended with a general agreement to disagree, and with an acknowledgment of a range of different problem definitions and different interpretations of what represented a good and appropriate action by a particular government official in response to his or her piece of that problem.

### Galvanizing and Sustaining Change

Focusing on small steps that individual participants can take may have a larger overall effect than a forced consensus around bigger steps forward. By nominating small steps for action, people can co-own the remedial plan and feel as though they are part of the solution rather than part of the problem. This is especially important in light of the anxiety the process evokes. The more exposed or indicted people feel by the approach, the more important it is to make them feel they are part of the solution and can take credit for it.

The Kafka Brigade had originally defined remedies at three different levels: case, category, and capacity. This distinction was helpful when we were conducting collective performance reviews because it emphasized the substantial difference between solving problems in particular cases and solving problems for similar cases. The separation of the case and category levels reduced anxiety for some of the participants, who worried that too much energy and too many resources (especially the time of all involved stakeholders) were being spent on just one case. We made it clear that there was a higher cause involved: structurally improving governance performance.

We found that in almost all cases, when we asked about remedies, participants were reluctant to come up with steps that they could implement themselves. For many of the public managers with whom we worked, the word "remedy" represented a grand plan to improve something structurally once and for all. This, however, was not precisely what we meant by remedy, because we developed this methodology to approach problem solving as an incremental process that people could commit to implementing within their organizations. Theoretically, these steps would add up to the best possible solution at the time. Often, individuals felt embarrassed to suggest something small because as an isolated step, it meant little to make a phone call in a difficult case, to change a form, or to coordinate more often with another agency. However, at the end of a session, when participants looked at a flip chart and saw fifteen to twenty apparently small steps suggested by individuals from different agencies, they could acknowledge that together, this could become a promising set of corrective actions with potential for an immediate impact on the whole category of cases similar to the one under discussion.

Even when participants committed to particular actions, however, there was no guarantee that they would be able to follow through. The problem that we identified, particularly in the check-back (that is, final) stage, was that many people said that they were "making progress." This euphemism usually meant they had been unable to take the steps they promised, which is an inevitable result of the fact that nobody acts in a vacuum. Even with some authority, participants still needed to convince—and sometimes even to train—others to comply with their new plans or to support their new interventions. The pressure of the collective performance review often generates enthusiasm and new commitments, but after the review has ended, participants return to their own organizations and divisions, and then the truly challenging work of convincing other people to cooperate and follow through begins. This last step can take longer than we anticipate or hope. A question that remains unanswered is, how do we ensure that people keep their promises? Is there any way we can maintain pressure on the process beyond what the check-back meetings create? How do we overcome what Kegan and Laskow Lahey (2009) have called "immunity to change" resulting from competing commitments?

### Reestablishing Accountability Focused on the Task

The dynamics of commitment are extremely important. We learned that we could better encourage people to use their discretionary authority to the fullest extent, and sometimes even move beyond the defined scope of their mandate or organizational boundaries, if we could say that the authorizer had agreed to address any accountability issues resulting from their contributions to the solution. The idea that the participants were being asked to do something they would not do otherwise, and had not done before, but that the rest would fall to someone else, both laid on extra pressure to accomplish something on their own and reassured them that the result of the collective performance review would not be limited to their own small piece of the puzzle. Together with action taken at higher levels, their contributions added value. Participants would see the value of collective action, and the active commitment of the sponsor and their fellow participants worked in an encouraging way on their perception of what was possible. We were unable to create this kind of contagious commitment in every case, but we found that when we were able to emphasize this dynamic of commitment, we could expect more reliable follow-through.

Authority can be used to focus attention and to sustain momentum in change processes. It is best used in a way that actively reforms the accountability system, so that change is not a matter of various ad hoc actions and commitments but rather an incremental transformation of structural and cultural conditions facing the organizations and officials involved. Although we attempted to achieve this level of transformation in all fourteen cases, we found that in only a few cases was this kind of result actually achieved. And in those cases only modest changes were made to the accountability system. We have not yet figured out how the approach can be changed or fine-tuned to initiate larger, more lasting modifications. But we did find that when authority was lacking, no structural improvements were made at all.

## Conclusion

Using the findings of our theoretical and empirical exploration, in this chapter I have answered the questions, What is bureaucratic dysfunction? What does dealing with bureaucratic dysfunction mean? I have discussed the most important issues and lessons that can be drawn from the entire inquiry. In the final chapter I will answer our central question: How can we effectively deal with bureaucratic dysfunction?

# 8

# Conclusions

*Believing in progress does not mean believing that any
progress has yet been made.*

FRANZ KAFKA, *The Blue Octavo Notebooks*,
1991 (1948)

The goal from the start of the Kafka Brigade's efforts has been to develop actionable ideas to reclaim some of the value that bureaucratic dysfunction strips away. In this book, I have used both bureaucratic theory and public value theory to explore the problem. Initially bureaucratic dysfunction was understood in terms of its consequences: a loss of value to the individual public sector client as well as the public at large. The *process* of dealing with bureaucratic dysfunction that the Kafka Brigade developed through action research may help reclaim some of the lost value. Analyzing and distilling lessons from this work has produced a set of principles that can guide remedial action and yield insights into the conditions under which they can be most effective.

What should an actor who wants to take on bureaucratic dysfunction pay attention to? Though the experiences of public sector clients were the point of departure, I sought to explore the problem from the perspectives of a variety of stakeholders, including the frontline professional, the manager, and the policymaker. To public sector clients, bureaucratic dysfunction manifests primarily as encounters gone wrong, ridden with red tape. Red tape means excessive regulation, unreasonable application of rules, cumbersome procedures, burdensome administrative requirements, unintelligible bureaucratic behavior, or any combination of these elements. The complex cases of red tape that the Kafka Brigade took on were both technically and politically thorny—the kinds of cases that often go unnoticed or remain unresolved. What we found underlying these complex cases of red tape was not only a lack of knowledge about the problem and its possible remedies but also a lack of consensus on (1) the existence of the "a problem" per se, (2) what exactly the problem was, and (3) how it should be solved.

Digging into the problem, we distinguished a variety of capacities in which people experience dysfunction in encounters with the government (including the eligible nonrecipient and the noncompliant obligatee, among others). This informed the development of conceptual tools for the diagnosis of problems labeled as red tape with sensitivity to the broader context of the situation and to underlying mechanisms of bureaucratic dysfunction. As discussed in chapter 2, there have been many attempts to "cut red tape" or "reduce administrative burdens" in practice, but these efforts have mainly treated the issue as a technical problem that required politically authorized *technical* solutions. What was still lacking was a more rigorous approach that acknowledged the political dimensions of the problem and the underlying mechanisms that cause and sustain red tape.

I started with a conceptual framework that integrated a variety of perspectives on bureaucratic dysfunction and then applied that framework to the results of empirical action research on fourteen cases of bureaucratic dysfunction, conducted by the Kafka Brigade in the Netherlands. This process yielded a generic *process solution* to the problem—consisting of guidelines to identify, define, diagnose, and remedy bureaucratic dysfunction.

In this concluding chapter, in addition to briefly revisiting the question of what bureaucratic dysfunction is and how we can deal with it effectively, I consider the important question of whom we mean by "we." In light of what we have learned about the problem and about solving it, where should we assign responsibility to act? Who, if any, are the actors in society that are best equipped to deal with the problem, and what should they do about it? I also discuss the conditions under which efforts to deal with bureaucratic dysfunction are most likely to find success, look at the limitations of this particular study, and offer suggestions for future research. Finally, we return to Franz Kafka, the mind and the muse that inspired this study, and take a moment to reflect.

## What Is Bureaucratic Dysfunction?

Bureaucratic dysfunction is a varied and heterogeneous phenomenon that manifests in many different ways and in many places, with different causes and consequences for different stakeholders. I have identified four distinct dimensions of the problem, each aligning with the perspective of a different kind of actor within the system:

|  |  |
|---|---|
| Red tape | Primarily from the *client's* perspective |
| Organizational culture | Primarily from the *professional's* perspective |
| Organizational structure | Primarily from the *public manager's* perspective |
| Flawed statecraft | Primarily from the *policymaker's* perspective |

These dimensions are neither mutually exclusive nor exhaustive. Bureaucratic dysfunction could be caused by action, inaction, mistakes, or miscues in any of these realms, and the symptoms cannot tell us the underlying cause. To keep an open mind as we examine a case of complex red tape, we need a process that helps us identify, define, and diagnose the problem. The process must be broad enough to cover the variety of dimensions yet focused enough to allow specific remedies to be devised. Using this process, the Kafka Brigade's action research uncovered some of the underlying mechanisms that were causing the problems in fourteen different cases. These mechanisms have been discussed extensively in chapters 5, 6, and 7.

The problem of bureaucratic dysfunction also is folded into the tangled relationships between people and government. People encounter the state in a variety of roles (for example, as citizens, recipients of public services, or obligatees), and accordingly, the state encounters citizens in various capacities (for example, as service provider, regulator, or enforcer). When encounters are service-plus-obligation hybrids, or when multiple agencies are involved in producing a service or enforcing a regulation, it is often unclear what is going on and what values, principles, or rules should guide the resolution of a problem.

Unclear or distorted relationships between the client and the state often lie at the root of complex red tape. Because it is mostly clients who experience and criticize red tape, most attempts to remedy the problem focus on service encounters in which there is a provider-client relationship between the government and people. But in all cases of red tape that we investigated, the underlying problems were related to the *multiplicity* of relationships between people and the government and to the fact that this multiplicity was not being acknowledged. The lines between service and obligation encounters are blurry. In government, service encounters are not focused solely on client satisfaction, and obligation encounters are not focused solely on compliance. Both types of encounters are ultimately focused on the production of public value and are a means to that end.

When City Hall issues permits for entrepreneurs, for example, it assists the business owner in the startup process. In this sense, it looks like a service encounter, but City Hall is also delivering obligations. The entrepreneur must comply with safety and zoning regulations. The public, in turn, reaps the benefits of local economic development and employment, and does not have to worry that the new business down the street poses a safety hazard. Conversely, when we look at one of the most onerous obligation encounters the state has with citizens—removing an abused and neglected child—the obligation imposed on parents to relinquish custody is simultaneously a service to the child. This action also upholds the public's commitment to human rights by protecting the rights of the most vulnerable members of society. While most public agencies have encounters with clients that involve elements of both service delivery and law enforcement—and all agencies are supposed to create some kind of public value through these encounters—very few manage to live up to all elements of the task to the same extent (Alford 2009; Moore 1995; Sparrow 2000). To complicate matters, clients often interact with more than one agency. Division of labor—or task fragmentation, depending how one views the phenomenon—has led to many different agencies focusing on different capacities of the same client: as car driver, patient, taxpayer, parent, resident, ex-convict. Clients tend to see government as a whole, but governments see clients as many different recipients or obligatees (Beecham 2006; Klievink 2011; Bardach 1998; Bogdanor 2005). This fragmentation adds to the complexity of creating productive encounters and improving social outcomes, increases the chances of errors, and creates patterns of dysfunction. The outcome is the nondelivery of services to eligible clients and the failure to impose duties on obligatees (false negatives), as well as the delivery of services to noneligible clients and the imposition of duties on nonobligatees (false positives). The more complex the situation, the more difficult it is to untangle the various relationships and deliver the correct services and obligations to the correct clients.

We have defined bureaucratic dysfunction as a mismatch between state capacity to deliver services and enforce regulations and client capacity to benefit from public services and comply with regulation. Small errors may make the difference between near matches and false positives or negatives. And mismatches can cause significant material and immaterial losses to individual clients, but also to the public at large, as a result of bad or suboptimal social outcomes. But there is a reason why bureaucratic dysfunction can simmer and go unnoticed and untreated for a long time: it can be very difficult to "triage" a case of bureaucratic dysfunction. Understanding the conditions under which recipients fall through the cracks and obligatees evade the arm of the law is important to ensure appropriate and productive client encounters and do right by the individual. But it is also important for another reason: since the government is supposed to achieve social outcomes of various sorts *through* its encounters with clients, it needs to worry about encounters gone wrong from the perspective of statecraft. Patterns of false positives and false negatives add up to policy failure; a lack of capacity to realize the correct service and obligation encounters limits the state's ability to deliver the desired social outcomes. Bureaucratic dysfunction is therefore not just a problem managing public service delivery or enforcing regulations but also a matter of public policy and governance. A mismatch affects not just a government's relationship with its clients but also its relationship with society at large.

## How Can We Effectively Deal with
## Bureaucratic Dysfunction?

In light of the variability and heterogeneity of the phenomenon, dealing with bureaucratic dysfunction requires a differentiated approach
that can combine various methods for detecting, understanding, and
(one hopes) resolving the problem. As described in chapter 7, dealing
with bureaucratic dysfunction is a process of identifying, defining,
diagnosing, and remedying problems (a process I have referred to with
the initialism IDDR):

- To **identify** something is to recognize or establish it as being a particular thing: What is it that we are looking to understand and
  solve? Do we notice a red tape problem if it occurs?
- To **define** something is to state or describe the exact nature, scope,
  or meaning of a particular thing: How can we understand a particular instance of red tape? What kind of bureaucratic dysfunction is
  going on?
- To **diagnose** something is to determine the nature of a problem by
  examining the symptoms: What are the symptoms of bureaucratic
  dysfunction? How can manifestations of red tape be attributed to
  underlying dysfunction?
- To **remedy** is to counteract something undesirable: What are the
  conceivable treatments for bureaucratic dysfunction? Can we cure
  the underlying dysfunction rather than simply treat the symptoms?

I call IDDR a "process" to acknowledge and emphasize that the
problem may not be "fixable" in the sense that there is a straightforward solution somewhere that simply needs to be found and applied.
Bureaucratic dysfunction can be understood as a combination of technical problems and adaptive challenges (Heifetz, Grashow, and Linsky 2009). However, we do not immediately know what parts of the
problem are technical—and can be fixed—and what parts require
more adaptive responses. And that is why IDDR is a *process of inquiry* and not a recipe for success. Herbert Kaufman wrote in his
1977 book *Red Tape*, "What we need is a detached clinical approach rather than heated attacks, the delicate wielding of a scalpel
rather than furious flailing about with a meat ax" (p.98). I believe
this study has developed the kind of detached clinical approach that

Kaufman advocates and combined it with insights from strategic management theory. We now know more about the phenomenon, its causes, and potentially effective remedies for it. We now have a scalpel in the form of a process solution to instances of bureaucratic dysfunction.

## Creating Capacity to Deal with Bureaucratic Dysfunction

The next question is, whose hands should be reaching out to grasp this tool? In light of the nature of the problem, it is not sensible to assign responsibility a priori to one actor or another. Below we discuss first what actors have traditionally been involved in dealing with bureaucratic dysfunction, and how. We then discuss how the institutional capacity to deal with the problem might be reconceived if a process-based solution were adopted.

### Special Units and Reform Agendas

In the past, most efforts to address bureaucratic dysfunction came from within government. Ever since the 1950s, governments from around the world have launched initiatives to deal with bureaucratic dysfunction. These efforts have been called, among other things, public sector reform agendas and deregulation initiatives (Barber 2007; Van Twist, Van der Steen, and Roosma 2010, p. 7; de Jong and Zuurmond 2010; Lindquist and Vincent 2011). Sometimes special units led the effort, such as the Prime Minister's Delivery Units in the UK (2002–06), the cabinet of the minister for administrative simplification in Belgium, and the Unit for Red Tape Reduction of the Ministry of the Interior in the Netherlands (2005–11). These units would then develop or utilize a variety of tools and programs to carry out their mission. More often, government efforts took the shape of general policies (for example, the famous National Performance Review in the United States under the Clinton administration, or the less famous 2004–06 reform program Alternative Government [Andere Overheid] in the Netherlands.) These programs promoted a general view of what had to be done and how to reduce red tape, but execution often depended on agencies and lower levels of government, as the initiatives were more about setting an agenda and promoting a general policy approach to the perceived problem of red tape.

## *Elected Representatives*

In some countries members of parliament (or Congress) play an important role in troubleshooting for constituents. In the United States, where there is no unified federal Ombudsman, members of Congress have staff dedicated to "constituent service," often referred to as "casework" (Petersen 2014). When people are having trouble navigating their way through various agencies, settling a dispute, getting through to a higher level official, or experiencing inordinately long wait times, a staff member can take on the role of "switch board operator," "mediator," "red tape cutter," or "expeditor (Lieber 2012). Elected representatives may have electoral motives to help constituents, but they will help anyone from "their" district or state, regardless if that person voted for them or not (and there would be no way of confirming that anyway, as voting is anonymous). The great benefit of having policymakers do problem-solving work would theoretically be that, confronted with the undesired outcomes of policy, they are better informed participants in the legislative process and better representatives of the countervailing power to the executive branch of government. In principle policymakers can identify patterns, define problems, diagnose underlying mechanisms, and nominate remedies for congressional action. In practice, casework in congressional offices is just that: helping to solve a case for a constituent with a problem who requests help. Members of Congress have limited staff capacity assigned to constituent services and caseworkers are not explicitly instructed to look at broader patterns or investigate to what extent people who did not ask for assistance are affected by the same problem that affected a constituent who did request help. Politics aside, if that is possible, there would be no fundamental reason for members of Congress not to pool resources, share data and expertise and join forces to engage in the work of dealing with bureaucratic dysfunction in a more concerted and systematic way.

## Nonstate Actors and the Public at Large

Government-mandated initiatives to address (perceived) bureaucratic dysfunction and efforts by elected representatives have not been the only responses to the problem. Initiatives have also come from the private and nonprofit sectors that have acted to reform the public sector, reduce red tape, and help clients experiencing problems in their encounters with government. These initiatives run the gamut from industries lobbying for less environmental and labor regulation (or at least more efficient enforcement of those regulations) (Nakamura and Church 2003; Howard 1994) to human rights activists critiquing the inertia and opacity of justice systems (Rhode 2004; de Jong and Rizvi 2008), and from the United Nations High Level Commission on Legal Empowerment of the Poor (United Nations 2008) to labor unions and political parties assisting members with bureaucratic paperwork. In the United States, a prominent lawyer and anti-red-tape activist has started a grassroots movement called Common Good that launched the Start Over campaign explicitly challenging the perceived overregulation that "suffocates America and destroys common sense" (Howard 2011). In the Netherlands, passionate critiques of excessive managerialism and red tape by organizations committed to promoting and protecting the role of the public sector professional have had a major impact on election campaigns in recent years and have also led to a variety of practical projects to change the professionals' predicament (Brink 2005; Jansen, Van den Brink, and Kole 2009). Finally, some media organizations do their part to address bureaucratic dysfunction: in the Netherlands, for example, a number of national newspapers have featured series of articles investigating "bureaucratic horror stories,"[1] and national broadcasting networks have produced TV shows that help "victims of the bureaucracy" seek redress with government agencies and private sector bureaucracies.[2] Sometimes these initiatives by nonstate actors have an effect on

---

1. Two national newspapers in the Netherlands, *NRC Handelsblad* and *De Volkskrant*, ran series of articles about excessive bureaucracy in 2009 and 2010.

2. *Breekijzer*, with Pieter Storms, aired from 1995 to 2002 (SBS6). *Kassa*, a consumer protection program (VARA) with Felix Meurders, has aired since 1989, and *De Ombudsman*, with Pieter Hilhorst, has aired from 2010 to 2012 (VARA).

government: some lobbies are very successful at influencing lawmakers, some watchdogs successfully get agencies to respond and take action to resolve issues of individual clients or larger systemic issues. In a sense the Kafka Brigade, as a social enterprise conducting action research with clients and government officials, falls into this category as well. The limitation of all these nonstate actors, of course, is that they typically have partial perspectives, specific interest or target groups, or insufficient capacity to take on all the problems that might be worth exploring. They also do not have the authority of the state to break through real institutional barriers. On the other hand, not being part of government can make it easier to put pressure on institutions or political executives through the media or through popular protest.

The public at large can also identify and articulate instances of bureaucratic dysfunction and nominate them for action. Individuals and organizations at all levels and in all sectors of society notice and nominate problems for discussion and remedial action. For example, in 2011 the Dutch government used social media as a tool to discover discontent about public services. A special unit at the Ministry of the Interior scans Twitter for problems by following the hashtag #redtape. This is one way to capitalize on the dispersed capacity for problem identification and problem solving. If the identification and articulation of problems is an important first step in effectively dealing with bureaucratic dysfunction, we need to acknowledge the actual and potential roles that nongovernmental actors can play in improving bureaucratic performance.[3]

## Auditors and Ombudsmen

Established institutions have also made efforts to recalibrate their problem-solving mechanisms. These institutions have traditionally been controlling mechanisms that kept the state "honest" and living up to principles of good governance and the rule of law (Hood 2004). The most common controlling mechanisms that modern welfare states employ are forms of oversight. Oversight may take the form

---

3. An interesting conceptual and empirical exploration of "dispersed democratic leadership" is found in Kane, Patapan, and Hart (2009).

of internal or external auditing, as well as independent inspections. When it comes to detecting and addressing bureaucratic dysfunction, auditors and inspectors interpret their roles in very different ways. Some confine their activities to classic accounting tasks, such as inspecting annual reports and checking expenditures against stated policy goals. Other, more innovative actors in the auditing and inspecting community have shifted their focus to investigating the link between organizational inputs and outputs and occasionally following these down the value chain to policy outcomes. An example of the latter is the Dutch Court of Audit, which has developed a mission statement that reaches beyond its formal constitutional mandate, taking responsibility for helping government learn about and improve its performance by strategically selecting research priorities based on perceived complexity and increased risk of dysfunction. It also strives to develop research methodologies that measure performance beyond financial accountability and operational efficiency (Rekenkamer 2010). This shift in the scope and focus of investigation reflects the realization that the traditional control mechanisms fail to grasp important aspects of government performance. A narrow focus on inputs and outputs does not allow one to learn about dysfunctional mechanisms that come into play further down the chain of policy implementation and value creation (de Jong 2009, p. 60).

Another important institution of democratic governance that focuses on problem solving is the Office of the Ombudsman. Whether the individual is appointed by the legislature, the executive, or an organization (or, less frequently, elected by constituents), the typical duties of an ombudsman are to investigate constituent complaints and attempt to resolve them, usually through recommendations (binding or not) or mediation. Ombudsmen sometimes also aim to identify systemic issues leading to poor service or breaches of rights. At the national level, most ombudsmen have a wide mandate to deal with the entire public sector, and sometimes also with elements of the private sector (for example, private service providers with government contracts).[4] The main challenge for any ombudsman is to define her strategic mission: the so-called ombudsman plan (Rowat 1985). In

---

4. Definition adapted from "Ombudsman" at Wikipedia.org.

a way, the real success of an ombudsman would be her redundancy: all complaints would be dealt with by (government) organizations themselves through effective complaints procedures and processes of appeal and redress governed by administrative law. In practice, many ombudsmen invest in the improvement of these "first-line" mechanisms, but they virtually never become redundant (Ziegenfuss and O'Rourke 2011). The reasons are several and varied: cases may require a truly independent third party to mediate a conflict; cases may be too complex because they involve a multitude of agencies; individual organizations may fail to recognize or act on patterns of complaints that amount to a larger problem of bureaucratic dysfunction. Ombudsmen face a strategic challenge in deciding how exactly to allocate their resources. Should they actively solicit complaints from people who are not very likely to complain or should they dedicate more resources to their so-called own motion research, focused on structurally changing practices (de Jong and Zuurmond 2007, p. 49)? In the former case, an ombudsman will be able to do microjustice on a large scale, at the individual case level. In the latter case, it will be advocating for justice on the macro (policy) level or at the meso (organization) level.

To some degree, their strategic choices are limited by their constitutional mandate. Just as Courts of Audit are not at liberty to challenge the ways that political choices regarding policy instruments affect outcomes for clients, ombudsmen are not at liberty to challenge the ways that ill-informed policy choices or organizational designs affect clients (de Jong and Zuurmond 2007, p. 49). Nevertheless, some ombudsmen (for example, the former Dutch ombudsman Alex Brenninkmeijer) have taken the position that the constitutional mandate of the office allows for a wider role interpretation. Subsequently, the Dutch National Ombudsman office has developed strategies and methodologies that focus on identifying patterns of bureaucratic dysfunction that transcend organizational and jurisdictional boundaries and attempt to resolve issues at higher levels of governance (De Nationale Ombudsman 2009).

## Problem-Solving Capacity Revisited

The actors discussed above are either actually or potentially involved in dealing with bureaucratic dysfunction (to a larger or lesser extent, for a longer or shorter period of time, and with variable focus and degrees of authority). Together, they form a potentially formidable problem-solving infrastructure for a society—that is, *if* they work together, push their envelopes, and transcend their own narrow definitions of bureaucratic dysfunction. As we have seen in our action research, institutions always develop a bias or a partial view on problems based on their particular mandate or disciplinary focus. The best solution may therefore not be a conventional institutional design. Assigning primary responsibility and allocating capacity for dealing with bureaucratic dysfunction to one organization or another would not be helpful. Depending on the circumstances of the particular problem, some institutions might be better positioned to do something about it than others. In some cases ombudsmen will have an institutional advantage; in other cases auditors might have a better shot at it. Sometimes problems are better solved from within, by civil servants themselves. At other times a fresh look and some prodding from nongovernmental actors might be preferable.

A process-based approach to dealing with the problem does not presuppose a designated actor or agent. The Kafka Brigade method and the ideas developed in this book can be used by any institution, social group, or individual willing and able to take on the responsibility to make change. Success will very likely depend, however, on the configuration of stakeholders that lend authority and commit resources. A good starting point would be to see how established institutions can strengthen focused cooperation using this approach. For example, ombudsmen and audit institutions could develop collaborative investigations, members of Congress can pool resources and take joint action, and various public agencies can team up to deal with complaints that fall through the cracks.

This research has yielded a set of guiding principles and tactics for anyone taking responsibility to make change. We know that identification, definition, diagnosis, and remedial action are the basic functions of the process, but it is useful to remember that these functions or tasks do not necessarily have to be carried out by one institution.

On the contrary, the process should probably be as inclusive and as collaborative as possible. Only then will it be possible to develop a more comprehensive and integral view of the causes and consequences of the problem and to mobilize the creative and managerial potential to remedy it. A process approach may not be as tangible or familiar as an institutional approach, but it would have to meet the same (or higher) standards of effectiveness. I have identified a number of actions and attitudes that define effectiveness in a process-based approach to dealing with bureaucratic dysfunction:

- *Identify, screen, and nominate problems for collaborative work:* Any actor who wants to take responsibility for a process-based approach to dealing with problems of bureaucratic dysfunction needs to make use of a variety of channels, radars, and antennae to detect problems. In other words, one has to organize distributed capacity to identify, screen, and nominate problems, utilizing a variety of mechanisms and actors.
- *Connect client encounters to social outcomes.* Any actor addressing bureaucratic dysfunction should consider the problem at hand from the perspective of both clients and the broader public. Without this dual perspective, the diagnosis is likely to remain incomplete and remedies are likely to be inadequate because they will fail to address the mechanisms that caused or sustained the problem. Using the encounter of the individual client (recipient or obligatee) as an entry point is a practical way to start; however, as one proceeds through the IDDR process, it is vital to consider the encounter and its difficulties in the context of public value creation and the achievement of social outcomes.
- *Acknowledge the merits of bureaucracy while reducing the limits*: Instead of dismissing the whole system because it has failed in one way or another, one should emphasize the values and benefits of bureaucracy. One way to do that is to appreciate fully the difficulties and dilemmas facing those running or working in bureaucracies. Acknowledging the constraints of bureaucracies helps overcome defensive routines and increases the willingness of people to explore what they can do *despite* these constraints. Success depends on productive working relationships between those inside and outside bureaucracies.

- *Create holding environments:* An actor who acknowledges the inherent fragmentation and competing perspectives within the system while also keeping people focused on their collective task in a pressure cooker environment is most likely to be successful. To do this, one needs convening power or the ability to use the convening power of other actors. This power can be derived from formal authority, but it can also come from reputation, celebrity, or connectedness in social networks. Holding environments are places confined by spatial and temporal limits, as well as by institutional boundaries.[5] In other words, in a holding environment people are compelled to deal with the problem and with each other in a certain venue at a certain time, convened by a certain institutional authority.

- *Reconnect policy to frontline professionals*: The approach should focus on mobilizing discontented professionals or managers rather than on controlling them. Many professionals have developed feelings of alienation from their work, their clients, or each other as a result of bureaucratic dysfunction. We often forget that civil servants too suffer from red tape, even if, or precisely because, they are the ones who have the most immediate and most frequent contacts with clients. Reconnecting with professionals means acknowledging their perspective, validating their professional values, and listening to their concerns and suggestions for improvement. Whatever actor is driving the process is not likely to succeed without support from the frontline professionals (and their managers) of the agencies involved. The capacity to keep the process going depends on the convener's ability to create a positive collaboration among all those involved and appealing to their professional knowledge, values, and aspirations.

- *Emphasize the political dimension of the work:* Bureaucratic dysfunction often appears as a result or manifestation of competing values. While most people feel that debating value is a prerogative of politicians, not civil servants, addressing bureaucratic dysfunction depends on engaging participants in deliberation about the

---

5. For more on the creation of holding environments for organizational learning, see Heifetz, Grashow, and Linsky (2009), Senge (1999, 2006), Kahn (2005), Heifetz and Linsky (2002), and Scharmer and Senge (2009).

values they are pursuing. There is a clear role for politicians here, but it is not their usual role. They should not be making the judgment call but rather allowing and encouraging the group of stakeholders to deliberate and decide on value. Their presence can be a forceful statement, particularly if they explain the role they may play in navigating the accountability issues and addressing jurisdictional, political, and legal obstacles. If they pledge commitment to the process and to contributing to the best possible outcomes, this can encourage others to do the same. Any actor driving the process should therefore develop productive relationships with politicians and use their authority in a way that stimulates rather than mutes value debates among the participants.

■ *Reshape accountability systems:* Sustainable success depends on the ability of those driving the process to transform accountability structures and accountability standards. If the structural issue is not addressed, the effectiveness of the approach will be contingent on individuals' willingness to exceed their authority or bend the rules. Reshaping accountability systems requires a kind of organizational learning that can transcend the boundaries of individual organizations. It requires mechanisms for acknowledging the limits of the current accountability system, articulating the public value lost under current circumstances, and unleashing problem-solving potential among the involved stakeholders. Only then can participants envision and devise a new accountability system geared toward improving the situation not just in one case but categorically. The approach we propose facilitates this kind of learning by bringing the public sector client as well as actors with political authority into a process of collaborative inquiry among representatives of the organizations involved.

■ *Promote distributed leadership through adaptive strategies:* Ultimately, it does not matter what actors take responsibility for the process, as long as they know that success depends on their ability to create ownership of the process and commitment to follow-up actions among all the actors involved. Since in most complex cases of bureaucratic dysfunction the overall accountability structure is fragmented, all stakeholders have their own perspective, task orientation, and discretionary authority. This means that even if parties agree on a problem definition and commit to remedial actions, no single stakeholder has the formal authority to move the process forward and hold stakeholders to their promises. However, the convening actor might have the capacity to instill a sense of commitment to the process in each stakeholder by appealing to shared value, shared interests, or simply the fact that the process itself has created a forum in which each of the members now have a responsibility. The bottom line is that in the absence of formal authority to coordinate the collaborative work, the convening actor needs to devise and apply strategies that mobilize leadership across the system in order for the system to adapt to the challenge at hand.

■ *Commit to relentless incrementalism:* It is essential to recognize that the work will never be done completely. To succeed in dealing with bureaucratic dysfunction means not just being able to make improvements but also being willing to accept that results may not last. As noted throughout this book, the problem cannot be solved definitively; it needs to be solved over and over again as it occurs in different places, in different ways, and at different times.[6] As long as governments use some form of bureaucratic organization to do business with clients and accomplish public goals, there will be errors and mistakes. And more or less frequently these problems will amount to structural patterns that some or all stakeholders will perceive as dysfunctional. Actors driving the process therefore need the mental and practical capacity to exercise relentless incrementalism in order to accomplish a positive net result.

To sum up the points enumerated above, given what we know about bureaucratic dysfunction and about dealing with it, it is not very likely that we can prevent it because in general, the causes cannot be removed. It is not very likely that a substantive universal remedy will be found because all instances of bureaucratic dysfunction are different. It is also not very likely that one particular actor will be best equipped or positioned to take responsibility for solving the problem because it can occur at any time and in any place, and it is hard to design a mechanism, institution, or policy that would detect

---

6. Here the children's game Whack-a-mole comes to mind. The goal is to hit moles that pop out of the ground with a stick so they retreat. But after they have disappeared, they reappear again and again. A skillful player notices the moles early, reacts quickly and effectively, and stays vigilant.

and address the problem on a systemwide basis. If we can never fix the problem in general, we might as well solve it as it appears. To do so, it is probably best to invest in distributed problem-solving capacities. We need many problem solvers at many levels and in many places. We depend on people who are able to identify and nominate problems for diagnosis and remedy and who are willing to convene and facilitate the process.

## Relevance and Urgency

Though there might never be a perfect match between people's capacity to benefit from services and comply with regulation and the state's capacity to deliver services and enforce regulation, we can keep working toward the ideal. The worldwide fiscal crisis provides one good reason to do so. Governments are cutting budgets and rationing services across the board. Addressing bureaucratic dysfunction is a way to reduce inefficiencies and increase the effectiveness of programs and operations. Since it seems only sensible to look for leaks before turning off the tap, taking bureaucratic dysfunction seriously might be wise for cash-strapped governments. Another reason to take red tape more seriously is that it affects the more vulnerable members of society disproportionately. Though all democratic societies invest in wealth distribution and social justice to some extent, addressing social inequality rarely drives strategies to reduce red tape. Increasing efficiency and effectiveness and reducing the costs of compliance are perfectly legitimate goals, but ignoring equity and fairness as an important value in public administration is a missed opportunity, both for affected individuals and groups and for governments.

A final reason to invest in more comprehensive and rigorous approaches to red tape reduction is the broader impact on organizational renewal and policy reform in the public sector. In most cases red tape is just the tip of the iceberg. It occurs in and around encounters between clients and governments. As such, it provides a point of departure for an investigation of how encounters can be improved. But the dysfunctional mechanisms that are uncovered in the process have consequences far beyond these encounters. If service delivery fails, clients may be dissatisfied. If these services are provided to clients to improve social outcomes that society as a whole benefits from, remedying the problem improves performance not only in terms of operational efficiency and equitable treatment but also in terms of policy effectiveness.

As governments struggle to redefine their roles in society, balance budgets, reform policies, restructure institutions, and so forth, they often focus on macrolevel policy design or institutional arrangements. Public sector reform in most countries has been a top-down exercise and has not demonstrated impressive results (Pollitt and Bouckaert 2000). Some have argued that fine-tuning the strategies and sustaining efforts will eventually yield results (Barber 2007). Others have given up hope that more of the same will produce different results (Ringen 2009). Because reform in the public sector is urgently needed but the large-scale, top-down reform agendas have made little progress, the time is ripe to invest more in pragmatic, bottom-up, collaborative approaches.

## Limitations and Suggestions for Future Research

A natural consequence of the fact that bureaucratic dysfunction manifests in a variety of different ways in different places is that real solutions will need to be "homegrown" or "tailor-made." Generic substantive solutions are of course desirable, in the sense that they provide clear-cut answers to perceived problems, but this study was not designed or intended to produce such results.[7]

However, we did produce a generic solution of a different kind. The research yielded insights into how practitioners may navigate through the messy practice of dealing with dysfunction. It produced some generic *process* solutions. It shows a way to engage in public problem solving that can be applied universally and that

---

7. To come back to the clinical metaphors we used in chapters 1 and 2, this study has not produced a generic "treatment" that will cure all instances of an illness. That would be a substantive solution, and such solutions would need to be rigorously tested on a large scale to guarantee universal application. Instead, this study has developed the equivalent of a diagnostic protocol that will help doctors identify the underlying illness and determine what kind of available treatments would ameliorate the condition of a patient in a particular case.

accommodates a wide range of different situations. It does not prescribe specific substantive solutions, but it does offer a detailed answer to the question of *how* one can begin to diagnose and remedy the problem. Practical application and further research will have to demonstrate the meaning, value, and validity of these process solutions.

Because we have looked only at Dutch cases, we cannot claim with certainty that the lessons from this study will apply to other countries. Comparative research should provide interesting insights into the wider applicability of these lessons. The diversity of cases in terms of location (different cities), policy area (both service delivery and law enforcement), and demographics and characteristics of affected individuals (such as ethnicity, age, and education) serves to maximize opportunities to explore.

To further advance knowledge about dealing with bureaucratic dysfunction in practice, it would be interesting to run experiments using the process-based approach (IDDR) with a variety of institutional actors, and identify additional factors for success and failure. It would also be interesting to do more longitudinal research on the medium- and long-term effects of the process-based approach. Finally, it would be valuable to further test and customize the approach for specific policy areas, such as health care, education, and social services. To make the lessons more easily applicable, it might be helpful to look at specific adaptations and configurations of the principles that could guide approaches in such particular areas.

## Epilogue

Some people find the writings of Franz Kafka frustrating, depressing, or even intimidating. Others find his work surreal, disorienting, and incomprehensible. Many people feel that Kafka's novels are about malicious governments suffocating innocent individuals with unreasonable regulation, defensive bureaucrats, and endless red tape. Few, however, notice that Kafka also conveys a lighter and more hopeful message in his work. Yes, individuals get disoriented in modern societies, and yes, government bureaucracies are not always helpful. However, the careful reader notices that it is not just the government's clients who are disoriented in Kafka's novels; it is also the frontline operators, the middle managers, the senior administrators—everyone is disoriented and wonders what is going on.[8] In fact, if seen from a distance, what looks like bureaucratic dysfunction up close in Kafka's work more closely resembles the action in Charlie Chaplin's slapstick movies: everyone is chasing and bothering everyone else while they try to figure out what is happening. The point is that Kafka does not write about dystopian bureaucratic systems but about the quest for humanity and agency within—and despite—those systems.

One of the most intriguing tales written by Kafka is "The Great Wall of China." It is written as a reflection by a midlevel manager of an army of construction workers on the construction of the wall. Looking back on the process of designing and building such an enormous structure, the narrator ponders what the leaders considered when they were conceiving the project. Why was the wall built in piecemeal fashion? Why did the construction armies build sections separately, leaving large gaps between them? Would the end result reflect the original plan at all? Would the rationale for building the wall—protection against the northern peoples—become obsolete by the time construction was finished? What does the way the project was managed tell us about the leaders and institutions of the empire? And what does the wall tell us about the people who obey, tolerate, and support the leaders? Kafka's narrator reflects:

> There was a great deal of mental confusion at the time . . . perhaps for the simple reason that so many people were trying as hard as they could to join together for a single purpose. Human nature, which is fundamentally careless and by nature like the whirling dust, endures no restraint. If it restricts itself, it will soon begin to shake the restraints madly and tear up walls, chains, and even itself in every direction. It is possible that even these considerations, which argued against building the wall in the first place, were not ignored by the leadership when they decided on piecemeal construction. We—and here I'm really speaking on behalf of many—actually first found out about it by spelling out the orders from the highest levels of management

8. See Kafka and Harman (1998) and Wagenbach (2003).

and learned for ourselves that without the leadership neither our school learning nor our human understanding would have been adequate for the small position we had within the enormous totality. In the office of the leadership—where it was and who sat there no one I asked knows or knew—in this office I imagine that all human thoughts and wishes revolve in a circle, and all human aims and fulfillments in a circle going in the opposite direction. But through the window the reflection of the divine worlds fell onto the hands of the leadership as they drew up the plans.[9]

The Great Wall is to China what bureaucracy has become to Western civilization: an expression of the ambiguous ambitions of a society and its leaders. Bureaucracy is a ubiquitous and inevitable phenomenon, and our relationship with it is fundamentally ambivalent. It is supposed to protect us, but it does so at a considerable cost. It serves society, but it does not serve all of society's members equally all of the time. As clients we get frustrated with bureaucracy at times, but from a public perspective we are often unclear about our values, interests, and preferences with regard to bureaucracy. And, in a way, we need to believe in the system because we have no real alternative. At the same time, we cannot ignore the many gaps and cracks in the wall—the persisting flaws of the bureaucracy. We do in fact see, in terms of various losses of value, the consequences of mismatches—the cracks—between states and clients.

And so we ask questions. Does the system serve the purpose we had in mind for it? What *did* we have in mind? Who had what in mind, exactly? Who are the leaders who designed the system, and where are they? Can we trust them to have thought everything through? Can we trust them to notice when things go wrong? When does bureaucratic dysfunction become a serious problem? Who should care about that? Do we, ordinary workers and citizens, need to care? What do we do about it?

All of these questions are asked implicitly and explicitly throughout Franz Kafka's work. They are questions about the possibility of human agency in a world governed by alienating institutions of our

9. Kafka (1971, pp. 235–47).

own making. These are the kinds of questions that I have found to be inspiring and informative when thinking about bureaucratic dysfunction, both academically and *in real life*. As human beings, our continued reflection about the merits and limits of the ways in which we organize ourselves as a collective defines us as builders, as leaders, and as citizens.

# References

Ackoff, Russell. 1978. *The Art of Problem Solving* (Hoboken, N.J.: Wiley).

Albrow, Martin. 1970. *Bureaucracy* (London: Pall Mall Press).

Alford, John. 2009. *Engaging Public Sector Clients: From Service-Delivery to Co-production* (London: Palgrave Macmillan).

Algemene Rekenkamer. 2003. *Tweede Kamer der Staten-Generaal: Vergaderjaar 2002–2003* (Sdu Uitgevers).

———. 2010. *Strategie Algemene Rekenkamer 2010–2015: Slagvaardig en Transparant, Presteren en Functioneren van het Openbaar Bestuur* (Den Haag: Rekenkamer).

Arentsen, Maarten, and Willem Trommel. 2005. *Moderniteit en Overheidsbeleid: Hardnekkige Beleidsproblemen en hun Oorzaken* (Amsterdam: Coutinho).

Argyris, Chris. 1993. *Knowledge for Action: A Guide to Overcoming Barriers to Organizational Change* (San Francisco: Jossey-Bass).

———. 2010. *Organizational Traps: Leadership, Culture, Organizational Design* (Oxford University Press).

Argyris, Chris, and Donald A. Schön. 1974. *Theory in Practice: Increasing Professional Effectiveness* (San Francisco: Jossey-Bass).

Ayres, Ian, and John Braithwaite. 1992. *Responsive Regulation: Transcending the Deregulation Debate* (Oxford University Press).

269

Balazs, Etienne. 1964. *Chinese Civilization and Bureaucracy: Variations on a Theme* (Yale University Press).

Barber, Michael. 2007. *An Instruction to Deliver: Tony Blair, Public Services and the Challenge of Achieving Targets* (London: Politico's).

Bardach, Eugene. 1998. *Getting Agencies to Work Together: The Practice and Theory of Managerial Craftsmanship* (Brookings Institution Press).

Bardach, Eugene, and Robert A. Kagan. 2002. *Going by the Book: The Problem of Regulatory Unreasonableness* (New Brunswick, N.J.: Transaction).

Bardach, Eugene, Robert A. Kagan, Lawrence S. Bacow, and Institute for Contemporary Studies. 1982. *Social Regulation: Strategies for Reform* (San Francisco, Calif.: Institute for Contemporary Studies).

Barzelay, Michael, and Babak J. Armajani. 1992. *Breaking through Bureaucracy: A New Vision for Managing in Government* (University of California Press).

Bazerman, Max H., and Ann E. Tenbrunsel. 2011. *Blind Spots: Why We Fail to Do What's Right and What to Do about It* (Princeton University Press).

Beecham, J. 2006. *Beyond Boundaries: Citizen-Centred Local Services for Wales* (Cardiff: Welsh Assembly).

Behn, Robert D. 2001. *Rethinking Democratic Accountability* (Brookings Institution Press).

Benington, John, and Mark H. Moore. 2011. *Public Value: Theory and Practice* (Basingstoke: Palgrave Macmillan).

Bjorkman, James W., Rob Van Eijbergen, Goos Minderman, and Hans Bekke. 2011. *Public Leadership and Citizen Value: The Wineland Papers 2010* (The Hague: Eleven International).

Blau, Peter Michael. 1956. *Bureaucracy in Modern Society,* Random House Studies in Sociology 12 (New York: Random House).

Bogdanor, Vernon. 2005. *Joined-up Government,* British Academy Occasional Paper 5 (Oxford University Press for the British Academy).

Bovens, M. A. P. 1998. *The Quest for Responsibility: Accountability and Citizenship in Complex Organisations* (Cambridge University Press).

Bovens, M. A. P., and Paul 't Hart. 1996. *Understanding Policy Fiascoes* (New Brunswick, N.J.: Transaction).

Bozeman, Barry. 2000. *Bureaucracy and Red Tape* (Upper Saddle River, N.J.: Prentice-Hall).

Bray, John N. 2000. *Collaborative Inquiry in Practice: Action, Reflection, and Making Meaning* (Thousand Oaks, Calif.: Sage).

Brink, Gabriel van den. 2005. *Beroepszeer: Waarom Nederland niet Goed Werkt* (The Hague: Boom).

Buchanan, David A., and Richard J. Badham. 1999. *Power, Politics, and Organizational Change: Winning the Turf Game* (London: Sage).

Burke, John P. 1986. *Bureaucratic Responsibility* (Johns Hopkins University Press).

Burrell, Gibson, and Gareth Morgan. 1979. *Sociological Paradigms and Organisational Analysis: Elements of the Sociology of Corporate Life* (London: Heinemann).

Caiden, Gerald E. 1991. "What Really Is Public Maladministration?" *Public Administration Review* 51, no. 6, pp. 486–93.

Cels, Sanderijn, Jorrit de Jong, and Frans Nauta. 2012. *Agents of Change: Strategy and Tactics for Social Innovation* (Brookings Institution Press).

Coen, Joel, and Ethan Coen. 1998. *The Big Lebowski* (Gramercy Pictures).

Conley, John M., and William M. O'Barr. 1990. *Rules versus Relationships: The Ethnography of Legal Discourse* (University of Chicago Press).

Corbin, J., and A. Strauss. 2007. *Basics of Qualitative Research: Techniques and Procedures for Developing Grounded Theory*, 3rd ed. (Thousand Oaks, Calif: Sage).

Crozier, Michel. 1964. *The Bureaucratic Phenomenon* [Phénomène bureaucratique] (University of Chicago Press).

de Jong, Jorrit. 2009. "Een dodehoekspiegel voor bestuurders: Kanttekeningen bij Feedbackmechanismen in het Openbaar Bestuur." *Bestuurskunde* 18, no. 1, p. 60–68

———. 2011. *De Diagnose en Behandeling van Overbodige Bureaucratie: Pleidooi voor een Klinische Benadering van een Hardnekkig Probleem* (Den Haag: Ministerie van Binnenlandse Zaken en Koninkrijksrelaties).

de Jong, Jorrit, Noor Huijboom, Marco Meesters, Joeri van der Steenhoven, and Arre Zuurmond. 2004. *Hollandse helden: Overheidsinnovatie volgens Uitvoerders* (Self-published).

de Jong, Jorrit, and Gowher Rizvi. 2008. *The State of Access: Success and Failure of Democracies to Create Equal Opportunities* (Brookings Institution Press).

de Jong, Jorrit, and Arre Zuurmond. 2007. Ongekende Klachten over het Doorgronden en Doorbreken van Kafkaiaanse Impasses, in

*Werken aan behoorlijkheid* (Den Haag: Boom Juridische Uitgevers), p. 49–72.

———. 2010. *Een aardig begin: De Aanpak van Overbodige Bureaucratie in Nederland (2003–2010)* (Den Haag: Ministerie van Binnenlandse Zaken en Koninkrijksrelaties).

de Jong, Steven. 2009. *De lastige burger: Dienstverlening in een Tijd
van Ontbrekend Burgerschap* (Culemborg: Van Duuren Media).

De Nationale Ombudsman. 2007. *Werken aan behoorlijkheid* (Den
Haag: Boom Juridische Uitgevers).

———. 2009. *De burger in de ketens: Samenvatting, verslag van de
nationale ombudsman over 2008* (The Hague: Bureau Nationale
Ombudsman).

de Tocqueville, Alexis. 2000. *Democracy in America* (Indianapolis, Ind.:
Hackett Publishing Company).

DeHart-Davis, Leisha, and Sanjay K. Pandey. 2005. "Red Tape and Public Employees: Does Perceived Rule Dysfunction Alienate Managers?"
*Journal of Public Administration Research and Theory* 15, no. 1.
pp. 133–48.

Dewey, John. 1954. *The Public and Its Problems* (New York: Henry
Holt).

Dick, Bob. 1999. *What Is Action Research?* Accessed online February
2014: http://www.scu.edu.au/schools/gcm/ar/whatisar.html

DiIulio, John J. 1994. *Deregulating the Public Service: Can Government Be Improved?* (Brookings Institution Press).

Docters van Leeuwen, Arthur, Wim Deetman, Ivo Opstelten, Marco
Pastors, and Roel In 't Veld. 2003. *Een kwestie van uitvoering:
Vernieuwingsagenda voor de presterende overheid* (The Hague:
Self-published).

Donahue, John D., and Richard Zeckhauser. 2011. *Collaborative Governance: Private Roles for Public Goals in Turbulent Times* (Princeton University Press).

Downs, Anthony, and RAND Corporation. 1967. *Inside Bureaucracy*
(Boston: Little, Brown).

Du Gay, Paul. 2000. *In Praise of Bureaucracy: Weber, Organization
and Ethics* (London: Sage).

———. 2005. *The Values of Bureaucracy* (Oxford University Press).

Engbersen, G. 2009. *Fatale Remedies: Over de Onbedoelde Gevolgen
van Beleid en Kennis* (Amsterdam University Press).

Etzioni-Halevy, Eva. 1983. *Bureaucracy and Democracy: A Political
Dilemma*, rev. ed. (London: Routledge and Kegan Paul).

Feldman, Allan. 1994. "Erzberger's Dilemma: Validity in Action Research and Science Teachers' Need to Know," University of Massachusetts, Amherst, School of Education, doi: 10.1002/sce.3730780106.

Ferlie, Ewan, Laurence E. Lynn, and Christopher Pollitt. 2005. *The Oxford Handbook of Public Management* (Oxford University Press).

Flyvbjerg, Bent. 2001. *Making Social Science Matter: Why Social Inquiry Fails and How It Can Succeed Again* (Cambridge University Press).

Foucault, Michel, and James D. Faubion. 2002. *Power,* vol. 3 of *Essential Works of Foucault, 1954–1984* (London: Penguin).

Freidson, Eliot. 2001. *Professionalism. The Third Logic* (Chicago University Press).

Freire, Paulo. 1998. *Pedagogy of Freedom: Ethics, Democracy, and Civic Courage* [Pedagogia de autonomia] (Lanham, Md.: Rowman & Littlefield).

———. 2000. *Pedagogy of the Oppressed* [Pedagogía del oprimido], 30th anniversary ed. (New York: Continuum).

Frissen, P. H. A. 2007. *De Staat van Verschil: Een Kritiek van de Gelijkheid* (Amsterdam: Van Gennep).

Fukuyama, Francis. 2004. *State-Building: Governance and World Order in the 21st Century* (Cornell University Press).

Ganz, Marshall. 2009. *Why David Sometimes Wins: Leadership, Organization, and Strategy in the California Farm Worker Movement* (Oxford University Press).

Gause, Donald C., and Gerald M. Weinberg. 1990. *Are Your Lights On? How to Figure Out What the Problem Really Is* (New York: Dorset House).

George, Alexander L., and Andrew Bennett. 2005. *Case Studies and Theory Development in the Social Sciences* (MIT Press).

George, Mike. 2003. *Lean Six Sigma for Service: How to Use Lean Speed and Six Sigma Quality to Improve Services and Transactions* (New York: McGraw-Hill).

Gerritsen, Erik, and Jeroen de Lange. 2007. *De Slimme Gemeente* (The Hague: Reed Business).

Gerth, H. H., and C. Wright Mills, eds. 1946. *From Max Weber: Essays in Sociology* (Oxford University Press).

Gilliam, Terry. 1985. *Brazil* (Embassy International Pictures).

Glazer, Amihai, and Lawrence S. Rothenberg. 2001. *Why Government Succeeds and Why It Fails* (Harvard University Press).

Goldsmith, Stephen, and William D. Eggers. 2004. *Governing by Network: The New Shape of the Public Sector* (Brookings Institution Press).

Goldsmith, Stephen, and Donald F. Kettl. 2009. *Unlocking the Power of Networks: Keys to High-Performance Government* (Brookings Institution Press).

Goodsell, Charles T. 2004. *The Case for Bureaucracy: A Public Administration Polemic*, 4th ed. (Washington, D.C.: CQ Press).

Gormley, William T., and Steven J. Balla. 2004. *Bureaucracy and Democracy: Accountability and Performance* (Washington, D.C.: CQ Press).

Greenwood, Davydd J., and Morten Levin. 2007. *Introduction to Action Research: Social Research for Social Change*, 2nd ed. (Thousand Oaks, Calif.: Sage).

Gregory, Robert. 2003. "All the King's Horses and All the King's Men: Putting New Zealand's Public Sector Back Together Again." *International Public Management Review* 4, no. 2, p. 41.

Grint, K. 2005. "Problems, Problems, Problems: The Social Construction of 'Leadership.'" *Human Relations* 58, no. 11, p. 1467.

———. 2008. "Wicked Problems and Clumsy Solutions: The Role of Leadership." *Clinical Leader* 1, no. 2, pp. 54–68.

Grumet, Gerald W. 2001. *Taming the Bureaucrat* (Bloomington, Ind.: Xlibris Corp.).

Hammer, Michael. 2001. *The Agenda: What Every Business Must Do to Dominate the Decade* (New York: Crown Business).

Hartley, Jean. 2008. *Managing to Improve Public Services* (Cambridge University Press).

Heifetz, Ronald, Alexander Grashow, and Marty Linsky. 2009. *The Practice of Adaptive Leadership: Tools and Tactics for Changing Your Organization and the World* (Harvard Business School Press).

Heifetz, Ronald A., and Martin Linsky. 2002. *Leadership on the Line: Staying Alive through the Dangers of Leading* (Harvard Business School Press).

Heller, Joseph. (1961) 1999. *Catch-22: A Novel* (New York: Simon & Schuster).

Herr, Kathryn, and Gary L. Anderson. 2005. *The Action Research Dissertation: A Guide for Students and Faculty* (Thousand Oaks, Calif.: Sage).

Herzfeld, Michael. 1992. *The Social Production of Indifference: Exploring the Symbolic Roots of Western Bureaucracy* (London: Berg).

Hofstede, Geert H., and Gert Jan Hofstede. 2005. *Cultures and Organizations: Software of the Mind*, rev. and exp. 2nd ed. (New York: McGraw-Hill).

Hood, Christopher. 1991. "A Public Management for All Seasons?" *Public Administration* 69 (Spring), pp. 3–19.

———. 2004. *Controlling Modern Government: Variety, Commonality, and Change* (Cheltenham: Edward Elgar).

Hoogwout, Marcel. 2010. *De Rationaliteit van de Klantgerichte Overheid: Een Onderzoek naar de Spanningen die de Invoering van het Klantdenken bij Gemeenten Veroorzaakt en de Manier waarop Gemeenten daarmee Omgaan* (Purmerend: Uitgeverij Reunion).

Hoppe, Rob, and Henk Van de Graaf. 2007. *Beleid en Politiek* (Muiderberg: Coutinho).

Howard, Philip K. 1994. *The Death of Common Sense: How Law Is Suffocating America* (New York: Random House).

———. 2011. "Common Good: Reform. Responsibility. Freedom" (http://commongood.org/).

Huber, John D., and Charles R. Shipan. 2002. *Deliberate Discretion? The Institutional Foundations of Bureaucratic Autonomy.* Cambridge Studies in Comparative Politics (Cambridge University Press).

Huijboom, Noor, and Jorrit de Jong. 2005. *Belgen Doen het Beter: Zes redenen om Morgen te Emigreren* (Amsterdam: Meulenhoff; Manteau).

Jackson, Patrick Thaddeus. 2006. "A Statistician Strikes Out: In Defense of Genuine Methodological Diversity," in *Making Political Science Matter: Debating Knowledge, Research, and Method* (New York University Press), pp. 86–97.

Jansen, T., Gabriel van den Brink, and J. Kole. 2009. *Beroepstrots: Een Ongekende Kracht* (Amsterdam: Boom).

Kafka, Franz. 1954. *Amerika* (New York: Schocken).

———. (1925) 1998. *The Trial,* translated by Breon Mitchell (New York: Schocken).

———. 1971. "The Great Wall of China," in: *The Complete Stories* (New York: Schocken)

———. 1991. *The Blue Octavo Notebooks* (Cambridge, Mass.: Exact Change).

Kafka, Franz, and Mark Harman. 1998. *The Castle: A New Translation, Based on the Restored Text* (New York: Schocken).

Kagan, Robert A. 2001. *Adversarial Legalism: The American Way of Law* (Harvard University Press).

Kahane, Adam. 2004. *Solving Tough Problems: An Open Way of Talking, Listening, and Creating New Realities* (San Francisco: Berrett-Koehler).

———. 2010. *Power and Love: A Theory and Practice of Social Change.* (San Francisco: Berrett-Koehler).

Kahn, William A. 2005. *Holding Fast: The Struggle to Create Resilient Caregiving Organizations* (Hove, East Sussex: Brunner-Routledge).

Kane, John, Haig Patapan, and Paul 't Hart. 2009. *Dispersed Democratic Leadership: Origins, Dynamics, and Implications* (Oxford University Press).

Kaplan, Robert S., and David P. Norton. 1996. *The Balanced Scorecard: Translating Strategy into Action* (Harvard Business School Press).

———. 2006. *Alignment: Using the Balanced Scorecard to Create Corporate Synergies* (Harvard Business School Press).

Kaufman, Herbert. 1977. *Red Tape: Its Origins, Uses, and Abuses* (Brookings Institution Press).

Kegan, Robert, and Lisa Laskow Lahey. 2009. *Immunity to Change: How to Overcome It and Unlock Potential in Yourself and Your Organization* (Harvard Business Press).

King, Gary, Robert O. Keohane, and Sidney Verba. 1994. *Designing Social Inquiry: Scientific Inference in Qualitative Research* (Princeton University Press).

Klievink, Bram. 2011. *Unraveling Interdependence. Coordinating Public-Private Service Networks* (Oisterwijk: BOX Press).

Kruiter, Albert Jan. 2010. *Mild despotisme: Democratie en verzorgingsstaat door de ogen van Alexis de Tocqueville* (Amsterdam: Van Gennep).

Kruiter, Albert Jan, Jorrit De Jong, Janine Van Niel, and Constant Hijzen. 2008. *De rotonde van hamed: Maatwerk voor mensen met meerdere problemen* (The Hague: NICIS Institute).

Laitin, David. 2003. "The Perestroikan Challenge to Social Science." *Politics & Society* 31, no. 1, pp. 163–84.

Lieber, R., "When to Call Your Elected Representatives for Help," *The New York Times*, October 19, 2012.

Lindblom, Charles Edward. 1990. *Inquiry and Change: The Troubled Attempt to Understand and Shape Society* (Yale University Press).

Lindquist, Evert, and Sam Vincent. 2011. *Delivering Policy Reform: Anchoring Significant Reforms in Turbulent Times*, edited by John Wanna (Australian National University Press).

Lipset, Seymour Martin, and Jason M. Lakin. 2004. *The Democratic Century*, The Julian J. Rothbaum Distinguished Lecture Series 9 (University of Oklahoma Press).

Lipsky, Michael. 1980. *Street-Level Bureaucracy: Dilemmas of the Individual in Public Services* (New York: Russell Sage Foundation).

———. 1984. "Bureaucratic Disentitlement." *Social Service Review* 58, pp. 3–27.

————. 2008. "Revenues and Access to Public Benefits," in *The State of Access: Success and Failure of Democracies to Create Equal Opportunities* (Brookings Institution Press), pp. 137–47.

Marx, Karl. 1977. *Critique of Hegel's "Philosophy of Right"* [Kritik des Hegelschen Staatsrechts], edited by Joseph J. O'Malley (Cambridge University Press).

Mashaw, Jerry L. 1983. *Bureaucratic Justice: Managing Social Security Disability Claims* (Yale University Press).

Meier, Kenneth, and Gregory Hill. 2005. "Bureaucracy in the Twenty-First Century," in *The Oxford Handbook of Public Management*, edited by Ewan Ferlie, Laurence Lynn, and Christopher Pollitt (Oxford: Scriptum Management), pp. 51–71.

Merton, Robert K. 1940. "Bureaucratic Structure and Personality," in *Classics of Public Administration*, edited by Jay M. Shafritz and Albert C. Hyde, 3rd ed. (Belmont, Calif.: Wadsworth), pp. 101–09.

Merton, Robert King. 1952. *Reader in Bureaucracy* (Glencoe, Ill.: Free Press).

Michels, Robert. (1911) 1962. *Political Parties: A Sociological Study of the Oligarchical Tendencies of Modern Democracy*, with an introduction by Seymour Martin Lipset, 2nd Free Press ed. (New York: Free Press).

Minderman, Goos. 2010. *De school als maatschappelijke onderneming* (Amsterdam: Zijlstra Center for Public Control and Governance).

Moore, Mark H. 1994. "Learning while Doing: Linking Knowledge to Policy in the Development of Community Policing and Violence Prevention in the United States," in *Integrating Crime Prevention Strategies: Propensity and Opportunity,* edited by P. O. Wikstrom (Stockholm: Swedish National Council for Crime Prevention), pp. 301–31.

————. 1995. *Creating Public Value: Strategic Management in Government* (Harvard University Press).

Mulgan, Geoff. 2009. *The Art of Public Strategy: Mobilizing Power and Knowledge for the Common Good* (Oxford University Press).

Nakamura, Robert T., and Thomas W. Church. 2003. *Taming Regulation: Superfund and the Challenge of Regulatory Reform* (Brookings Institution Press).

The Netherlands. Nationale Ombudsman. 2007. *Werken aan behoorlijkheid: De nationale ombudsman in zijn context* (Den Haag: Boom Juridische Uitgevers).

Niskanen, William A. 1971. *Bureaucracy and Representative Government* (Chicago: Aldine, Atherton).

Noordegraaf, Mirko. 2000. *Attention! Work and Behavior of Public Managers amidst Ambiguity* (Delft: Eburon).

———. 2008. *Professioneel Bestuur: De Tegenstelling tussen Publieke Managers en Professionals als "Strijd om Professionaliteit"* (Den Haag: Uitgeverij Lemma).

Organization for Economic Cooperation and Development (OECD). 2007. *Cutting Red Tape: Administrative Simplification in the Netherlands* (Paris: OECD).

———. 2010. *Cutting Red Tape: Why Is Administrative Simplification So Complicated? Looking Beyond 2010* (Paris: Edward Elgar).

Osborne, David, and Ted Gaebler. 1992. *Reinventing Government: How the Entrepreneurial Spirit Is Transforming the Public Sector* (New York: Plume).

Peters, B. Guy. 2003. "Dismantling the Weberian State," in *Governing Europe*, edited by Jack Hayward and Anand Menon (Oxford University Press), pp. 113–27.

Petersen, R. Eric. 2014. *Casework in a Congressional Office: Background, Rules, Laws, and Resources* (Washington, D.C.: Congressional Research Office).

Pollitt, Christopher, and Geert Bouckaert. 2000. *Public Management Reform: A Comparative Analysis* (Oxford University Press).

Pommer, Evert, Hetty Van Kempen, and Evelien Eggink. 2008. *De staat van de publieke dienst: Het oordeel van de burger over de kwaliteit van overheidsdiensten* (Den Haag: Sociaal en Cultureel Planbureau).

Popper, Karl. 1999. *All Life is Problem Solving.* (New York: Routledge).

Pressman, Jeffrey L., and Aaron B. Wildavsky. 1984. *Implementation: How Great Expectations in Washington Are Dashed in Oakland: Or, Why It's Amazing That Federal Programs Work at All, This Being a Saga of the Economic Development Administration As Told by Two Sympathetic Observers Who Seek to Build Morals on a Foundation of Ruined Hopes*, 3rd ed. (University of California Press).

Raad voor Maatschappelijke Ontwikkeling. 2008. *De ontkokering voorbij: Slim organiseren voor meet regelruimte* (Amsterdam: SWP).

Radin, Beryl. 2006. *Challenging the Performance Movement: Accountability, Complexity, and Democratic Values* (Georgetown University Press).

Rawls, John, and Erin Kelly. 2001. *Justice as Fairness: A Restatement* (Belknap Press of Harvard University Press).

Reason, Peter, and Hilary Bradbury. 2008. *The Sage Handbook of Action Research: Participative Inquiry and Practice*, 2nd ed. (London: Sage).

Rhode, Deborah L. 2004. *Access to Justice* (Oxford University Press).

Ringen, Stein. 2009. *The Economic Consequences of Mr. Brown: How a Strong Government Was Defeated by a Weak System of Governance* (Oxford: Bardwell Press).

Rittel, Horst W. J., and Melvin M. Webber. 1973. "Dilemmas in a General Theory of Planning." *Policy Sciences* 4, pp. 155–69.

Roemer, John E. 1996. *Theories of Distributive Justice* (Harvard University Press).

———. 1998. *Equality of Opportunity* (Harvard University Press).

Rose-Ackerman, Susan. 1999. *Corruption and Government: Causes, Consequences, and Reform* (Cambridge University Press).

Rowat, Donald. 1985. *The Ombudsman Plan: The Worldwide Spread of an Idea* (Lanham, Md.: University Press of America).

Salamon, Lester M., and Odus V. Elliott. 2002. *The Tools of Government: A Guide to the New Governance* (Oxford University Press).

Scharmer, Otto C., and Peter Senge. 2009. *Theory U, Leading from the Future As It Emerges: The Social Technology of Presencing* (San Francisco: Berrett-Koehler).

Schön, Donald A. 1987. *Educating the Reflective Practitioner: Toward a New Design for Teaching and Learning in the Professions* (San Francisco: Jossey-Bass).

Schuck, Peter H., and Richard Zeckhauser. 2006. *Targeting in Social Programs: Avoiding Bad Bets, Removing Bad Apples* (Brookings Institution Press).

Scott, James C. 1998. *Seeing Like a State: How Certain Schemes to Improve the Human Condition Have Failed* (Yale University Press).

Sen, Amartya Kumar. 1992. *Inequality Reexamined* (Harvard University Press).

———. 1999. *Development As Freedom* (New York: Knopf).

Senge, Peter M. 1999. *The Dance of Change: The Challenges of Sustaining Momentum in Learning Organizations* (New York: Currency/Doubleday).

———. 2006. *The Fifth Discipline: The Art and Practice of the Learning Organization* (New York: Currency/Doubleday).

Shafritz, Jay M., and Albert C. Hyde. 1992. *Classics of Public Administration,* 3rd ed. (Fort Worth, Tex.: Harcourt Brace).

Simon, Herbert Alexander. (1945) 1997. *Administrative Behavior: A Study of Decision-making Processes in Administrative Organizations,* 4th ed. (New York: Free Press).

Smith, Steven Rathgeb, and Michael Lipsky. 1993. *Nonprofits for Hire: The Welfare State in the Age of Contracting* (Harvard University Press).

Sparrow, Malcolm K. 1994. *Imposing Duties: Government's Changing Approach to Compliance* (Westport, Conn.: Praeger).

———. 2000. *License to Steal: How Fraud Bleeds America's Health Care System*, updated ed. (Boulder, Colo.: Westview Press).

———. 2008. *The Character of Harms: Operational Challenges in Control* (Cambridge University Press).

Sparrow, Malcolm K., and Brookings Institution. 2000. *The Regulatory Craft: Controlling Risks, Solving Problems, and Managing Compliance* (Brookings Institution Press).

Stone, Deborah. 1984. *The Disabled State* (Temple University Press).

———. 2008. *The Samaritan's Dilemma: Should Government Help Your Neighbor?* (New York: Nation Books).

Stringer, Ernest T. 2007. *Action Research*, 3rd ed. (Thousand Oaks, Calif.: Sage).

Tamanaha, Brian Z. 2004. *On the Rule of Law: History, Politics, Theory* (Cambridge University Press).

———. 2007. *Law As a Means to an End: Threat to the Rule of Law* (Cambridge University Press).

Tolman, Charles W. 1996. *Problems of Theoretical Psychology.* (Concord, Ontario: Captus Press).

Tonkens, Evelien. 2003. *Mondige burgers, getemde professionals: Marktwerking, vraagsturing en professionaliteit in de publieke sector* (Utrecht: NIZW).

United Nations. 2008. *Legal Empowerment of the Poor* (New York: United Nations).

van Egten, Caren. 2011. "Public Value through Collaboration in the Netherlands," in *Public Leadership and Citizen Value: The Winelands Papers*, edited by James W. Bjorkman, Rob Van Eibergen, Goos Minderman, and Hans Bekke (The Hague: Eleven International), pp. 13–14.

van Twist, Mark, Martijn van der Steen, and Femke Roosma. 2010. "Alleviating Administrative Pain: Learning from Complaints and Problem Reports," in *Improving Public Administration: An English Summary of Five Papers for the Trends in Troubleshooting Conference on 4 November 2010* (Den Haag: Ministry of the Interior and Kingdom Relations), pp. 7–11. https://lirias.kuleuven.be/bitstream/123456789/287107/2/Improving+public+administration+definitief.pdf.

von Hayek, Friedrich A. 1994. *The Road to Serfdom*, 50th anniversary ed., with an introduction by Milton Friedman (University of Chicago Press).

Wagenbach, Klaus. 2003. *Kafka* (Harvard University Press).

Walzer, Michael. 1983. *Spheres of Justice: A Defense of Pluralism and Equality* (New York: Basic Books).

———. 2004. *Politics and Passion: Toward a More Egalitarian Liberalism* (Yale University Press).

Weber, Max. 1922. *Wirtschaft und Gesellschaft* (Tübingen: J. C. B. Mohr).

———. [1919] 2004. *Politics as Vocation* (Cambridge, Mass.: Hackett).

Weick, Karl E., and Kathleen M. Sutcliffe. 2007. *Managing the Unexpected: Resilient Performance in an Age of Uncertainty*, 2nd ed. (San Francisco: Jossey-Bass).

Wilson, James Q. 1989. *Bureaucracy: What Government Agencies Do and Why They Do It* (New York: Basic Books).

World Bank. 2009. *Doing Business 2010, Comparing Regulation in 183 Economies: Reforming through Difficult Times* (Washington, D.C.: Palgrave MacMillan).

Yin, R.K. 2003. *Case Study Research. Design and Methods*, 3rd ed. (Thousand Oaks, Calif.: Sage)

Ziegenfuss, James, and Patricia O'Rourke. 2011. *The Ombudsman Handbook: Designing and Managing an Effective Problem-solving Program* (London: McFarland).

Zuurmond, Arre. 1994. *De infocratie: Een theoretische en empirische herorientatie op Weber's Ideaaltype in het informatietijdperk* (Den Haag: Uitgeverij Phaedrus).

Zuurmond, Arre, and Jorrit de Jong. 2010. *De professionele professional: De andere kant van het debat over ruimte voor professionals* (Den Haag: Ministerie van Binnenlandse Zaken en Koninkrijksrelaties).

# Index